The Revolution from Within

J. Krishnamurti

HOHM PRESS
Prescott, Arizona

Published, under license, by

Krishnamurti Foundation of America
PO Box 1560
Ojai, California, 93024

Cover design by: Zac Parker, Kadak Graphics, Prescott, Arizona
Interior layout and design: Becky Fulker, Kubera Book Design, Prescott, Arizona

Library of Congress Cataloging-in-Publication Data

Krishnamurti, J. (Jiddu), 1895-1986.
The revolution from within / J. Krishnamurti.
    p. cm.
ISBN 978-1-935387-05-3 (alk. paper)
1. Philosophy. 2. Religion. 3. Psychology. I. Title.
B5134.K751 2009b
181'.4--dc22
                                         2009016089

HOHM PRESS
PO Box 2501
Prescott, Arizona 86302
www.hohmpress.com

Excerpted from *The Collected Works of J. Krishnamurti*
Vols: VII, VIII, IX, X & XI; copyrighted material, The Krishnamurti
Foundation of America

This book was printed in the U.S.A. on recycled, acid-free paper using
soy ink.

Contents

Contents

Foreword
Changing Oneself, Changing the World
David Skitt

Running like a gold thread throughout these talks Krishnamurti gave in the nineteen-fifties is the subject of change. Most of us would agree with the postulate in science that change is the only permanent factor of the universe, and evolutionary biology tells us that the survival of a species, including our own, depends on genetic changes that best adapt to the demands of a constantly changing environment. The changes that occur in our bodies are also ones that we take for granted.

We have no difficulty then in acknowledging change in what we call matter. But what about change in the nature of the mind and in human behaviour? We know that there is often widespread support for our politicians to change, but this usually ends up in replacing them. Yet such is the power of the very word *change* that where no democratic process prevails or is discredited, whole societies can be overthrown by revolutionaries simply chanting the word like a mantra. The results, in the twentieth century, proved, as we know, to be calamitous. Trying to change society while leaving the individuals who constitute society unchanged is something that we now see as a very dangerous error.

Foreword

Bringing the notion of change closer to home, to personal relationships, most of us have said or heard it said, 'You can't change human nature.' Or, 'You have to take me as I am.' Or, 'He [or she] will never change'. And when we do change occasionally, it seems mostly to be under the pressure of events or at the urging of others.

So there seems to be something of a discordance here. The physical universe changes all the time. And a species, including the human one will have a better chance of surviving if it changes genetically in a way that fits the environment. But we seem to assume that a change in the human mind, particularly of a fundamental kind, though found desirable when we look around us and within ourselves, is impractical or too demanding. We may even find it somewhat disturbing. Also, we have no clear sense of how far such a change may go.

How does Krishnamurti approach this issue? Perhaps disconcertingly for someone reading him for the first time, he states as 'obvious' that if we are a serious human being we must be deeply concerned with bringing about a radical transformation of our relationships, our way of thinking, and understanding of religion. Now, first of all, he asks, do we *see* that such a transformation is essential? If we do not, he argues, we need simply to observe the state of the world, its conflict, violence, confusion, and massive and avoidable human suffering. What, he asks, is the responsibility of a human being who sees that?

Well, a critic might object, I'm just an ordinary person, and all that nastiness going on out there has nothing to do with me. Krishnamurti challenges that objection head-on. First, he says, we cannot afford to be 'ordinary' any more,

the challenge of the world is too great. Second, psychologically speaking, none of us are on the sidelines of the
world, we are all in the thick of it—'we *are* the world.'
Human problems are not personal but universal.

So what can bring about a radical change in our minds?
Krishnamurti approaches this question by inviting us to
first observe our state of mind as it is *now*, to watch it
without condemnation or judgement—'like a child that
one loves . . . wandering into the depths of one's mind
without calculation or intention.' Only when aware of the
limitations of thought, of the known, of its time-bound
quality, of the stunted shaping of us by the past and by
our cultural and religious conditioning, can there be a new
state of mind.

This is only one of the many aspects of psychological
transformation that are covered in these talks, and clearly
this preface can only single out a few. But again and again
Krishnamurti maintains that change cannot be brought
about by any act of will, of wanting to *be* or *become* somebody or something. There is irrefutable logic here—if my
mind malfunctions, does not work well in certain ways,
then what I project as an objective will inevitably reflect
this. So clear observation of one's mind, seeing 'what is', is
a first and essential step.

This ability to see 'what is' in oneself, another, and in
life as a whole, releases, Krishnamurti says, 'a creative fire.'
'One has to understand "what is", before one can perceive
that which is other than "what is."'

To undertake this psychological journey is 'hard work.'
It requires 'a great deal of enquiry, penetration, and self-
knowledge.' It is also meditation, which is 'something you

have to do as you breathe, as you think, as you live.' But it is a pilgrimage open to us all. 'If we can take this journey together, and simply observe as we go along the extraordinary width and depth and beauty of life, then out of this observation may come a love . . . which is a state of being free of all demand . . . and we may perhaps be awakened to something far more significant than the boredom and frustration, the emptiness and despair of our daily lives.'

A first-time reader of Krishnamurti may be surprised to find that he often asks more questions of us than he gives answers. He invites us to 'test out' in daily life what he says and to find out for ourselves whether it is true or not. So there is no telling us what to do, no parading of assertions that have a take-it-or-leave-it quality, no usurping of our own ability to unravel the tangle that our lives may be. In times when human life is trivialized and brutalized in so many ways, it is as though Krishnamurti declares its true worth and extraordinary potential. And perhaps what is needed for its survival?

David Skitt is a respected editor of several books by J. Krishnamurti, and a trustee of the Krishnamurti Foundation, Brockwood Park, Hampshire, Great Britain.

First Talk in Ojai
3 August 1952

Perhaps we can continue with what we were considering yesterday—the problem of change, of fundamental or radical transformation, and how it is to be brought about. I think it is very important to go into this question fully, not only this morning, but in the subsequent talks that are going to take place. I do not know if you have further considered the matter; but the more one regards the problem, the more one takes it into consideration, the vaster and more complicated one discovers it to be. We see the importance and the absolute necessity of changing—changing ourselves in our relationships, in our activities, in the process of our thinking, which includes the mere accumulation of knowledge. Yet when one considers the implications of change, one sees how, though we attempt to change ourselves, there is no radical transformation. I am using the word 'transformation' in its simple meaning, not in any grandiose sense, the super-physical, and all the rest of it.

We see the necessity of change, not only in world politics, but in our own religious attitude, in our social relationships, in our individual, everyday contacts with the familiar, with each other; but the more we attempt to change on the small scale, the more superficial our thinking becomes and the greater the mischief in action. The closer we look at the problem, the more we are aware of this. Seeing the necessity of change, we project ideals, and according to that pattern we hope to transform ourselves. I am narrow, petty, superstitious, shallow, and I project the ideal of something vast, significant, deep; and I am continually struggling, adjusting, moulding myself according to that pattern. Now, is that change? Let us look at it a little closely. When I project an ideal and try to live up to that ideal, constantly adapting myself to a particular pattern of thought, does that process bring about the fundamental change which you and I recognize as essential? But first of all, do we in fact recognize that it is essential to bring about a fundamental change in our orientation, in our outlook, in our values, in our contacts, in the manner of our behaviour in the way of our thinking? Do we see the importance of that? Or do we merely accept it as an ideal and try to do something about it?

Surely, it is obvious to any person who is at all thoughtful that there must be a revolution in our thinking and in our action because everywhere there is chaos, misery. In our selves and outwardly there is confusion, there is an incessant striving without any release, any hope; and perhaps, being aware of it, we think that by creating an ideal, a projection outside of us of something which we are not, or by following an example, a leader, a saviour, or a particular religious teaching, we can bring about a fundamental change. Of course, in following a pattern, certain superficial modifications take place, but obviously that does not bring about a radical transformation. And yet most of our existence is spent in that way—trying to live up to something, trying to bring about a change in our attitude, to change according to the pattern which we have projected as an ideal, as a belief.

Now, let us find out if the pursuit of an ideal really does bring about a change in us, or only a modified continuity of what has been. I do not know if this is a problem to you. If you are satisfied with merely trying to live up to an ideal, then there is no problem—though that has its own problem of constant conflict between what you are and what you should be. This struggle, this ceaseless effort to adjust to a pattern, is still within the field of the mind, is it not? Surely, there is a radical transformation only when we can jump, as it were, from the process of time into something which is not of time. We will go into that as we discuss.

For most of us, change implies the continuation of ourselves in a modified form. If we are dissatisfied with a particular pattern of ideas, of rituals, of conditioning, we throw it aside and pick up the same pattern in a different milieu, a different colour, with different rituals, different words. Instead of Latin it is Sanskrit, or some other language, but it is still the old pattern repeated over and over and over again; and within this pattern we think we are moving, changing. Because we are dissatisfied with what we are, we go from one teacher to another. Seeing confusion about us and in ourselves, seeing perpetual wars, ever-increasing destruction, devastation and misery, we want some haven, some peace; and if we can find a refuge that gives us a sense of security, a sense of permanency, with that we are satisfied.

So, when the mind projects an idea and clings to it, struggles towards it, surely that is not change, that is not transformation, that is not revolution, because it is still within the field of the mind, the field of time. To clear away all that, we must be conscious of what we are doing, we must be aware of it. And it must be cleared away, must it not? Because, with all that burden, with all that impetus of the mind, obviously we cannot find the other; and without experiencing the other, do what we will, there will be no change. But what generally happens? We say that individually we can do nothing, we are helpless, therefore let us do something politically to bring about peace in the world; let us have faith in the vision of one world, of a classless society, and so on and so on. The intellect worships that vision, and to carry out that vision we sacrifice ourselves and others. Politically, that is what is happening. We say that, in order to end wars, we must have one society, and to create that society we are willing to destroy everything—which is using wrong means to a right end. All this is still within the field of the mind.

Also, are not all our religions man-made, that is, mind-made? Our rituals, our symbols, our disciplines, though they may temporarily alleviate, bring about an uplift, a feeling of well-being, are they not all within the field of time? When we regard the political and religious ideals by means of which we hope to bring a change, to educate and discipline ourselves to be less selfish, to be less ambitious, to be more considerate, more virtuous, to renounce, not to acquire so much and so on—when we look at this whole pattern, do we not see that it is a process of the mind? The mind, which is also the will, is the source of effort, of intentions, of conscious and unconscious motives, it is the centre of the 'me' and the 'mine', and whatever it may do, however far it may endeavour to go, can that centre ever bring about a fundamental change within itself?

I want to change, but not superficially, because I see that in the process of superficial change there is mischievous action taking place. So, what am I to do? Isn't that your problem also, if you are really serious about all this? One may be a communist, one may be a socialist, one may be a reformer or a religious person, but that is the core of our problem, is it not? Though we may have a hundred explanations of man, of his responses and activities, or of the universe, until we change fundamentally, no explanation has any value. I see that, not just casually, I see the importance of a radical change in myself. And how is that to be brought about? There is revolution only when the mind has ceased to function within the field of time, for only then is there a new element which is not of time. It is that new element which brings about a deep, lasting revolution. You can call that element God, Truth, or what you will—the name you give to it is of no importance. But until I touch it, until I have a sense of that which will cleanse me completely, until I have faith in that which is not self-induced, not of the mind, obviously every change is a mere modification, every reformation has to be further reformed, and so on—infinite mischief.

So, what is one to do? Have you ever asked yourself this question? Not that I am asking you or you are asking me; but if we are at all intelligent, if we are at all aware of our own problems and those of the world, isn't this the first question to put to ourselves? Not what kind of beliefs, religions, sects, new teachers we should have— they are all so utterly empty and futile. But surely, this is the fundamental question that one ought to put to one-self—how to bring about a change which is not of time, which is not a matter of evolution, which is not a matter of slow growth. I can see that if I exercise will, control, if I discipline myself, there are certain modifications; I am better or worse, I am changed a little bit. Instead of being bad tempered or angry or vicious or jealous I am quiet; I have repressed all that, I have held it down. Every day I practise a certain virtue, repeat certain words, go to a shrine and repeat certain chants, and so on and so on. They all have a pacifying effect; they produce certain changes but these changes are still of the mind, they are still within the field of time, are they not? My memory says, 'I am this, and I must become that.' Surely, such activity is still self-centred; though I deny greed, in seeking non-greed I am still within the self-enclosing process of the 'me'. And I can see that it leads nowhere, do what I will; though there may be change, as long as my thinking is held within the process of the 'me', there is no freedom from struggle, pain.

I do not know if you have enquired into this. The problem of change is very important, is it not? And can this change be brought about through a process of thinking, through disciplines, through rituals, through various forms of sacrifice, immolation, denial, suppression?—which, if you observe, are all tactics, designs of the mind. However much the self, the 'me', struggles to be free, can it ever be free? Whatever effort it makes, can it ever absolve itself from its own activities? If it cannot, then what is it to do?

you see the problem as I see it. You may translate
ently in words, but that is the core of our problem.

Now, since we do not see any outlet, any way of release from the process of the 'me', we begin to worship reason, the intellect. We reject everything else and say that the mind is the only important thing, the more intellectual, the more cunning, the more erudite, the better. That is why knowledge has become so important to us. Even though we may be worshippers of God, essentially we have denied God, because our gods are the images of our own minds; our rituals, our churches—the whole business is still within the field of the mind. We say, 'Since there is only the mind, let us make man according to the mind, according to reason.' Our society, our relationships, everything we do conforms to the pattern of the mind; and whoever does not conform is either liquidated or otherwise denied.

Seeing all this, are we not concerned to find out how we can jump over that intangible barrier between the process of time and the timeless, between the projections of the mind and that which is not of the mind? If that is really an earnest question which we have put to ourselves, if it has become an urgent problem, then surely we will lay aside the obvious activities of the mind: the ideals, the rituals, the churches, the accumulation of knowledge—we will completely wash them out of our system. It is through negation that we will find the other thing, not through direct approach, and I can negate only when I begin to understand the ways of my own mind and see that I seek refuge, that I am acquisitive, that there is not a single moment when the mind is really quiet. The incessant chattering, the images, the things that I have acquired and hold on to, the words, the names, the memories, the escapes—of all that I have to be aware, have I not? Because, with that burden, which is of time, how can I experience something which is timeless? So I must purge myself completely of all that, which means I must be alone—not alone in an ivory tower, but there must be that aloneness in which I see all the processes, the eddies of the mind. Then, as I observe, as I become more and more aware and begin to put aside without effort the things of the mind, I find that the mind becomes quiet; it is no longer curious, searching, groping struggling, creating and pursuing images. All those things have dropped away, and the mind becomes very quiet, it is as nothing. This is the thing that cannot be taught. By listening a hundred times to this statement, you are not going to get it; if you do, then you are mesmerized by words. It is a thing that must be experienced, that must be directly tasted, but it's no good hovering at the edge of it.

So, when the mind is still, not made still by self-discipline, by control, by greed to experience something which is not of the mind, when the mind is really still, then you will find that there comes a state which brings a revolution in our outlook, in our attitude. This revolution is not brought about by the mind, but by something else. For this revolution to take place, the mind must be quiet; it must be literally as nothing, stripped, empty; and I assure you, it is not an easy job. That emptiness is not a state of day-dreaming; you cannot get it by merely sitting still for ten hours or twenty-four hours of the day and trying to hold on to some thing. It can come only when the mind has understood its own processes, the conscious as well as the unconscious—which means one must be everlastingly aware. And the difficulty for most of us is inertia. That is another problem which we will not go into now. But the moment we begin to inquire and see the importance of change, we must go into all this. That means we must be willing to strip ourselves of everything to find the other; and when once we have even a slight glimmering of the other, which is not of the mind, then that will operate. That is the only revolution, that is the only thing that can give us hope, that can put an end to wars, to this destructive relationship.

Question: How is one who is superficial to become serious?

Krishnamurti: Let us find out together. First of all, we must be aware that we are superficial, must we not? And are we? What does it mean to be superficial? Essentially, to be dependent, does it not? To depend on stimulation, to depend on challenge, to depend on another, to depend psychologically on certain values, certain experiences, certain memories—does not all that make for superficiality? When I depend on going to church every morning, or every week, in order to be uplifted, in order to be helped, does that not make me superficial? If I have to perform certain rituals to maintain my sense of integrity, or to regain a feeling which I may once have had, does that not make me superficial? And does it not make me superficial when I give myself over to a country, to a plan, or to a particular political group? Surely, this whole process of dependence is an evasion of myself; this identification with the greater is the denial of what I am. But I cannot deny what I am; I must understand what I am, and not try to identify myself with the universe, with God, with a particular political party, or what you will. All this leads to shallow thinking, and from shallow thinking there is activity which is everlastingly mischievous, whether on a worldwide scale, or on the individual scale.

So, first of all, do we recognize that we are doing these things? We don't; we justify them. We say, 'What shall I do if I don't do these things? I'll be worse off; my mind will go to pieces. Now, at least, I am struggling towards something better.' And the more we struggle, the more superficial we are. So I have to see that first, have I not? And that is one of the most difficult things—to see what I am, to acknowledge that I am stupid, that I am shallow, that I am narrow, that I am jealous. If I see what I am, if I recognize it, then with that I can start. Surely, a shallow mind is a mind that escapes from what it is; and not to escape requires arduous investigation, the denial of inertia. The moment I know I am shallow, there is already a process of deepening—if I don't do anything about the shallowness. If the mind says, 'I am petty, and I am going to go into it, I am going to understand the whole of this pettiness, this narrowing influence', then there is a possibility of transformation; but a petty mind, acknowledging that it is petty and trying to be non-petty by reading, by meeting people, by travelling, by being incessantly active like a monkey, is still a petty mind.

Again, you see, there is a real revolution only if we approach this problem rightly. The right approach to the problem gives an extraordinary confidence which I assure you moves mountains—the mountains of one's own prejudices, conditionings. So, being aware of a shallow mind, do not try to become deep. A shallow mind can never know great depths. It can have plenty of knowledge, information, it can repeat words—you know, the whole paraphernalia of a superficial mind that is active. But if you know that you are superficial, shallow, if you are aware of the shallowness and observe all its activities without judging, without condemning, then you will soon see that the shallow thing has disappeared entirely without your action upon it. But that requires patience, watchfulness, not an eager desire for a result, for a reward, for achievement. It is only a shallow mind that wants an achievement, a result. The more you are aware of this whole process, the more you will discover the activities of the mind, but you must observe them without trying to put an end to them, because the moment you seek an end, you are again caught in the duality of the 'me' and the 'not-me'—which is another problem.

Question: I read the Buddha because it helps me to think clearly about my own problems, and I read you and some others in the same way. You seem to suggest that such help is superficial and does not bring about a radical transformation. Is this a casual suggestion on your part, or do you mean to indicate that there is something very much deeper which cannot be discovered through reading?

Krishnamurti: Do you read in order to be helped? Do you read in order to confirm your own experience? Do you read in order to amuse yourself, to relax, to give your mind, this constantly active mind, a rest? The questioner says he reads because it helps him to solve his problems. Are you really helped by reading?—it does not matter who it is. When I go out seeking help, am I helped? I may

find temporary relief, a momentary crack through which I
can see the way; but surely, to find help, I must go within
myself, must I not? Books can give you information about
how to move towards the door which will solve your
problems, but you must walk, must you not? You see, that
is one of our difficulties—we want to be helped. We have
innumerable problems, devastating, destructive problems
in which we are caught, and we want help from somebody: the psychologist, the doctor, the Buddha, whoever it
is. The very desire to be helped creates the image to which
we become a slave; so, the Buddha, or Krishnamurti, or x
becomes the authority. We say, 'He helped me once, and
my goodness, I am going back to him again'—which indicates the shallow mind, the mind that is seeking help.
Such a mind created its own problems and then wants
somebody else to solve them, or it goes to somebody to
help it to uncover the process of its own thinking. So,
unconsciously, the one who seeks help creates the authority: the authority of the book, the authority of the State,
the authority of the dictator, the authority of the teacher,
of the priest, you know, the whole business of it. And can
I be helped, can you be helped? I know we would like to
be. Fundamentally, can you and I be helped? Surely, it is
only by understanding ourselves patiently, quietly, unob-
trusively, that we begin to discover, experience something
which is not of our own creation, and it is that which
brings about help, which begins to clear the field of our
vision. But you cannot ask for that help; it must come to
you darkly, uninvited. But when we are suffering, when
we are in real psychological pain, we want somebody to
give us a hand; and so the church, the particular friend,

the teacher, or the State, becomes all-important. For that help, we are willing to become slaves.

So we have to go into this problem of how we are caught in our own sorrows, we have to understand and clear it up for ourselves; for Reality, God, or what you will, is not to be experienced through another. It must be experienced directly, it must come to you without any intermediary; but a mind that is seeking help, that is petitioning, that is asking, begging—such a mind can never find the other, because it has not understood its own problems, it has not studied the process of its own activities. It is only when the mind is quiet that there is light. That light is not to be worshipped by the mind; the mind must be utterly silent, not asking, not hoping for experience. It must be completely still. Only then is there a possibility of that light which will dispel our darkness.

Second Talk in Ojai
9 August 1952

The last two times we met, we were considering the problem of change and I would like, this afternoon, to go into the question of power, and whether power, as we know it, can bring about a fundamental psychological transformation within oneself. The difficulty in going into this problem lies, I think, in understanding the usage of words. That is one of our major difficulties, is it not? Words like God, love, discipline, power, communist, American, Russian, have a very specific psychological significance in our lives, and when they are touched upon, we react nervously, emotionally; there is a psychological response. So, if we are to go further into this problem of change, I think we also have to consider the fact that certain words have a psychological influence on each one of us. We have built about ourselves so many verbal barriers, and it is very difficult to transcend those barriers and see the significance that lies beyond the word. After all, words are a means of communication; but if particular words cause a neurological or psychological reaction in us, then it becomes very difficult to communicate. And surely, this is another of our difficulties—that in trying to understand the problem of change, we have to strip ourselves of all ideals; because, conformity to a particular pattern, however reasonable, however logical and well thought out, is not a change at all, is it? Change implies a complete transformation, not the continuity of a modified thought. So there are many factors to be considered in this whole problem of how to bring about a fundamental change, not only psychologically, within ourselves, but also outwardly.

I see the necessity of certain changes in myself; and I can either deal with the problem superficially or go into it very profoundly and find out what are its implications. When I see that I have to change, that it is a necessity, I generally exercise the will, do I not? Any process of change implies resistance, the application of effort, which is will. With that we are familiar. That is, I perceive in myself a state which is socially not good, or a state which brings conflict within me, and I want to go beyond it; I want to break down that particular quality or condition, so I suppress it, or I discipline myself to resist it, which necessitates a certain power of the will. We are accustomed to that process, are we not? So we think power in different forms—social, political, economic, inward, spiritual and so on—is a necessity.

Now, is not this whole process of will a self-centred activity in which there is no release from the condition in which I am caught, in which the mind is held, but only a covering up and a continuity of the same thing in a modified form? And our education, our reforms, our religious thinking, our psychological struggles are all based on this process, are they not? I am this, and I want to become that, and in becoming that, I must employ a certain force of will;

there must be resistance, control. And is not this process of control, of discipline, a self-centred activity which engenders a sense of power? The more you discipline, control yourself the more there is of a certain concentrated activity, but is not that activity still within the field of the self, of the 'me' and the 'mine'? And is Reality, God, or what you will, the outcome of self-centred activity? Yet do not all your religious books, your teachers, the various sects to which you belong—do they not all imply, fundamentally, that change can be brought about through compulsion, through conformity, through the desire for success, that is, to achieve a certain result? But is not that whole process an activity of the 'me' in its desire to be something more? And can we, realizing it, bring that process to an end?

I do not know if you see the problem as I see it. All this activity, however reasonable, however noble or well calculated, is still within the field of the mind; it is the activity of the self, the result of desire, of the 'me' and the 'mine', is it not? And can the self, that consciousness which is always within the limits of the mind and therefore always in conflict—can that self ever go beyond itself? Will that self not always create conflict between individuals, and therefore between groups, between nations?

Now, it seems to me very important to understand this, but is it a problem to each one of us? We see that a radical change is necessary in society, in ourselves, in our individual and group relationships, and how is it to be brought about? If change is through conformity to a pattern projected by the mind, through a reasonable, well-studied-out plan, then it is still within the field of the mind; therefore, whatever the mind calculates becomes the end, the vision, for which we are willing to sacrifice ourselves and others. If you maintain that, then it follows that we as human beings are merely the creation of the mind, which implies conformity, compulsion, brutality, dictatorships, concentration camps—the whole business. When we worship the mind, all that is implied, is it not? If I realize this, if I see the futility of discipline, of control, if I see that the various forms of suppression only strengthen the 'me' and the 'mine', then what am I to do? Have you ever put yourself that question? I see that to exercise any power over myself is evil, it is merely a continuation of the 'me' in a different form, and I also see that the 'me' must entirely cease if there is to be peace in the world and in myself. The 'me' as a person, as an entity, as psychological process of accumulation, the 'me' that is always struggling to become something, the 'me' that is assertive, dogmatic, aggressive, the 'me' that is kind, loving—that is the centre from which arise all conflicts, all compulsion, all conformity, all desire for success, and it is only in bringing it to an end that there is a possibility of peace within myself and outwardly. When I realize this, what am I to do? How am I to put an end to the 'me'?

Now, if this is a serious problem to each one of us, what is our response to it? Naturally, we cannot all give our replies, but we can see that any movement of the self in order to become better, nobler, any movement of suppression, any desire for success, must come to an end. That is, the mind, which is the centre of the 'me', has to become very quiet, has it not? The mind is the centre of sensation, it is the result of memory, the accumulation of time, and any movement on the part of the mind to become

17

something is still within the limits of the 'me', of sensation. And can the mind, which is sensation, which is memory, which is tradition, which is the calculating machine of the 'me', which is everlastingly seeking security, hiding behind words—can that mind, out of its own desire, by any exercise of its own will, come to an end? Can it cease by its own volition?

So I must study my own mind, I must be aware of all its reactions—just be aware of my mind, without any desire to transform it. Is that not the first necessary step?—if I can use that word 'step' without introducing the idea of time. To be aware of the process of my mind without condemnation, to observe the fact without judgement, to be merely aware of 'what is'—is it possible to do that? Some may say 'yes', some may say 'no'—but what others say about this matter is of very little importance, is it not? You have to experiment with this, experience it; and is it possible to experience without building up images, symbols? That is, we generally experience only the things that we recognize, do we not? We are conscious of experiencing only when we recognize the experience, and if we are not capable of recognizing it, there is no experience. So the factor of recognition is essential to what we call experience. Now, is God, Truth, or what you will, a matter of recognition? If I can recognize something, it implies that I have already experienced it before, does it not? That which I have experienced before becomes a memory; and when there is a desire for the continuation of that experience, I project that memory and recognize it, experience it. That is, through memory, through recognition, through experience, I build the centre of the 'me'.

So, for most of us, it is extremely arduous to go into this problem of change and really bring about a transformation within ourselves. Can I change if I am constantly experiencing through the process of recognition, whether on the verbal level or the psychological level? That is, when I meet you for the first time, I do not know you, but the second time I meet you, I have certain memories of you; there is like or dislike, pain or pleasure. So, through the dictates of pain and pleasure, I say I have met you; there is a process of recognition. That recognition is established verbally or psychologically, and if I am to go beyond and discover a state which is not mere recognition, recollection, memory, must not the centre of the 'me', which is the process of recognition, come to an end? There is this entity as the 'me' which is everlastingly craving experience, seeking more of what it has known, whether outwardly or psychologically, and as long as the 'me' continues to exist, whatever I experience only strengthens the 'me', does it not? Therefore I create more and more problems, endless conflict. And is it possible for the mind to be so still that the process of recognition ceases? After all, that is creation, is it not?

Please, in listening to these talks it seems to me that what is important is not to accept all this, but to let the significance of the words penetrate and see whether they have any validity, any truth. It is that quality of truth which liberates, not the verbal denial or assertion, and so it is very important to listen rightly, that is, not to be caught in words, in the logic of certain statements, or in your own experiences. You are here to find out what another says, and to find out you must listen, and to listen rightly is one of the most difficult things to do, is it not? Because, when I use words like 'experience', 'truth' and so on, you immediately have certain responses—certain images, symbols come up, and if the mind gets caught in those symbols, you cannot go beyond.

So our problem is how to free the mind of this self-centred activity, not only at the level of social relationships, but also at the psychological level. It is this activity of the self that is causing the mischief, the misery, both in our individual lives and in our life as a group, as a nation, and we can put an end to it only if we understand the whole process of our own thinking. Can thought bring about a vital change? Up to now we have relied on thought, have we not? The political revolution, whether of the right or the extreme left, is the result of thought. And can thought fundamentally change man, change you and me? If you say it can, then you must see all the implications—that man is the product of time, that there is nothing beyond time, and so on and on. So, if I am to create a fundamental change in myself, can I rely on thought as an instrument to bring about that transformation? Or, can there be a fundamental change only when there is the ending of thought? My problem, then, is to experiment, to find out, and I can find out only through self-knowledge, through knowing myself, watching, being aware in moments when I'm off guard. It is only when I begin to understand the process of my own thinking that I can find out whether or not there is a possibility of a fundamental change; until then, mere assertion that I can or cannot change is of little significance. Though we see the importance of a radical change in the world and in ourselves, there is very little chance of such a change as long as we do not understand the thinker and his thought. The economist and the politician are never revolutionary. It is only the truly religious person that is revolutionary, the man who is seeking Reality, God, or what you will. Those who merely believe, who follow a pattern, who belong to a particular society, sect or group—they are not seekers, therefore they are not real revolutionaries. We can bring about a transformation within ourselves only when we understand the process of our own thinking.

Question: What do you mean by ambition? Would you consider any improvement of oneself ambitious? At what point does ambition begin?

Krishnamurti: Do we not know when we are ambitious? When I want something more, when I want to assert myself, when I want to become something, is that not ambition? Can we say where it begins and where it ends? Is not all self-improvement a form of ambition? I may not be ambitious in this world, I may not want to be a leader with great political power, or a big businessman with a lot of property, position, but I may be very ambitious spiritually. That is, I want to become a saint, I want to be free from all pride. Is not the very assertion of wanting to be something, the beginning of ambition? The desire not to be ambitious—is that not self-improvement, and therefore self-centred activity? If I am proud and, seeing the implications of pride, I cultivate humility, is not that cultivated humility a self-centred activity? And is that not ambition?

And if you are not to cultivate humility, then what are you going to do with pride? How is one to deal with

21

it? The very desire to get rid of one thing in order to be something else—is that not a self-centred activity, which is ambition? Please see how extremely difficult it is, when you know what you are, not to struggle to be something else. This process of struggle, this trying to become great, or humble, or generous, is called evolution, is it not? I am this, and I am going through a struggle to be come that. From thesis I proceed to antithesis, and out of that create synthesis. This process is called growth, evolution, is it not? Now, in that is implied self-centred activity, the improving of the self, the 'me'. But can the 'me' ever be improved? It may be improved within its own field, but if I want to go beyond and find out if there is something which is not of the 'me', will self-improvement help to bring about that discovery? So, being ambitious, what am I to do? Should I suppress ambition? And is not the very suppression of ambition a form of ambition which negatively strengthens the 'me' and in which there is a certain sense of power, dominance?

I see that I am ambitious, and what am I to do? Is it possible to be free from it?—which does not mean that I must become non-ambitious. Is it possible to be free from ambition? I can think it out logically, see the conflicts, the ruthlessness, the brutality of ambition in my relationships, and so on. And will that help me? Will explanations of the perniciousness of ambition help me to be free from ambition? Or, is there only one way, which is to see all the implications of ambition without condemnation, just to be aware of the fact that I am ambitious, not only at the conscious level, but at the deeper levels of my own thinking? Surely, I must be completely aware of it, without any resistance, because the more I struggle against it, the more vitality I give it. Ambition has become a habit with me, and the more I resist a habit, the stronger it becomes. Whereas, if I am aware of it, merely see the fact of it, does that not bring about a radical change? I am no longer concerned with suppressing ambition, or with putting it aside, nor am I satisfied with any explanation—I am directly concerned with the fact of ambition. So, when I look at it, what do I see? Is ambition mere habit? Am I caught in the habit of a society which is based on ambition, on success, on being somebody? Am I stimulated by challenge, by the sense of achievement, and without that stimulation do I feel lost, and so I depend on stimulation? Is it not possible to be aware of all this, to see the implications of it and not react—just see the fact? And will that perception not bring about a radical change? If I acknowledge that I am ambitious and see the implications of it, not only at the verbal level, but also inwardly which means that I am aware of the influence of habit, sensation, tradition, and so on, then what has happened? My mind is quiet with regard to that fact, is it not? My mind does not react to it anymore—it is a fact. And the quiet acceptance of 'what is' is a release from that fact, is it not?

Please do not accept this. Experiment with it and you will see. First be aware that you are ambitious, or whatever it is, and then see all your reactions to it, whether those reactions are habitual, traditional, verbal. Merely to oppose the verbal responses by another series of words, will not free you, or if it is tradition, in the mere cultivation of a new tradition or habit you will not find release. The very desire to suppress ambition is a trick of the mind to be something else—which is part of ambition. So, when the mind sees that any movement it makes with regard to a particular quality is part of the process of its own sustenance and security, what can it do? It cannot do anything; therefore, it is immediately quiet with regard to that quality. It is no longer related to it. But this is an arduous task, is it not?

A revolutionary inward change is essential, and if we are to understand the problem of change, we must go into all this and study the problem of the 'me' from different angles.

Third Talk in Ojai
23 August 1952

I think it is possible, in talking, to expose oneself and one's own inward thoughts, and if we can do that this evening, perhaps it will be worthwhile; for then this will not be a lecture, a talk to which you are listening, but an exposing of the problems and difficulties that one confronts in going into the question of transformation, this inward revolution which is so essential. We see around us the disintegration of the world, and we are aware of our own extraordinary processes of deterioration as we grow older—lack of energy, the settling into grooves of well-established habit, the pursuit of various illusions and so on—all of which creates a barrier to the understanding of our own fundamental and radical change.

In considering this problem of change, which we have been doing for the last three weeks, it seems to me that the question of incentive is very important. For most of us, change implies an incentive. I need an incentive to change. Most of us require an incentive, an urge, a motive, a purpose, a vision, or identification with a particular belief, utopia, or ideology, do we not? And does incentive bring about a radical change? Is not incentive merely a projection of one's own desires, idealized or personified, or put away in the future in the hope that by pursuing that self-projection, we can somehow bring about a change? Is not this problem of change very profound, and can it be solved by the superficial incentives which societies offer, which religious organizations dangle before us? Can a fundamental transformation be brought about by the revolutionary ideologies which give logical reasons for change and offer the incentive of a better world, a heaven on earth, a society in which there are no class distinctions? We identify ourselves with these incentives and give our lives for the things which they promise, and does that bring about a radical change? That is the problem, is it not?

I do not know how much you have thought about all this, or how deeply you have gone into the question of changing oneself, but unless we understand from what point of view, from what centre the transformation must take place, it seems to me that mere superficial changes, however beneficial socially and economically, will not resolve our extraordinarily complex problems. The incentives, the beliefs, the promises, the utopias—to me, all these are very superficial. There can be a radical change only at the centre, only when there is complete self-abnegation, complete self-forgetfulness, the complete putting aside of the 'me', the self. Until that is done, I do not see how a fundamental transformation can take place. And is this radical change at the centre brought about through an incentive of any kind? Obviously not. And yet all our thinking is based on incentive, is it not? We are continually struggling to gain a reward, to do good, to live a noble life, to advance, to achieve. So, is it not important to find out what this self is that wants to grow, to improve?

What is the self, the 'me'? If you were asked, what would be your response to that question? Some would say, perhaps, that is the expression of God, the higher self enclosed in material form, the immense manifested in the particular. And probably others would maintain that there is no spiritual entity, that man is nothing but a series of responses to environmental influences, the result of racial, climatic and social conditioning. Whatever the self may be, should we not go into it, understand it, and find out how it can be transformed at the centre?

What is the self? Is it not desire? Please, I would like to suggest these things for you to observe, not to contradict or accept, because I feel the more one is capable of listening, not so much with the conscious mind, but unconsciously, effortlessly, the more there is a possibility of our meeting and proceeding together further and more deeply into the problem. If the conscious mind merely examines an idea, a teaching, a problem, then it does not go beyond its own level, which is very superficial, but if one can listen, not with the conscious mind, as it were, but with a mind that is relaxed, observing, and is therefore able to see what is beyond the words, the symbols, the images, then there is a possibility, I think, of a quickening of direct experience and understanding, which is not a process of conscious analysis. I think we can do that at these talks if we do not meet idea by idea. What I am saying is not a set of ideas to be learnt, to be repeated, to be read over, or communicated to others, but if we can meet each other, not at the conscious, reasoning level, which we can do later, but at that level where the conscious mind is neither opposing nor struggling to understand, then there is a possibility,

I think, of seeing something which is not merely verbal, not merely intellectual.

So, what is the self that needs fundamental transformation? Surely, it is there that a change must take place, not on the superficial level; and in order to bring about a radical change there, must we not find out what this self is, the 'me'? And can we ever find out what the 'me' is? Is there a permanent 'me'? Or, is there a permanent desire for something, which identifies itself as the 'me'?

Please don't take notes, do please listen. When you take notes you are not really listening; you are more concerned with putting down what you hear so that you can read it over tomorrow, or convey it to your friends, or print it somewhere. What we are trying to do is something quite different, is it not? We are trying to find out what this thing is which we call the self, the centre of the 'me', from which all activity seems to spring; for if there is no transformation there, mere change on the periphery, on the outside, on the surface, has very little meaning.

So I want to find out what this centre is, and whether it is possible to really break it up, transform it, tear it away. What is the self with most of us? It is a centre of desire manifesting itself through various forms of continuity, is it not? It is the desire to have more, to perpetuate experience, to be enriched through acquisition, through memories, through sensations, through symbols, through names, through words. If you look very closely, there is no such thing as a permanent 'me' except as memory, the memory of what I have been, of what I am and what I should be; it is the desire for more—the desire for greater knowledge, greater experience, the desire for a continued identity, identity with the body, with the house, with the land, with ideas, with persons. This process goes on not only at the conscious level but also in the deeper, unconscious layers of the mind, and so the self, the centre of the 'me' is sustained and nourished through time. But none of that is permanent, in the sense of a continuity, except through memory. In itself it is not a permanent state, but we try to make it permanent by clinging to a particular experience, a particular relationship, or belief—not consciously, perhaps, but unconsciously we are driven to it through various desires, urges, compulsions, experiences.

So all this is the 'me', is it not? It is the self, the 'I', which is ever wanting the 'more', which is never satisfied, everlastingly groping for further experience, further sensation, cultivating virtue in order to strengthen itself at the centre; therefore it is never virtue, but only the expansion of itself in the guise of virtue. So, that is the 'me', the 'I'; it is the name, the form, and the feeling behind the symbol, beyond the word, which, in its struggle to acquire, to hold, to expand or to be less, creates an acquisitive society in which there is contention, competition, ruthlessness, war, and all the rest of it.

Unless there is a transformation at the centre, not substitution, but a radical uprooting of the 'me', no fundamental change is possible. Realizing this, how is one to bring about a deep inner change? That is the problem, is it not?—for a serious person, not for the superficial who are seeking some comforting illusion, gurus, teachers, and all the rest of the nonsense. So, how can that centre transform itself? Sirs, people who see that a change must take place, and do not know how it should come about, are easily caught by incentives, are they not? They are distracted by ideological utopias, by the Masters, by worship, by churches, by organizations, by saviours, and so on and on and on; but when I put aside all distractions because they will not transform the centre, and I am concerned only with the transformation of the centre—when I really see the urgency, the necessity of that, then all these superficial reformations have very little significance.

Now, when all incentives, pursuits and desires have been put aside, is one then capable of transforming the centre? You and I are considering this problem as two individuals, I am not addressing a group. You see the problem, do you not? There must obviously be a change, not at the superficial or abstract level, but at the very centre; there must be a new flow, a new state of being which is not of time, of memory; there must be a change which is not the result of any theory or belief, whether of the left or of the right, a change which is not the conditioning of a believer or a non-believer. I see this complex problem; and how is it possible for a spontaneous change to take place at the centre—a change which is not the result of compulsion, of discipline which are mere substitutions? I do not know if you have put the question to yourself in this manner; and if you have, what do you find, how are you to bring about that change, that transformation? Is the understanding of these distractions, incentives, pursuits, desires, merely verbal, intellectual, superficial, or is it real—real in the sense that incentives no longer have any value, and therefore they have dropped away? Or, knowing their immature promptings, are you still playing with them?

So I have first to find out what is the state of my mind that sees the problem and tries to seek an answer, have I not? Am I making myself clear? There is the problem, which we all know, and of which we are fully aware at different moments of our existence; there are occasions when we see the significance, the depth of it. And as we discuss it together, what is the state of one's mind that is looking at the problem? Isn't that important? The state of the mind as it approaches the problem is very important, because that state of mind is going to find the answer. So I first see the problem, and then I have to see what the state of my mind is that looks at the problem. Please, these are not first and second steps—the problem is a whole, a total process. It is only in putting it verbally that it has to be broken up in this way. If we approach the problem in stages, first seeing the problem, then enquiring what the state of the mind is, and so on and on, we shall get lost, we shall wander further and further away from the central issue. So it is very important for me to be fully aware of the whole state of my mind as I approach the problem.

First of all, I do not know if I want to have a fundamental change, if I want to break all the traditions, values, hopes, beliefs that have been built up. Most of us do not, obviously. Very few want to go so deeply and fundamentally into the problem. They are quite satisfied with substitutes, with a change of belief, with better incentives. But, going beyond that, what is the state of my mind? And is the state of the mind different from the problem? Is not the problem the state of the mind? The problem is not apart from the mind. It is my mind that creates the problem, my mind being the result of time, of memory, the seat of the 'me', which

31

is everlastingly craving for the 'more', for immortality, for continuity, for permanency here and in the hereafter. So, can the mind detach itself from the problem and look at the problem? It can abstractly, logically, with reason—but actually, can it separate itself from the thing it has created and of which it is a part? This is not a conundrum, this is not a trick. It is a fact, is it not? My mind, seeing its own insufficiency, its own poverty, proceeds to acquire properties, degrees, titles, the everlasting God, so it strengthens itself in the 'me'. The mind, being the centre of the 'me', says, 'I must change', and it proceeds to create incentives for itself, pursuing the good and rejecting the bad.

Now, can such a mind see the problem and act upon the problem? And when it does act, is it not still within the field of incentives, of desires, of time, of memory? So, is it not important for me to find out how my mind looks at the problem? Is the mind separate from the problem, as the observer apart from the observed, or is the mind itself the totality of the problem? With most of us, that is the point, is it not? I am observing the problem of how to dissolve radically and deeply that centre which is the 'me', so the mind says, 'I am going to dissolve it.' That is, the mind, the 'I', separates itself as the observer and the observed, and then the observer acts upon the observed, the problem. But the observer is the creator of the problem, the observer is not separate from the problem. He himself is the problem. So, what is he to do? If we can really feel this out, just stay with the problem and not try to find an answer, a quick solution, or reach for a quotation from some teacher or book, or rely on our past experience; if we can simply be aware of this total problem without judgement, then I think we will find the answer—not an answer at the verbal level, but a solution which is not invented by the mind.

So my problem is this, and I hope it is yours also—I see that a fundamental revolution must take place at the centre, not on the surface. Change on the surface has no meaning. Becoming better, nobler, acquiring more virtue, having much or little property—these are all superficial activities of a very superficial mind. I am not talking about those changes; I am concerned only with a change at the centre. I see that the 'me' must be completely dissolved. So I enquire what the 'me' is, I become aware of the 'me', not as a philosophical abstraction, but from day to day. From moment to moment I see what the 'me' is—the 'me' that is always watching, observing, gathering, acquiring, rejecting, judging, hating, breaking up, or coming together in order to be more secure. The change has to take place there; that centre has to be rooted out completely. And how is that to happen? Can the mind, which is the creator of the problem, abstract itself from the problem and then act upon it in the name of God, in the name of the higher self, for a utopia, or for any other reason? And when it does that, has it dissolved the centre? Obviously it has not. Therefore my problem is: Can the mind bring about a fundamental revolution through dialectics or through knowledge of historical processes? This is an important question, is it not? Because, if a radical change can take place at the centre, then my whole life has a different significance; then there is beauty, then there is happiness, then there is creation, then there is quite a different state of being; there is love, which is everlasting forgiveness.

So, can that state be brought about by the mind? If you say, 'no', you are not aware of the problem. That is a very quick, a very superficial answer. And if you say, 'I must look to God, to some high spiritual state which will transform all this', again you are relying on words, on symbols, on a projection of the mind. So, what is one to do? Is this not a problem to you? Looking at this complex problem of the 'me', with all its darkness, its shadows and lights, its tensions and stresses, can I, the observer, affect this thing that is observed? Please listen to the problem, don't look for an answer or try to solve it; just listen to it, let it soak into you, as the soft rains that enrich the earth. If you are really with the problem, if it is your daily concern from moment to moment to see how that change can be brought about, and if you are negatively putting aside those things which you have thought to be positive, then I think you will find the element that comes into being so darkly, without your knowing. This is not a promise. Don't smile as though you had understood.

So, what we have to do, surely, is to be aware of the totality of this problem, not merely consciously, but especially unconsciously; we have to be aware of it inwardly, deeply. The superficial mind can give reasons, explanations, it can logically work out certain problems, but when we are concerned with a profound problem, the superficial approach has little value. And we are concerned with a very profound problem, which is how to bring about a change, a revolution at the centre. Without that fundamental transformation, mere changes on the surface have no meaning, and reforms need constant reform. If we can look at this problem as a whole, taste it, smell it, unconsciously absorb it, then we shall be familiar with all the activities and tricks of the 'me'; we shall see how the observer is separating himself from the observed, rejecting this and accepting that. The more we know of this total process, the less the superficial mind will act. Thought is not the dissolver of the problem. On the contrary, thought must come to an end. It is the observer who judges, justifies, accepts and rejects, all of which is the process of thinking. Thought has created our problem—the thought that seeks the more in property, in things, in relationship, in ideas, in knowledge; and with that thought we are trying to solve the problem. Thought is memory, and the calming of memory is the stilling of the mind, and the more the mind is still, the deeper it will understand this problem and resolve the centre.

Question: Does not this process of constant self-awareness lead to self-centredness?

Krishnamurti: It does, does it not? The more you are concerned about yourself, watching, improving, thinking about yourself, the more self-centred you are, are you not? That is an obvious act. If I am concerned with changing myself, then I must observe, I must build a technique which will help me to break up that centre. There is self-centredness as long as I am consciously or unconsciously concerned with a result, with success, as long as I am gaining and putting aside—which is what most of us are doing. The incentive is the goal I am pursuing; because I want to gain that end, I watch myself. I am unhappy, I am miserable, frustrated, and I feel there is a state in which I can be happy, fulfilled, complete, so I become aware in order to gain that state. I use awareness to get what I want, so I am self-centred. Through awareness, through self-analysis, through reading, studying, I hope to dissolve the 'me', and then I shall be happy, enlightened, liberated, I shall be one of the elite—and that is what I want. So, the more I am concerned with gaining an end, the greater is the self-centredness of thought. But thought is ever self-enclosing anyhow, is it not?

So—what? To break down the self-centredness, I must understand why the mind seeks an end, a goal, a particular result. Why does my mind go after a reward? Why? Can it function in any other way? Is not the movement of the mind from memory to memory, from result to result? I have acquired this, I don't like it, and I am going to get something else. I don't like this thought, but that thought will be better, nobler, more comforting, more satisfying. As long as I am thinking, I can think in no other terms; for the mind moves from knowledge to know ledge, from memory to memory. Is not thinking self-centred in its very nature? I know there are exceptions, but we are not discussing the exceptions. In our everyday life, are we not consciously or unconsciously pursuing an end, gaining and avoiding, seeking to continue, putting aside anything that is disturbing, that is insecure, uncertain? In seeking its own certainty, the mind creates self-centredness; and is not that self-centredness the 'me', which then watches over and analyses itself? So, as long as we seek a result, self-centredness must exist, whether in an individual, in a group, in a nation or a race. But if we can understand why the mind seeks a result, a satisfying end, why it wants

to be certain—if we understand that, then there is a possibility of breaking down the walls that enclose thought
as the 'me'. But that requires an astonishing awareness of
the total process, not only of the conscious, but also of
the unconscious levels, an awareness from moment to moment in which there is no gathering, no accumulation, no
saying, 'Yes, I have understood this, and I am going to use
it for tomorrow', a spontaneity which is not of the mind.
Only then is there a possibility of going beyond the self-
enclosing activities of thought.

First Talk in Bombay
4 March 1953

I think it may be said that most of our lives are very confused, and being confused and in constant struggle we try to find a way out of the confusion. So we turn to anyone who can give us help. When we are economically strained, we turn to the economist or the politician, and when there is confusion psychologically, inwardly, we turn to religion. We turn to another to find a way, a method, out of our confusion, out of our misery. And I would like, if I can this evening, to find out if there is a method, a way to overcome our sufferings through any accumulation of knowledge or experience; or, if there is quite a different process, quite a different attitude, quite a different way that is far more important than the search for a system, a technique, or the cultivation of a particular habit.

So, if I may, I would like to quietly and hesitatingly explore this question; and, in this exploration, you are going to take part also, because it is also your problem. The problem is a way out, a system, to help me fundamentally to resolve the cause, the substance or the very nature of the mind that creates the problem. Is that possible through any form of accumulation, both of knowledge and of experience? Knowledge is the outward accumulation which is the gathering of technical knowledge, and the inward accumulation of psychological experience the 'knowing', the capacity to know. Will these actually help to bring about complete freedom—not a momentary alleviation but a total freedom—from this constant battle within myself? Because, it is this battle, this conflict, this incessant uncertainty, that creates outward activities which produce mischief, which produce chaos, which bring about the expression of personal ambition—the desire to be somebody, the aggressive attitude towards life.

I think it is very important to understand whether by the cultivation of any particular attitude or by the development of any particular knowledge or technique, suffering can come to an end? Or can suffering come to an end only with a mind that is not seeking, that does not know, that is not gathering? Most of us have certain attitudes towards life, certain values with which we approach our activities, which create the pattern which we have established, culturally, outwardly or inwardly; and we say, 'I know, I know what to do.' Do we know what we know? And should we not very earnestly endeavour to probe into the question of what we call 'knowledge', whether we can know anything at all, and whether it is fallacious thinking to say, 'I know'? Is it not very important to find out, when a mind says 'I know', what it does know? And will that knowledge at any time, dissipate the conflicting process of the mind which creates such innumerable conflicts within one, so many frustrations, fears?

The problem is: Can knowledge dissipate suffering? We know that technological knowledge at one level can dissipate suffering when the body is ill physically, psychologically. At one level knowledge is essential, is necessary. Knowledge is also necessary when we are concerned with the evil of poverty. We have the technological knowledge to put an end to poverty, to have plenty, to have sufficient clothing and shelter. Scientific knowledge is essential to make life more easy, purely on the physical level. But the knowledge that we accumulate, the knowledge that the mind gathers, in order to be free, in order not to have suffering—the practices, the techniques, the meditations, the various adjustments the mind makes in order not to have conflict—will they bring about the cessation of conflict? You read various books and try to find a method, a way of life, a purpose of life, or you go out to find it from another, and according to that purpose you act; you try to live, but the suffering goes on, the conflict goes on.

The constant adjustment of 'what is' to 'what should be' is the deteriorating factor of struggle. So our life inwardly is full of tears, turmoil and suffering and there must be a way of meeting life not with the accumulated knowledge of experience, but a different way in which this battle is not going on. We know how we meet life, how we meet the challenge always with knowledge, with experience, with the past. That is, I say, 'I know', 'I have accumulated experience', 'Life has taught me', so I always begin with knowledge, with a certain residue of experiences, and with that, I meet my suffering. The suffering is the conflict between 'what is' and 'what should be'. We know the inward nature of suffering—the death of someone, the suffering of poverty, the psychological inward frustration, the insufficiency, the struggle to fulfil and the everlasting pain of fear; and we meet suffering always with knowledge, do we not? So I say, 'I know what to do', 'I believe in reincarnation, in karma, in some experience, in some dogma', and with this, I meet the everyday occurrences of life.

Now, I want to question that knowledge, that thing with which we say we meet life. There is never a sense of complete humility in a mind that says, 'I know.' But there is a complete humility which says, 'I do not know.' And is that not an essential state, an absolute necessity when you meet life, when you meet a problem, when you meet suffering, when you meet death? That sense of humility is not induced, is not cultivated, is not brought about, is not put together. It is the feeling that you do not know.

What do you know? What do you know of death? You see bodies being burnt, relations dying; but what do you know except the things that you have learnt, the beliefs? You do not know what is the unknown. Can the mind which is the result of time, which is the result of accumulation, which is the result of the total past, can such a mind know the unknown, namely 'What is after death'? Hundreds of books have been written about what is after death, but the mind does not know.

So, is it not essential in order to discover anything true, to have that complete sense of humility of not knowing? Then only is there a possibility of knowing. It is only when I do not know what God is, there is God.

But I think I know. I have already tasted the idea of what God is—not God, but the idea of God. I have sought him out, I have suffered; therefore I go to the guru, to the book, to the temple. My mind has already got a glimpse of what is Reality; I know, I have a little experience, I have

41

read, I have tasted. So there is, in essence, vanity, a strange
sense of vanity which is based on knowing. But what I
know is only a memory, an experience—which is a conditioned response an everyday movement of life. So I start
with vanity: 'I know God speaks to me', 'I have knowledge', 'I have visions', and I call that wisdom—which is
absurd. I organize schools of thought, I gather, and there
is never a moment when I can honestly say with complete
humility, with complete integration that 'I do not know.'
Because, I think I know. But what I know is the past accumulation of experience, of memory; and that does not
solve my problem of suffering, nor the problem of how to
act in life with all its confusion, its contradictions, its pulls,
its influences and urges.

Can your mind which is already contaminated by vanity, by knowledge, by experience, can such a mind be completely free? Can it have that feeling of complete humility?
Not to know is humility, is it not? Please follow, please
listen. When you realize that you do not know, then you
are beginning to find out. But the state of not-knowing-
ness cannot be cultivated. The state of not-knowing comes
only with complete humility. Then when such a mind has
a problem, it is not-knowing, and the problem gives the
answer—which means the mind that is giving answers
must completely, totally, inwardly, deeply, profoundly be
without vanity, in a state of complete not-knowing. But
the mind objects strongly to that state. Watch your own
minds, sirs. You will see how extraordinarily difficult it is
for it to face itself and to say, 'I do not know.' The mind objects to that statement because it wants something to lean
on. It wants to say, 'I know the way of life', 'I know what

love is', 'I have suffered', 'I know what it means'—which is really a mind clothed in its own knowledge. Therefore it is never innocent. It is the innocent mind, the mind that says, 'I do not know', which has no vanity, no trimmings; it is such a mind that can find the Real which is the true answer. It is only a mind that says 'I do not know', which receives that which is Truth.

When the mind enquires the way to freedom, the way to Truth, the way of any psychological technique, all that it is concerned with is the accumulation of knowledge by which it hopes to dispel this constant struggle within itself. But that knowledge does not dissolve it. You know that, don't you? From your books, from the experiences of your everyday life, you know sufficiently, but has that prevented you from suffering?

Is it not possible for a mind to be completely in a state of not-knowing, so that it is capable of sensitivity, so that it can receive? Is not the highest form of thinking the completely negative state of the mind in which there is no accumulation, in which therefore there is complete poverty of mind—poverty in the most dignified, profound sense? It is new soil, it is a mind in which there is no knowledge; therefore it is the unknown. It is only then the unknown can come to the unknown. The known can never know the unknown. Sirs, this is not just a statement, but if you listen to it, if you listen to the real meaning of it, you will know the truth of it. But the man of vanity, the man of knowledge, the scholar, the man who is pursuing a result, can never know the unknown; therefore he cannot be a creative being. And at the present time it is the creative being—the man who is creative—that is essential in our daily life, not a man who has a new technique, a new panacea. And there can be no creativeness if there is already a residue of knowledge. The mind must be empty to be creative. It means, the mind must be totally and completely humble. Then only is there a possibility of that creativity to come into being.

Question: In a world that needs collective action, why do you emphasize the freedom of the individual?

Krishnamurti: Is not freedom essential for co-operation? Must you not be free in order to co-operate with me or I with you? And does freedom come into being when you and I have a common purpose? When you and I intellectually, verbally, theoretically establish a common purpose, a common aim, and you and I work together, are we really working together? Does the common end bind us? You think I have a common aim, but when I have a common aim, am I free? I have established an aim, a purpose, because of my knowledge, because of my experience, of my erudition, and I say that is the purpose of man. When I have established it, has that aim not caught me? Am I not a slave to it? Therefore, is there creativeness? To be creative, we have to be free of common purpose.

Is collective action possible, and what do we mean by collective action? There can be no collective action because we are individuals. You and I cannot paint a picture together. There is no collective action, there is only collective thinking, is there not? It is collective thinking that brings us together, to act together. So what is important is not collective action but collective thinking.

Now, can there be collective thinking? And what do we mean by collective thinking? When do we all think alike? When we all are communists, when we are all socialists, Catholics, then all of us are being conditioned to a certain pattern of thought, all of us are acting together. And what happens when there is collective thinking? What happens? Does it not involve concentration camps, liquidation, control of thought, so that you must not think differently from the party, from the whole which the few have established? So collective thinking leads to more misery; collective thinking leads to destruction of people, to cruelty, to barbarity. What is necessary is not collective thinking, but to think rightly—not according to the right, not according to the communist, socialist, but to know how to think, not what to think.

We think that by conditioning the mind to what to think, there would be collective action. But that only destroys human beings, does it not? When we know what to think, has not all creative investigation, the sense of complete freedom come to an end? So our problem is not collective action or collective thinking, but to find out how to think. And this cannot be learnt from a book. The way to think, which is thinking, can only be found in relationship, in self-knowledge. And there cannot be self-knowledge if you have no freedom, if you are afraid you are going to lose a job, if you are afraid of what your wife, your husband, your neighbour says.

So in the process of self-knowledge there comes freedom. It is this freedom that will bring about collective action, not the conditioned mind that is made to act. Therefore there is no collective action in any form of compulsion, coercion, reward, or punishment. It is only when you and I are capable of finding what is Truth through self-knowledge, that there can be freedom; then there is a possibility of real collective action.

There is no collective action when there is common purpose. We all want a happy India, a cultured India, a cultured world; we all say that is our aim; we know that, we repeat it, but are we not throwing it away all the time? We all say there must be brotherhood, there must be peace and love of God; that is our common aim; and are we not destroying each other though we profess we have a common purpose? And when the leftist says there must be collective action through collective thinking, is he not destroying, bringing about misery, war, destruction? So a common purpose, a common idea, the love of God, the love of peace, does not bring us together.

What brings us together is love which comes into being with self-knowledge and freedom. The 'myself' is not a separate unit; I am in relationship with the world; I am the total process. So, in understanding the total process which is the 'me' and which is the 'you', there is freedom. This self-knowledge is not the knowledge of 'me' as a separate entity. The 'me' is a total 'me' of everyone of us, because I am not isolated; there is no such thing; no being can exist in isolation. The 'myself' is the total process of humanity, the 'myself' is 'you', in relation with one another. It is only when I understand that 'myself', there is self-knowledge; then in that self-knowledge there is freedom. Then the world becomes our world—not your world, or a Hindu world, or a Catholic world, or a communist world. It is our world, yours and mine, in which to live happily, creatively. That is not possible if we are conditioned by an idea, if we have a common end for all of us. It is only in freedom which comes with the understanding of the 'me' which is the total process of man, that there is a possibility of collective thought and action.

That is why it is important in a world that is torn apart by religions, by beliefs, by political parties, that this should be very clearly understood by each one of us. Because, there is no salvation in collective action; that way lies more misery, more destruction and more wars; it ends in tyranny. But most of us want some kind of security. The moment the mind seeks security, it is lost. It is only the insecure that are free, but not the respectable, not the man who is secure. Please listen to this. In any enriching of the mind, in any belief, in any system, there is never freedom. And because the mind is secure in some form or pattern of action, because of its bondage, it creates action which produces more misery. It is only the free mind—that is, when you understand the process of the self, the 'me' with all its contents, the mind is free—that can create a new world. Then that is our world; it is a thing we can build together, not create to the pattern of some tyranny, of some god. Then you and I can work; then it is our world to be built, to be nurtured, to be brought into being.

Question: When I see and hear you, I feel myself before an immeasurable sea of stillness. My immediate response to you is reverence and devotion; surely that does not mean that I establish you as my authority. Is it not so?

Krishnamurti: Sir, what do we mean by reverence and devotion? Reverence and devotion surely is not to something. When I am devoted to something, when I reverence somebody, then I create an authority, because that reverence and devotion, unconsciously, deep down, gives me comfort, a certain sense of gratification; therefore I depend upon it. As long as I am devoted to somebody, as long as there is reverence towards something, I am a slave, there is no freedom.

Is reverence, devotion, not capable of existence by itself? That is you reverence a tree, a bird, the child in the street, the beggar, or your servant; the reverence is not to something, it is not to somebody, but it is in yourself, the feeling of respecting. The respect of somebody—is that not based on fear? Is not the feeling of respecting more important and essential than respect to some deity, to some person? If that feeling exists then there is equality. The equality which the politicians, the lawyers, the communists, are trying to establish is not equality, because inequality will always exist when you have a higher capacity, better brains, more gifts than I. But when I have that respect, not to somebody but the respect in itself, then that inherent respect is love, not love of something. When I am conscious that I am revering something outside of me, a person or an image, then there is no love; then there is the division between you whom I revere and me who am lowly.

So devotion and reverence surely are inherent when I begin to understand the whole process of life. Life is not merely the 'me' in action but the life of the animal, the life of nature, the child begging in the street. How often do we look at a tree? Do you ever look at a tree or a flower? And when you do, is there a sense of reverence—not to the flower that is going to fade away, but to the beauty of the flower, to that strange thing that is life? This means really the complete sense of being humble without any sense of begging. Then your mind in itself is still; then you do not have to see somebody who is still. And in that stillness there is no you and I, there is only stillness. And it is in that stillness you will find that there is respect, not in something but in itself. Life is then extraordinarily vital, there is no authority, the mind is completely still.

Question: When I am aware of my thoughts and feelings, they disappear. Later, they catch me unawares and overwhelm me. Can I ever be free from all the thoughts that plague me? Must I always live between depression and elation?

Krishnamurti: Sir, what is the way of thought? What is thinking? I am asking you a question; I am sure you have an answer. Your mind immediately jumps and answers. It does not say, 'I do not know, I am going to find out.' Watch your own mind and you will find an answer to this.

What is thinking, not right thinking and wrong thinking but this whole process of thinking? When do you think? Only when you are challenged. When you are asked a question, you begin to respond according to the background, according to your memory, according to your experience. So thinking is the process of response to a challenge, such as, 'I am unhappy, I want to find a way out', so I begin to enquire. 'I want to find a way out'—that is my problem, that is my question. If I do not find the answer

49

outside, then I begin to enquire within myself. I depend on my experience, on my knowledge, and my knowledge, my experience, always responds—which is, to find a way out. So I start the process of thinking.

Thinking is the response of the past, the response to the past. I do not know the way to your house and you tell me because you know it. I ask you what God is, and you immediately respond, because you have read, your mind is conditioned, and that condition responds. Or if you do not believe in God, you will respond also according to your conditioning. So thinking is a process of verbalization to the reaction of the past.

Now the question is: Can I be aware of the past and thereby put an end to thinking? The moment I think fully, focus fully, there is no thinking. Observation of an idea, of an action—the concentration on something—still implies thinking because you are concentrating, in which there is exclusion. The mind is focussed, concentrated on an idea, writing a letter, in thinking out a problem; in that concentration, there is exclusion. In that, there is a process of thinking, conscious or unconscious.

But when there is total awareness—awareness not of an idea, not the concentration on an idea, but the awareness of the whole problem of thinking—there is no concentration; there is awareness without exclusion. When I begin to enquire how to be rid of a particular thought, what is implied in it?

Please follow this and you will see what I mean by awareness. There is a particular thought that is disturbing you, and you want to get rid of it. And so you proceed to find a way out of resisting that particular thought.

But you want to keep the pleasant thoughts, the pleasant memories, the pleasant ideas. You want to get rid of those thoughts that are painful, and hold on to things which are pleasurable, which are satisfying you, which give you vitality, energy, and drive. So when you want to get rid of one thought, you are at the same time holding on to the things that give you pleasure, memories which are delight-ful, which give you energy; and then what happens? You are concerned not with the total process of thinking, but only how to hold on to the pleasant and how to get rid of the unpleasant. But here we are concerned with the whole, with the total process of thinking—not with how to get rid of a certain thought. If I can understand the whole past and not just how to get rid of a particular past, then there is the freedom of the past, not of a particular past.

But most of us want to hold on to the pleasant and put away the unpleasant. That is a fact. But when we are enquiring into the whole question of the past from which there is thinking, then we cannot look at it from the point of view of the good thought and the bad thought, what is the good past and what is the unpleasant past. Then we are only concerned with the past, not with the good and the bad.

Now, can the mind be free from the past, free from thought—not from the good or bad thought? How do I find out? Can the mind be free from a thought, thought being the past? How do I find out? I can only find out by seeing what the mind is occupied with. If my mind is oc-cupied with the good or occupied with the bad, then it is only concerned with the past, it is occupied with the past. It is not free of the past. So, what is important is to find out how the mind is occupied. If it is occupied at all, it is always occupied with the past, because all our consciousness is the past. The past is not only on the surface, but on the highest level, and the stress on the unconscious is also the past. So can the mind be free from all its occupations? Watch your own minds, sirs, and you will see.

Can the mind be free from occupation? This means—can the mind be completely without being occupied, and let memory, the thoughts good and bad, go by, without choosing? The moment the mind is occupied with one thought, good or bad, then it is concerned with the past. It is just like the mind sitting firmly on the wall watching things go by, never occupied with anything as memory, thought, whether it is good, pleasant or unpleasant—which means, the total freedom of the past, not just the particular past. If you really listen—not just merely verbally, but really, profoundly—then you will see that there is stability which is not of the mind, which is the freedom from the past.

Yet, the past can never be put aside. There is a watching of the past as it goes by, but not occupation with the past. So the mind is free to observe and not to choose. Where there is choice in this movement of the river of memory, there is occupation, and the moment the mind is occupied, it is caught in the past: and when the mind is occupied with the past, it is incapable of seeing something real, true, new, original, uncontaminated.

A mind that is occupied with the past—the past is the whole consciousness that says, 'this is good', 'that is right', 'this is bad', 'this is mine', 'this is not mine'—can never know the Real. But the mind unoccupied can receive that which is not known, which is the unknown. This is not an extraordinary state of some yogi, some saint. Just observe your own mind; how direct and simple it is. See how your mind is occupied. And the answer, with what the mind is occupied, will give you the understanding of the past, and therefore the freedom from the past.

You cannot brush the past aside. It is there. What matters is the occupation of the mind—the mind that is concerned with the past as good or evil, that says, 'I must have this' or 'I must not have this', that has good memory to hold on to and bad memory to let go. The mind that is watching the thing go by, without choice, is the free mind that is free from the past. The past is still floating by; you cannot set it aside; you cannot forget the way to your home. But the occupation of the mind with the past—in that there is no freedom. The occupation creates the past, and the mind is perpetually, everlastingly, occupied with good words, with virtue, with sacrifice, with the search for God, with happiness; such a mind is never free. The past is there; it is a shadow constantly threatening, constantly encouraging and depressing. So, what is important is to find out how the mind is occupied—with what thought, with what memory, with what intention, with what purpose.

Question: Talk to us of meditation.

Krishnamurti: Are you not meditating now? Meditation is when the mind, not knowing, not desiring, not pursuing, is really enquiring, when the mind is really probing, not towards any particular idea, not to any particular image, to any particular compulsion; when the mind is merely seeking—not an answer, not an idea, not to find some-thing. When do you seek? Not when you know the answer, not when you are wanting something, not when you are seeking gratification, not when you want comfort. Then, it is no longer seeking. It is only when the mind, under-standing the whole significance of comfort and of wanting security, puts aside all authority, only when the mind is free, that it is capable of seeking. And is not that the whole process of meditation? Therefore, is not the seeking itself devotion, is not the seeking itself reverence?

So meditation is the stillness of the mind, when it is no longer wanting, vibrating, searching out in order to be satisfied. It is not meditation when it is repeating words, cultivating virtue. A mind which is cultivating virtue, re-peating words, chanting—such a mind is not capable of meditation; it is self-hypnosis, and in self-hypnosis you can create marvellous illusions. But a mind that is capable of real freedom—freedom from the past—is a mind that is not occupied; therefore it is extraordinarily still. Such a mind has no projections; such a mind is in the state of meditation. In that meditation there is no meditator—I am not meditating, I am not experiencing stillness—there is only stillness. The moment I experience stillness, that moment it becomes memory; therefore it is not stillness; it is gone. When a mind is occupied with something that is gone, it is caught in the past.

So in meditation there is no meditator; therefore there is no concentrator who makes an effort to meditate, who sits cross-legged and shuts his eyes to meditate. When the meditator makes an effort to meditate, what he then meditates on is his own projection, his own things clothed in his own ideas. Such a mind cannot meditate; it does not know what meditation means.

But the man who understands the occupation of his mind, the man who has no choice in his occupation, such a man will know what is stillness—the stillness that comes from the very beginning, the freedom. Freedom is not at the end; it is at the very beginning. You cannot train a mind to be free. It has to be free from the very beginning. And in that freedom the mind is still, because it has no choice; it is not concentrating, it is not absorbed in anything. And in that stillness, that which is unknown is concentrating.

First Talk in London
9 April 1953

Again this evening I would like to talk over with you the question of renewal, of being reborn—not in an afterlife, a next life, but whether it is possible to bring about the complete regeneration of consciousness, a rebirth, not a continuity but a complete revolution. It seems to me that is one of the most important questions to go into and to consider—if it is possible for the mind which is the only instrument we have of perception, of understanding, of investigation, of discovery, to be made completely new. And if we can discover it, if we do not merely listen to words but actually experience that state of renewal, of complete regeneration, something new—then it may be possible to live the ordinary life of everyday routine, of trials, fears, mistakes, and yet bring to these mistakes and fears a quite different significance, a different meaning. So it may be worthwhile this evening to talk over this question—whether there can be a complete transformation of the unconscious. In understanding that, we may be able to find out what is the true function of the mind.

Now as I talk, perhaps it would be worthwhile if you would not merely listen to the words, but actually experience the significance of the words by observing your own minds, not only following what I am saying but watching the operation of your own mind as it is functioning when you listen. Because, I think, if we can go into this question we may find the key to this creativeness, to this complete state in which the unknown, the unknowable, can come into being.

What we now know of life is a series of struggles, of adjustments, of limitations, of continual compulsions; that is our life. And in that process there is no renewal; there is nothing new taking place. Occasionally there is a hint from the unconscious; but that hint is translated by the conscious mind and made to conform to the pattern of our everyday convenience. What we do know is struggle, a constant effort to achieve a result. And will strife, struggle, the conflict between the thesis and the antithesis, hoping to find a synthesis—will that struggle bring about this quality of something new, original, clear, uncorrupt?

Our life is a routine, a wasting away, a death—the death of continuity, not the death that brings a new state. We know this; this is our life; conscious or unconscious. And it is possible for this mechanical mind, the mind that is the result of time, that is made up of experience, memory, and knowledge—which are all a form of continuity, the mechanism of the known—is it possible for such a mind completely to renew itself and become innocent, uncorrupted? Can the mind, my mind and your mind, which is caught in various habits, passions, demands, urges, which is forever following a series of convenient pleasant habits, or struggling to break down habits that are not pleasant—can such a mind put aside its activities and be the unknown?

Because, it seems to me, that is one of the major problems of our existence— how to be able to die to everything of the past? Can that take place? Can the mind die to all the past, the memory, the longings, the various conditionings, the fears, the respectabilities? If not, there is no hope, is there? Because then, all that we know is the continuity of the things that have been, which we are continually establishing in the mind, in consciousness. The mind is constantly giving birth, through memory, through experience, through knowledge, to a state of continuity. That is all I know. I want to continue, either through property, through family, or through ideas; I want this continuity to go on. And can the mind which is seeking security, seeking permanency either in pleasure or in strife, or trying to go beyond its own fears and so establish a state of permanency, which is the reaction of its own desire for continuity—can such a mind come to an end?

Because, what continues can never renew, can never give birth to something new. And yet, deep down in all of us there is the desire to live, to continue, to be as we are, only modified, better, more noble, having greater significance in life through our actions, our relationships. So the function of the mind, as we know it, is to give birth to continuity, to bring about a state in which time plays a very extraordinarily important part as a means of becoming. And so we are constantly making an endeavour, struggling, striving to maintain this continuity. And that continuity is the 'me', the 'I', the ego. That is the function of our mind up to now; that is all we know.

Now, can such a mind which is so embedded in time put an end to itself, and be in that state in which the unknown is? The mind is mechanical, because memory is mechanical, experience is mechanical, and knowledge, though it may be stimulating, is still mechanical, and the background of the mind is of time; can such a mind cease to think in terms of time, in terms of becoming, in terms of the 'me'? The 'me' is the idea, the idea being memory, the experience, the struggle, the fears. Can that mind come to an end, without desiring to come to an end?

When the mind desires to arrive at an end, it can intellectually come to that state; it can hypnotize itself to that state. The mind is capable of any form of illusion, but in that illusion there is no renewal.

So the problem is: Knowing the function of the mind as it is, can such a mind renew itself? Or, is such a mind incapable of seeing the new, or receiving the new, the unknown, and therefore all that it can do is to be completely silent? And it seems to me that is all that it can do. Can the mind, which is so restless, discursive, wandering all over the place, gathering, rejecting—please follow your own mind—can such a mind immediately come to an end and be silent?

Because, in that silence there is the renewal, the renewal that is not comprehensible by the mind of time. But when the mind is silent, freed from time, it is altogether a different mind in which there is no continuity of experience, because there is no entity that is accumulating. In that silence, in that state, there is creativity, the creativity of God or Truth. That creativity is not continuous, as we know it. But our mind, the mind that is mechanical, can only think in terms of continuity and therefore it asks of Truth, of God, that it should be continuous, constant, permanent.

But the mechanical mind, the ordinary mind, the mind that we use every day, cannot experience the other; such a mind can never renew itself; such a mind can never know the unknowable.

But if the mind that is the continuous mind—the mind of time, the mind that functions in memory, in knowledge, in experience—if such a mind can come to that silence, that extraordinary stillness, then in that there is the creativity of Truth. That Truth is not for all time; it is only from moment to moment, for in it there is no sense of accumulation.

And so creativeness is something which is never, in terms of the ordinary mind, continuous. It is always there; but even to say 'it is always there' is not true. Because the idea that it is always there gives it a permanency. But a mind that can be silent will know that state which is eternally creative. And that is the function of the mind, is it not? The function of the mind is not merely the mechanical side of it, not merely how to put things together, how to struggle, how to break down and again be put together. All that is the everyday mind; the plain mind, where there are hints from the unconscious but where the whole process of consciousness is in the net of time—the mind that is constantly reacting, which it should; otherwise we are dead entities. We cannot dispense with such a mind. Such a mind is born of technique, and the more you pursue technique—the 'how', the method, the system—the less there is of the other, the creative. Yet we have to have technique; we must know how to do things. But when that mechanical mind—the mind of memory, experience, knowledge—exists by itself and functions by itself, irrespective of the other, it obviously must lead to destruction. For, intellectuality, without that creativeness of Reality, has no meaning; it only leads to war, to further misery, to further suffering. And so, is it possible for that creative state to be, while at the same time, the mechanical, technical mind is yet going on? Does the one exclude the other?

There is only exclusion of the Real, surely, when the intellect which is the mechanical becomes all-important; when ideas, beliefs, dogmas, theories, the inventions of the intellect, become all-important. But when the mind is silent, and that creative Reality comes into being, then the ordinary mind has quite a different meaning; then the ordinary mind also is in continuous revolt against technique, the 'how'; then such a mind will never ask for the 'how'; then it is not concerned with virtue, because Truth is beyond virtue. The silent mind, the mind that is utterly still, knowing, being the unknown, that creativity of the Real, does not need virtue. For, in that, there is no struggle. It is only the mind that is struggling to become which needs virtue.

So, as long as we give emphasis to the intellect, to the mind of knowledge, of information, of experience and memory, the other is not. One may occasionally catch glimpses of the other; but that glimpse is immediately translated in terms of time, of demanding further experience, and so strengthening memory. But if, seeing all this— this whole process of consciousness—the mind naturally is no longer caught in the net of beliefs, ideas, then there is a stillness, a silence, an unpremeditated silence; not a silence that is put together by will, by resistance. Then in that silence there is that creative Reality which cannot be measured, which cannot be made as an end to be got hold of by the mechanical mind. In that state there is happiness of a kind the mechanical mind can never understand.

This is not mysticism, a thing from the East. But, on the contrary, this is a human thing, wherever one is and whatever the clime. If one can really observe this whole process of consciousness, the function of the mind as we know it, then, without any struggle, that extraordinary stillness of the mind comes into being. And in that there is creative reality.

Many questions have been sent in. And I hope those who have sent them will forgive if all are not answered; there are too many of them. But each evening we have tried to answer the representative ones. And if your particular question is not answered, perhaps in listening to the other questions which have been answered you may solve or understand your own problem.

As I said, it is very important to know how to listen, to listen to everything—not only to me, which is not very greatly important. But if one knows how to listen, then there is no authority, then there is no imitation. For in that listening there is great freedom. The moment I am incapable of listening, then I create resistance, and to break down that resistance I need further authorities, further compulsions. But if one knows how to listen without interpretation, without judgement, without twisting, without always bringing to it one's reactions, the reactions of one's conditioning, if one can put aside all that and listen to everything, listen to one's wife, one's children, one's neighbour, to the ugly newspapers, to all the things that are taking place about us—then everything has an extraordinary significance, everything is a revelation.

We are so caught up in our own judgements, in our own prejudices, in what we want to know; but if one can listen, it reveals a great deal. If we can really quietly listen to everything that is happening in our consciousness, to our own impulses, the various passions, the envies, the fears, then that silence of which I spoke earlier comes into being.

Question: How is collective action possible when there are so many divergent individual interests?

Krishnamurti: What do we mean by collective action? Let us take that up first, and then see if we have fundamentally divergent interests which come into conflict with the collective action.

What do we mean by collective action? All of us doing something together, creatively doing things together, building a bridge together, painting together, writing a poem together, or cultivating the farm together? Collective action, surely, is only possible when there is collective thinking. We do not mean collective action; we mean collective thinking, which will naturally produce an action in which we all conform.

Now, is collective thinking possible? That is what we all want. All the governments, all the religions, organized philosophies, beliefs, all of them want collective thought. We must all be Christians, or communists, or Hindus; then the world will be perfect. Now, is collective thinking possible? I know it is made possible now through education, through social order, through economic compulsion, through various forms of disciplines, nationalism, and so on; collective thinking is made possible, in which you are all English or Germans or Russians or what you will. Through propaganda, through education, through religion, there are various elastic frames in which we all think alike. And because we are individuals with our peculiar idiosyncrasies, with our peculiar drives and urges and ambitions, the framework is made more and more solid, so that we do not wander away from it; and if we do, we are liquidated, we are excommunicated, we are thrown out of the party—which means losing the job.

So we are all held together, whether we like it or not, by the framework of an ideology. And the more that work becomes solid, firm, the more we are happy, relieved, because responsibility is taken away from us. So every government, every society, wants to make us all think alike. And we also want to think alike, because we feel secure in thinking alike, don't we?, we feel safe. We are always afraid lest we do not create the right impression, afraid of what people will say about us, because we all want to be respectable.

And so collective thinking becomes possible. And out of it, when there is a crisis, we all come together, as in wars, or when we all are threatened religiously, politically, or in any other way.

Now, is such a conditioning of the individual creative? Though we may yield to this conditioning, we are inwardly never happy, there is always a resistance because in that yielding to the collective, there is no freedom; the freedom of the individual becomes merely verbal. And the individual, because he is so held by conventions, by tradition, is always expressing himself, wanting to fulfil himself through ambition. So society again curbs him, and there is a conflict between the individual and society, an everlasting war.

And is it not possible to have one vocation for all of us, not divergent aptitudes, divergent interests, but one true interest for all of us, which is the understanding of what is true, what is real? That is the true vocation, surely, of all of us—not that you become an engineer or a sailor, or a soldier, or a lawyer—the true vocation, surely, of each one of us, is to find that Reality. Because, we are human beings, suffering, enquiring; and if we can have that true vocation, by right education from the very beginning, through freedom and so on, if we can find that Reality, then we shall in freedom co-operate together, and not have collective thought everlastingly conditioning us and making us act together. If we as human beings can find that Reality, then only is true creative action possible.

Question: How can our poor faulty human love become incorruptible?

Krishnamurti: Can that which is corruptible become non-corruptible? Can that which is ugly become beautiful? Can the stupid become very intelligent? Can I, who become aware that I am stupid, struggle to become intelligent? Is not the very struggle to become intelligent, stupid? Because, fundamentally I am stupid, though I may learn all the clever tricks; still, in essence, I am stupid. Similarly, if my love is corruptible, I want to make it pure, incorruptible. I do not think it is possible. The very becoming is a form of corruption. All that I can do is to be aware of the whole implication of this love, with its envies, jealousies, anxieties, fears, its bondage, its dependence. We know that; we know what we mean when we say we love, the enormous background that lies behind that word. And we want the whole of that background to become incorruptible—which means, again, the mind making something out of love, trying to give the timeless a quality of time. Is that possible?

Please, see this. Because the mind knows the pain of love, the anxiety, the uncertainty, the separation, the fear, the death, it says it must change it, it wants to make love into something that cannot be corrupted. Does not the very desire to change it make love into something which is of the mind, which is sensation? The mind cannot make something which is already corrupt into something noble; and that is what we are always trying to do, are we not? I am envious, and I want to be non-envious; and so I struggle, because the mind feels the suffering of envy, and wants to transform it. I am violent, and it is painful; so the mind wants to transform violence into non-violence—which is still within the field of time. And so there is never a freedom from violence, from envy, from the decay of love. As long as the mind makes of love something which is of time, there must always be corruption.

Then, is human love not possible? One will find that out if one really understands the significance of how the mind corrupts love. It is the mind that destroys. Love is not corrupt. But the mind that feels that it is not being loved, that feels isolated, that is conditioned, it is that mind which destroys love. We love with our minds, not with our hearts. One has to find out what this means. One has to enquire, to go into it, not just repeat the words.

But one cannot comprehend it without understanding the whole significance of the function of the mind. One must come to understand the whole consciousness of the 'me' that is so afraid of not being loved, or, having love, is so anxious to hold the love that depends on another for its sustenance; that is all part of that mind. The 'me' that says 'I must love God, Truth', and so creates the symbol, and goes to church every day, or once a week, or whenever you will, is still a part of the mind. Whatever the mind touches, with its mechanical memory, experience and knowledge, it corrupts.

So it is very important, when we are faced with a problem of such a kind, to find out how to deal with it. One can only deal with it and bring about that quality which is incorruptible when the mind, knowing its function, comes to an end. Then only, surely, is love incorruptible.

Question: Are there not as many ways to Reality or God as there are individuals? And is not yoga or discipline one of the ways?

Krishnamurti: Is there a path to the unknowable? There is always a path to the known, but not to the unknown. If we really saw that once, felt it in our hearts and minds, really saw the truth of it, then all the heavens that religions promise, and our own desire to find a path through which Reality can be found, would be broken down.

If Reality is the known—as you know your way home, to your house—then it is very simple; you can make a path to it. Then you can have a discipline, then you can bind yourself to it with various forms of yogas, disciplines, beliefs, so as not to wander away. But is Reality something known? And if it is known, is it the real? Surely, Reality is something from moment to moment, which can only be found in the silence of the mind. So there is no path to Truth, in spite of all the philosophies, because Reality is the unknowable, unnameable, unthinkable. What you can think about Truth is the outcome of your background, of your tradition, of your knowledge. But Truth is not knowledge, is not of memory, is not of experience. If the mind can create a God, as it does, surely it is not God, is it?, it is merely a word. The mind can only think in words, in symbols, in images. And what the mind creates is not the Real.

The word is all we know. And to have faith in that God which the mind has created obviously gives us certain strength. That is all we know. We have read, we have been conditioned as Christians, or Buddhists, as communists, or what you will—and that conditioning is all we know. There is a path always to the known, but not to the unknown. And can any discipline lead us to that—discipline being resistance, suppression, sublimation, substitution? We want to find a substitute for the real. Because we do not know how to allow the Real to come into being, we think it will come through control, through virtue. So we cultivate virtue, which is again the mechanical habit of the mind, and thus make of virtue something which gives, not freedom by respectability, a safeguarding from fear.

When we use discipline there is no understanding. Surely, a mind that is disciplined, controlled, shaped, can never be a free mind—free to enquire, to find out, to be silent. Because, all that it has learned is to strengthen the process of thought, which is the reaction of memory, reaction according to a conditioned demand, hoping thereby it will achieve some happiness, which it calls Truth.

So, can we not see all this, how consciousness, the mind, operates; how the 'me' is everlastingly seeking, gathering, accumulating, in order to be secure, and projecting heaven, or God, which is its own creation, which is the urge to be safe, to be singularistic? Such a mind obviously cannot come upon truth. A mind that is suppressed, that has never looked within itself, that is always fearful of what it may find within itself, and so always escaping, running away from 'what is', such a mind obviously can never find the unknown.

For the unknown comes into being only when the mind is no longer searching, no longer asking, petitioning. Then the mind, fully comprehending the whole process of itself, naturally comes to that silence in which there is creative Reality.

First Talk in Ojai
4 July 1953

I think it is particularly important to understand the question of what is knowledge. Most of us seem so eager for knowledge; we are always acquiring, not only property, things, but also ideas. We go from one teacher to another, from one book, from one religion, from one dogma to another. We are always acquiring ideas, and this acquisition we think is important in the understanding of life. So I would like, if I may, to go into the problem and see whether this additive process of the mind does bring about freedom, and whether knowledge can solve any human problem. Knowledge may solve superficial, mechanical problems, but does it free the mind fundamentally so that it is capable of directly perceiving what is true? Surely, it is very important to understand this question, because in understanding it perhaps we shall revolt against mere methodology, which is a hindrance except in achieving some mechanical result. I am talking about the psychological process of the mind, and whether it is possible to bring about individual creativeness—which is naturally of the greatest importance, is it not? Does the acquisition of knowledge, as we conceive it, bring about creativeness? Or, to be capable of that state which is creative, must the mind be free from the whole additive process?

Most of us read books, or go to talks, in order to understand; when we have a problem, we study, or we go to somebody to discuss it, hoping thereby that our problem will be solved, or that we will see something new. We are always looking to others, or to experience, which is essentially knowledge, in the hope of resolving the many problems that confront us. We turn to the interpreters, those who say they understand a little more—the interpreters, not only of these talks, but also of the various sacred books. We seem to be incapable of tackling the problem directly for ourselves without relying on anyone. And is it not important to find out whether the mind, in its process of accumulation, is ever able to resolve any psychological, spiritual problem? Must not the mind be totally unoccupied if it is to be capable of perceiving the truth of any human conflict?

I hope you will have the patience to go into this problem, not merely as I describe it, but as each one of us is involved in it. After all, why are you here? Obviously, some are merely curious, so we won't concern ourselves with those. But others must be very serious; and if you are serious, what is the intention behind that seriousness? Is it to understand what I am saying—and, not understanding, to turn to another to explain what has been said, thereby bringing about the process of exploitation? Or, are you listening to find out if what I say is true self, not because I say it, or because someone else explains it? Surely, the problems which we discuss here are your problems, and if you can see and understand them directly for yourself, you will resolve them.

We all have many problems and there must obviously be a change, but is change brought about by the process of the mind? I am talking of fundamental change, not of mere sociological or economic reform. Surely, it is the mind that has created our problems, and can the mind resolve the problems it has created? Does the resolution of these problems lie in acquiring more knowledge, more information, in learning new techniques, new methods, new systems of meditation, in going from one teacher to another? All that is clearly very superficial, and is it not important to find out what makes the mind superficial, what brings about superficiality? With most of us, that is the problem, is it not? We are very superficial, we do not know how to go deeply into our conflicts and difficulties, and the more we turn to books, to methods, to practices, to the acquisition of knowledge, the more superficial we become. That is an obvious fact. One may read innumerable books, attend highly intellectual talks, gather vast stores of information; but if one does not know how to delve within oneself and discover the truth, understand the whole process of the mind, surely all one's efforts will only lead to greater superficiality.

So, is it possible for you, while listening, not merely to remain at the superficial, verbal level, but to uncover the process of your own thinking and go beyond the mind? What I am saying is not very complicated. I am only describing that which is taking place within each one of us, but if you live at the verbal level and are satisfied with the description without directly experiencing, then these talks will be utterly useless. Then you will turn to the interpreters, to those who offer to tell you what I am talking about—which is so utterly silly. It is much better to listen directly to something than to turn to someone else to tell you what it is all about. Cannot one go to the source without interpretation, without being guided to discover what the source is? If one is guided to discover, it is no longer discovery, is it?

Please see this point. To discover what is true, what is real, no guidance is necessary. When you are guided to discover, it is not discovery: you merely see what someone has pointed out to you. But if you discover for yourself, then there is quite a different experience which is original, unburdened by the past, by time, by memory, utterly free of tradition, dogma, belief. It is that discovery which is creative, totally new; but to come to that discovery, the mind must be capable of penetrating beyond all the layers of superficiality. And can we do it? Because all our problems—political, social, economic, personal—are essentially religious problems; they are reflections of the inward, moral problem, and unless we solve that central problem, all other problems will multiply. That problem cannot be resolved by following anybody, by reading any book, by practising any technique, In the discovery of Reality, methods and systems are utterly valueless, because you have to discover for yourself. Discovery implies complete aloneness, and the mind cannot be alone if it is living on explanations, on words, if it is practising a method or depending on someone else's translation of the problem.

So, realizing that from childhood our education, our religious training, our social environment, have all helped to make us utterly superficial, can the mind put aside its superficiality, this constant process of acquisition, negative or positive—can it put all that aside and be, not blank, but unoccupied, creatively empty, so that it is no longer creating its own problems and seeking the resolution of what it has created? Surely, it is because we are superficial that we do not know how to go very deeply, how to reach great depths within ourselves, and we think we can reach great depths by learning or by listening to talks.

Now, what is it that makes the mind superficial? Please don't merely listen to me, but observe, be aware of your own thinking when a question of that kind is put to you. What makes the mind superficial? Why cannot the mind experience something that is true, beyond its own projections? Is it not primarily the gratification which each one of us is seeking that makes the mind superficial? We want at any price to be gratified, to find satisfaction, so we seek methods to achieve that end. And is there such a thing as satisfaction, ever? Though we may be temporarily satisfied, and change the object of our satisfaction depending on our age, is there satisfaction at any time? Desire is constantly seeking to fulfil itself, so we go from one satisfaction to another, and getting caught in each new satisfaction, with all its complications, we again become dissatisfied and try to disentangle ourselves. We cling to persons, pursue teachers, join groups, read books, take up one philosophy after another, but the central desire is always the same—to be satisfied, to be secure, to become somebody, to achieve a result, to gain an end. Is not that whole process one of the primary causes of the mind's superficiality?

And is not the mind superficial because we think in terms of acquisition? The mind is constantly occupied with acquiring, or with putting aside, denuding itself of what it has acquired. There is tension between acquisition and denudation, and we live in that tension; and does not that tension contribute to shallowness of mind?

Another factor which brings about shallowness is the mind's ceaseless occupation with its own troubles, or with some philosophy, or with God, ideas, beliefs, or with what it should do or should not do. As long as the mind is absorbed, concerned, taken up with something, is it not superficial? Surely, only the unoccupied mind, the mind that is totally free, not caught in any problem, that is not concerned with itself, with its achievements, with its pains, with its joys and sorrows, with its own perfection—only such a mind ceases to be shallow. And cannot the mind live from day to day, doing the things it has to do, without this preoccupation?

For most of us, with what is the mind occupied? When you observe your own mind, when you are aware of it, what is it concerned with? With how to make itself more perfect, how to be healthy, how to get a better job, whether it is loved or not loved, whether it is making progress, how to get out of one problem without falling into another—it is concerned with itself, is it not? In different ways it is everlastingly identifying itself with the greatest, or with the most humble. And can a mind occupied with itself ever be profound? Is it not one of our difficulties, perhaps the major difficulty, that our minds have become so extraordinarily shallow? If any difficulty arises, we rush to somebody to help us; we have not the capacity to penetrate, to find out: we are not investigators into ourselves. And can the mind investigate, be aware of itself, if it is occupied with any problem? The problems which we create in our superficiality demand, not superficial responses, but the understanding of what is true; and cannot the mind, being aware of the causes of superficiality in itself, understand them without struggling against them, without trying to put them aside? Because the moment we struggle, that in itself becomes another problem, another occupation which merely increases the superficiality of the mind.

Let me put it this way: If I realize that my mind is superficial, what am I to do? I realize its superficiality through observation. I see how I turn to books, to leaders, to authority in various forms, to Masters, or to some yogi—you know the many different ways in which we seek to be satisfied. I realize all that. Now, is it not possible to put all that aside without effort, without being occupied with it, without saying, 'I must put it aside in order to go deeper, be more thoughtful'? This concern to become something more—is it not the constant occupation of the mind, and a primary cause of superficiality? That is what we all want—to understand more, to have more property, to have better brains, to play a better game, to look more beautiful, to be more virtuous—always the more, the more, the more. And as long as the mind is occupied with the 'more', can it ever understand 'what is'?

Please listen to this. When the mind is pursuing the 'more', the 'better', it is incapable of understanding itself as it is; because it is always thinking of acquiring more, of going further, achieving greater results, it cannot understand its actual state. But when the mind perceives what it actually is without comparison or judgement, then there is a possibility of being deep, of going beyond. As long as

one is concerned with the more at any level of consciousness, there must be superficiality; and a superficial mind
can never find what is Real, it can never know Truth, God.
It can concentrate on the image of God; it can imagine,
speculate and throw up hopes, but that is not Reality. So
what is needed, surely, is not a new technique, a new social
or religious group, but individuals who are capable of going beyond the superficial; and one cannot go beyond the
superficial if the mind is occupied with the 'more' or with
the 'less'. If the mind is concerned with having more property or less property, if property is its occupation, then obviously it is a very superficial, silly mind; and the mind that
is occupied with becoming more virtuous is equally silly,
because it is concerned with itself and its acquisitions.

So the mind is the result of time, which is the process of the 'more'; and cannot the mind be aware of this
process and be what it is without trying to change itself?
Surely, transformation is not brought about by the mind.
Transformation comes into being when the Truth is seen;
and Truth is not the 'more'. Transformation, which is the
only real revolution, is in the hands of Reality, not within
the sphere of the mind.

Is it not important, then, for each one of us, not merely
to listen to these talks, but to be aware of ourselves and
remain in that state of awareness without looking to interpreters or leaders, and without desiring something more?
In that state of awareness, in which there is no choice, no
condemnation or judgement, you will see what is taking
place, you will know the process of the mind as it actually
is, and when the mind is thus aware of itself, it becomes
quiet, it is unoccupied, still. It is only in that stillness that

there is a possibility of seeing what is true, which brings
about a radical transformation.

*Question: Why is it that in this country we seem to feel so little
respect for anybody?*

Krishnamurti: I wonder in what country one feels respect
for another? In India they salute most profoundly, they
give you garlands, flowers—and ill-treat the neighbours,
the servants, the animals. Is that respect? Here, as in
Europe, there is respect for the man with an expensive car
and a big house; there is respect for those who are considered superior, and contempt for others. But is that the
problem? We all want to feel equal to the highest, do we
not? We want to be on a par with the famous, the wealthy,
the powerful. The more a civilization is industrialized the
more there is the idea that the poor can become the rich,
that the man living in a cabin can become the president,
so naturally there is no respect for anyone; and I think if
we can understand the problem of equality we may then
be able to understand the nature of respect.

Now, is there equality? Though the various governments, whether of the left or of the right, emphasize that
we are all equal, are we equal? You have better brains,
greater capacity, you are more gifted than I; you can paint,
and I cannot; you can invent, and I am only a labourer.
Can there ever be equality? There may be equality of op-
portunity, you and I may both be able to buy a car; but
is that equality? Surely, the problem is not how to bring
about equality economically, but to find out whether the
mind can be free from this sense of the superior and the

inferior, from the worship of the man who has much, and the contempt for the man who has little. I think that is the problem. We look up to those who can help us, who can give us something, and we look down on those who cannot. We respect the boss, the man who can give us a better position, a political job, or the priest, who is another kind of boss in the so-called spiritual world. So we are always looking up and looking down; and cannot the mind be free from this state of contempt and false respect?

Just watch your own mind, your own words, and you will discover that there is no respect as long as there is this feeling of superiority and inferiority. And do what the government may to equalize us, there can never be equality, because we all have different capacities, different aptitudes; but what there can be is quite a different feeling, which is perhaps a feeling of love, in which there is no contempt, no judgement, no sense of the superior and the inferior, the giver and the taker. Please, these are not mere words; I am not describing a state to be desired, and being desired gives rise to the problem, 'How am I to get there?'—which again only leads to superficial attitudes. But when once you perceive your own attitude and are aware of the activities of your own mind, then perhaps a different feeling, a sense of affection comes into being; and is it not that which is important?

What matters is not why some people have respect and others do not, but to awaken that feeling, that affection, that love, or what name you will, in which this sense of the high and the low will totally cease. And that is not a utopia; it is not a state to be striven after, something to be practised day after day until you ultimately arrive. I think it is important merely to listen to it, to be aware of it as you would see a beautiful picture, or a lovely tree, or hear the song of a bird; and if one listens truly, the very listening, the very perception does something radical. But the moment the mind interferes, bringing in its innumerable problems, then the conflict arises between 'what should be' and 'what is'; then we introduce ideals and the imitation of those ideals, so we never discover for ourselves that state in which there is no desire to be more and therefore no contempt. As long as you and I are seeking fulfilment, there is no respect, there is no love. As long as the mind wants to fulfil itself in something, there is ambition; and it is because most of us are ambitious in different directions, at different levels, that this feeling, not of equality, but of affection, of love, is impossible.

I am not talking of something superhuman, but I think if one can really understand ambition, the desire to become more, to fulfil, to achieve, to shine, if one can live with it, know for oneself all its implications, look at it as one would look at oneself in a mirror, just to see what one is without condemnation—if one can do that, which is the beginning of self-knowledge, of wisdom, then there is a possibility of this affection coming into being.

Question: Is fear a separate, identifiable quality of the mind, or is it the mind itself? Can it be discarded by the mind, or does it come to an end only when the mind ceases altogether? If this question is confusing, can it be asked differently: is fear always an evil to be overcome, and is it never a necessary blessing in disguise?

Krishnamurti: The question has been asked, and let us try to find out, you and I together, what fear is and whether it is possible to eradicate it. Or, as the questioner suggests, it may be a blessing in disguise. We are going to find out the truth of the matter, but to do that, though I may be talking, you must investigate your own fears and see how fear arises.

We have different kinds of fear, have we not? Fear exists at different levels of our being; there is the fear of the past, fear of the future, and fear of the present, which is the very anxiety of living. Now, what is this fear? Is it not of the mind, of thought? I think of the future, of old age, of poverty, of disease, of death, and of that picture I am afraid. Thought projects a picture which awakens anxiety in the mind, so thought creates its own fear, does it not? I have done something foolish, and I don't want my attention called to it, I want to avoid it, I am afraid of the consequences. This is again a thought process, is it not? I want to recapture the happiness of youth; or perhaps I saw something yesterday in the mountain sunlight which has now escaped me, and I want to experience that beauty again; or I want to be loved, I want to fulfil, I want to achieve, I want to become somebody; so there is anxiety, there is fear. Thought is desire, memory, and its responses to all this bring about fear, do they not? Being afraid of tomorrow, of death, of the unknown, we begin to invent theories, that we shall be reborn, that we shall be made perfect through evolution, and in these theories the mind takes shelter. Because we are everlastingly seeking security, we build churches around our hopes, our beliefs and dogmas, for which we are prepared to fight, and all this is

81

still the process of thinking, is it not? And if we cannot resolve our fear, our psychological block, we turn for help to somebody else.

As long as I am thinking in terms of achieving, fulfilling, of not becoming, of dying, I am always caught in fear, am I not? The process of thinking as we know it, with its self-enclosing desire to be successful, not to be lonely, empty—that very process is the seat of fear. And can the mind which is occupied with itself, which is the product of its own fears, ever resolve fear?

Suppose one is afraid, and one knows the various causes that have brought about fear. Can that same mind, which has produced fear, put aside fear by its own effort? As long as the mind is occupied with fear, with how to get rid of it, with what to do and what not to do in order to surmount it, can it ever be free from fear? Surely, the mind can be free from fear only when it is not occupied with fear—which does not mean running away from fear, or trying to ignore it. First, one must be fully aware that one is afraid. Most of us are not fully aware, we are only vaguely aware of fear, and if we do come face to face with it, we are horrified; we run away from it and throw ourselves into various activities which only lead to further mischief.

Because the mind itself is the product of fear, whatever the mind does to put away fear only increases it further. So, can one just be aware of one's fear without being occupied with it, without judging or trying to alter it? To be aware of fear without condemnation does not mean accepting it, taking it to your heart. To be aware of fear without choice is just to look at it, to know there is fear and to see the truth of it; and seeing the truth of fear dissolves fear. The mind cannot dissolve fear by any action of its own; in the face of fear it must be very quiet, it must know and not act. Please listen to this. One must know that one is afraid, be fully conscious of it, without any reaction, without any desire to alter it. The alteration, the transformation, cannot be brought about by the mind; it comes into being only with the perception of truth, and the mind cannot perceive what is true if it is concerned with fear, if it condemns or desires to be rid of it. Any action of the mind with regard to fear only increases fear, or helps the mind to run away from it. There is freedom from fear only when the mind, being fully aware of its own fears, is not active towards them. Then quite a different state comes into being which the mind cannot possibly conceive or invent. That is why it is so important to understand the process of the mind, not according to some philosopher, analyst, or religious teacher, but as it is actually going on in yourself from moment to moment in all your relationships—when you are quiet, when you are walking, when you are listening to somebody, when you are turning on the radio, reading a book, or talking at table. To be fully aware of oneself without choice is to keep the mind astonishingly alert, and in that awareness there is self-knowledge, the beginning of wisdom. The mind that struggles against fear, that analyses fear, will never resolve fear, but when there is passive awareness of fear, a different state comes into being in which fear does not exist.

First Talk in Amsterdam
26 May 1955

Perhaps you would kindly listen to rather a difficult problem with which I am sure most of us are concerned. It is a problem we are all confronted with—the problem of change—and I feel one must go into it rather fully to understand it comprehensively. We see that there must be change. And we see that change implies various forms of exertion of will, effort. In it is also involved the question of what it is we are changing from and what it is we want to change to. It seems to me that one must go into it rather deeply and not merely be contented with a superficial answer. Because the thing that is involved in it is quite significant, and requires a certain form of attention, which I hope you will give.

For most of us it is very important to change; we feel it is necessary for us to change. We are dissatisfied as we are—at least, most of the people are who are at all serious and thoughtful—and we want to change; we see the necessity of change. But I do not think we see the whole significance of it, and I would like to discuss that matter with you. If I may suggest it, please listen, not with any definite conclusion, not expecting a definite answer, but so that by going into the matter together, we may understand the problem comprehensively.

Every form of effort that we make in order to bring about a change implies, does it not?, the following of a certain pattern, a certain ideal, the exertion of will, a desire to be achieved. We change, either through circumstances, forced by environment, through necessity, or we discipline ourselves to change according to an ideal. Those are the forms of change that we are aware of—either through circumstances, which compel us to modify, to adjust, to conform to a certain pattern, social, religious, or family, or we discipline ourselves according to an ideal. In that discipline there is a conformity, the effort to conform to a certain pattern of thought, to achieve a certain ideal.

The change that is brought about through the exertion of will—with this process we are, most of us, familiar. We all know of this change through compulsion, change through fear, change made necessary by suffering. It is a modification, a constant struggle in order to conform to a certain pattern which we have established for ourselves, or which society has given us. That is what we call 'change', and in that we are caught. But, is it change? I think it important to understand this, to somewhat analyse it, to go into the anatomy of change, to understand what makes us want to change. Because all this implies, does it not?, either conscious or unconscious conformity, conscious or unconscious yielding to a certain pattern, through necessity, through expediency. And we are content to continue in modified change, which is merely an outward adjustment—putting on, as it were, a new coat of a different colour, but inwardly remaining static. So I would like to talk it over, to find out if that effort really brings about a real change in us.

Our problem is how to bring about an inward revolution which does not necessitate mere conformity to a pattern, or an adjustment through fear, or making great effort, through the exertion of the will, to be something. That is our problem, isn't it? We all want to change, we see the necessity of it, unless we are totally blind and completely conservative, refusing to break the pattern of our existence. Surely, most of us who are at all serious are concerned with this—how to bring about in ourselves and thereby in the world a radical change, a radical transformation. After all, we are not any different from the rest of the world. Our problem is the world problem. What we are, of that we make the world. So, if as individuals we can understand this question of effort and change, then perhaps we shall be able to understand if it is possible to bring about a radical change in which there is no exertion of will.

I hope the problem is clear. That is, we know that change is necessary. But into what must we change? And how is that change to be brought about? We know that the change which we generally think is necessary is always brought about through the exertion of will. I am 'this', and I must change into something else. The 'something else' is already thought out, it is projected—it is an end to be desired, an ideal which must be fulfilled. Surely, that is our way of thinking about change—as a constant adjustment, either voluntarily, or through suffering, or through the exertion of will. That implies, does it not?, a constant effort, the reaction of a certain desire, of a certain conditioning.

And so the change is merely a modified continuity of what has been.

Let us go into it. I am something, and I want to change. So I choose an ideal, and according to that ideal I try to transform myself, I exert my will, I discipline, I force myself; and there is a constant battle going on between what I am and what I should be. With that we are all familiar. And the ideal, what I think I should be—is it not merely the opposite of what I am? Is it not merely the reaction of what I am? I am angry, and I project the ideal of peace, of love, and I try to conform myself to the ideal of love, to the ideal of peace; and so there is a constant struggle. But the ideal is not the real: it is my projection of what I would like to be—it is the outcome of my pain, my suffering, my background. So the ideal has no significance at all; it is merely the result of my desire to be something which I am not. I am merely struggling to achieve something which I would like to be, so it is still within the pattern of self-enclosing action. That is so, is it not? I am 'this', and I would like to be 'that', but the struggle to be something different is still within the pattern of my desire.

So, is not all our talk about the necessity of change very superficial, unless we first uncover the deep process of our thinking? So long as I have a motive for change, is there a real change? My motive is to change myself from anger into a state of peace. Because I find that a state of peace is much more suitable, much more convenient, more happy, therefore I struggle to achieve that. But it is still within the pattern of my own desire, and so there is no change at all—I have only gathered a different word, 'peace' instead of 'anger', but essentially I am still the same. So the problem

is, is it not?, how to bring about a change at the centre—
and not to continue this constant adjustment to a pattern,
to an idea, through fear, through compulsion, through environmental influence. Is it not possible to bring about a
radical change at the very centre itself? If there is a change
there, then naturally any form of adjustment becomes unnecessary. Compulsion, effort, a disciplining process according to an ideal, is then seen as totally unnecessary and
false—because all those imply a constant struggle, a constant battle between myself and what I should be.

Now, is it possible to bring about a change at the
centre?—the centre being the self, the 'me' that is always
acquiring, always trying to conform, trying to adjust, but
remaining essentially the same. I hope I am making the
problem clear. Any conscious, deliberate effort to change
is merely the continuity, in a modified form, of what has
been, is it not? I am greedy, and if I deliberately, consciously set about to change that quality into non-greed, is not
that very effort to be non-greedy still the product of the
self, the 'me', and therefore there is no radical change at
all? When I consciously make an effort to be non-greedy,
then that conscious effort is the result of another form
of greed, surely. Yet on that principle all our disciplines,
all our attempts to change, are based. We are either consciously changing, or submitting to the pattern of society, or being pushed by society to conform—all of which
are various forms of deliberate effort on our part to be
something or other. So, where there is conscious effort to
change, obviously the change is merely the conformity to
another pattern; it is still within the enclosing process of
the self, and therefore it is not a change at all.

So can I see the truth of that; can I realize, understand, the full significance of the fact that any conscious effort on my part to be something other than what I am only produces still further suffering, sorrow and pain? Then follows the question: Is it possible to bring about a change at the centre, without the conscious effort to change? Is it possible for me, without effort, without the exertion of will, to stop being greedy, acquisitive, envious, angry, what you will? If I change consciously, if my mind is occupied with greed and I try to change it into non-greed, obviously that is still a form of greed—because my mind is concerned, occupied, with being something. So, is it possible for me to change at the centre this whole process of acquisitiveness, without any conscious action on the part of my mind to be non-acquisitive?

So our problem is: Being what I am—acquisitive— how is that to be transformed? I feel I understand very well that any exertion on my part to change is part of a self-conscious endeavour to be non-greedy, non-acquisitive—which is still acquisitiveness. So, what is to be done? How is the change at the centre to be brought about? If I understand the truth that all conscious effort is another form of acquisitiveness, if I really understand that, if I fully grasp the significance of it, then I will cease to make any conscious effort, will I not? Consciously I will stop exercising my will to change my acquisitiveness. That is the first thing. Because I see that any conscious effort, any action of will, is another form of acquisitiveness, therefore, understanding completely, there is the cessation of any deliberate practice to achieve the non-acquisitive state.

J. Krishnamurti

If I have understood that, what happens? If my mind is no longer struggling to change acquisitiveness, either through compulsion, through fear, through moral sanctions, through religious threats, through social laws and all the rest of it—then what happens to my mind? How do I then look at greed? I hope you are following this, because it is very interesting to see how the mind works. When we think we are changing, trying to adjust, trying to conform, disciplining ourselves to an ideal, actually there is no change at all. That is a tremendous discovery; that is a great revelation. A mind occupied with non-acquisitiveness is an acquisitive mind. Before, it was occupied with being acquisitive, now it is occupied with non-acquisitiveness. It is still occupied, so, the very occupation is acquisitiveness.

Now, is it possible for the mind to be non-occupied? I hope you are following this, because, you see, all our minds are occupied—occupied with something, occupied with God, with virtue, with what people say or don't say, whether someone loves you or doesn't love you. Always the mind is occupied. It was occupied before with acquisitiveness, and now it is occupied with non-acquisitiveness—but it's still occupied. So the problem is really: Can the mind be unoccupied? Because if it is not occupied, then it can tackle the problem of acquisitiveness, and not merely try to change it into non-acquisitiveness. Can the mind which has been occupied with acquisitiveness, can it, without turning to non-acquisitiveness—which is another occupation of the mind—put an end to all occupation? Surely it can, but only when it sees the truth that acquisitiveness and non-acquisitiveness are the same state of occupation. So long as the mind is occupied with something, obviously there cannot be a change. Whether it is occupied with God, with virtue, with dress, with love, with cruelty to animals, with the radio—they're all the same. There is no higher occupation or lower occupation; all occupation is essentially the same. The mind, being occupied, escapes from itself; it escapes through greed, it escapes through non-greed. So, can the mind, seeing all this complex process, put an end to its own occupation?

I think that is the whole problem. Because, when the mind is not occupied, then it is fresh, it is clear, it is capable of meeting any problem anew. When it is not occupied, then, being fresh, it can tackle acquisitiveness with a totally different action. So our question, our enquiry, our exploration, then is—can the mind be unoccupied? Please do not jump to conclusions. Do not say it must then be vague, blank, lost. We are enquiring, therefore there can be no conclusion, no definite statement, no supposition, no theory, no speculation. Can the mind be unoccupied? If you say 'How am I to achieve a state of mind in which there is no occupation?', then that 'how to achieve' becomes another occupation. Please see the simplicity of it, and therefore, the truth of the whole matter.

It is very important for you to find out how you are listening to this, how you are listening to these statements. They are merely statements, which you should neither accept nor reject; they are simply facts. How are you listening to the fact? Do you condemn it? Do you say, 'It is impossible'? Do you say 'I don't understand what you are talking about, it's too difficult, too abstract'? Or, are you listening to find out the truth of the matter? To see the truth without any distortion, without translating the fact into your own particular terminology or your own fancy—just to see clearly, just to be fully conscious of what is being said, is sufficient, Then you will find that your mind is no longer occupied, therefore it is fresh, and so capable of meeting the problem of change entirely, totally differently.

Whether change is brought about consciously or unconsciously it is still the same. Conscious change implies effort, and unconscious endeavour to bring about a change also implies an effort, a struggle. So long as there is a struggle, conflict, the change is merely enforced, and there is no understanding; and therefore it is no longer a change at all. So, is the mind capable of meeting the problem of change—of acquisitiveness, for example—without making an effort, just seeing the whole implication of acquisitiveness? Because you cannot see the whole content of acquisitiveness totally so long as there is any endeavour to change it. Real change can only take place when the mind comes to the problem afresh, not with all the jaded memories of a thousand yesterdays. Obviously, you cannot have a fresh, eager mind if the mind is occupied. And the mind ceases to be occupied only when it sees the truth about its own occupation. You cannot see the truth if you are not giving your whole attention, if you are translating what is being said into something which will suit you, or translating it into your own terms. You must come to something new with a fresh mind, and a mind is not fresh when it is occupied, consciously or unconsciously.

This transformation really takes place when the mind understands the whole process of itself; therefore self-knowledge is essential—not self-knowledge according to some psychologist or some book, but the self-knowledge that you discover from moment to moment. That self-knowledge is not to be gathered up and put into the mind as memory, because if you have gathered it, stored it up, any new experience will be translated according to that old memory. So self-knowledge is a state in which everything is observed, experienced, understood, and put away—not put away in memory, but cast aside, so that the mind is all the time fresh, eager.

Question: The world in which we live is confused, and I too am confused. How am I to be free of this confusion?

Krishnamurti: It is one of the most difficult things to know for oneself, not merely superficially but actually, that one is confused. One will never admit that. We are always hoping there may be some clarity, some loophole through which there will come understanding, so we never admit to ourselves that we are actually confused. We never admit that we are acquisitive, that we are angry, that we are this or that; there are always excuses, always explanations. But to know, really, 'I am confused'—that is one of the most important things to acknowledge to oneself. Are we not all confused? If you were very clear, if you knew what is true, you wouldn't be here, you wouldn't be chasing teachers, reading books, attending psychological classes, going to churches, pursuing the priest, the confession, and all the rest of it. To know for oneself that one is confused is really an extraordinarily difficult thing.

That is the first thing—to know that one is confused. Now, what happens when one is confused? Any endeavour—please follow this—any endeavour to become non-confused is still confusion. (Murmur of amusement). Please, listen quietly, and you will see. When a confused mind makes an effort to be non-confused, that very effort is the outcome of confusion, is it not? Therefore, whatever it does, whatever pursuit, whatever activity, whatever religion, whatever book it picks up, it is still in a state of confusion, therefore it cannot possibly understand. Its leaders, its priests, its religions, its relationships, must all be confused. That is what is happening in the world, is it not? You have chosen your political leaders, your religious leaders, out of your confusion.

If we understand that any action arising out of confusion is still confused, then, first we must stop all action—which most of us are unwilling to do. The confused mind in action only creates more confusion. You may laugh, you may smile, but you really do not feel that you are confused and that therefore you must stop acting. Surely, that is the first thing. If I have lost myself in a wood, I don't go round chasing all over the place, I just stop still. If I am confused, I don't pursue a guide, keep asking someone how to get out of confusion. Because any answer he gives, and I receive, will be translated according to my confusion, therefore it will be no answer at all. I think it is most difficult to realize that whenever one is confused, one must stop all activity, psychologically. I am not talking of outward activity—going to business and all the rest of it—but inwardly, psychologically, one must see the necessity of putting an end to all search, to all pursuits, to all desire to change. It is only when the confused mind abstains from any movement that out of that stopping comes clarity.

But it is very difficult for the mind, when it is confused, not to seek, not to ask, not to pray, not to escape—just to remain in confusion, and enquire what it is, why one is confused. Only then will one find out how confusion arises. Confusion arises when I do not understand myself, when my thoughts are guided by the priests, by the politicians, by the newspapers, by every psychological book that one reads. Contradiction—in myself and in the people I am trying to follow—arises when there is imitation, when there is fear. So it is important, if we would clear up confusion, to understand the process of confusion within oneself. For that, there must be the stopping of all pursuits, psychologically. It is only then that the mind, through its own understanding of itself, brings about clarity, so that it is aware of the whole process of its own thoughts and motives. Such a mind becomes very clear, simple, direct.

Question: Will you please explain what you mean by awareness.

Krishnamurti: Just simple awareness! Awareness of your judgements, your prejudices, your likes and dislikes. When you see something, that seeing is the outcome of your comparison, condemnation, judgement, evaluation, is it not? When you read something you are judging, you are criticizing, you are condemning or approving. To be aware is to see, in the very moment, this whole process of judging, evaluating, the conclusions, the conformity, the acceptances, the denials.

Now, can one be aware without all that? At present all we know is a process of evaluating, and that evaluation is the outcome of our conditioning, of our background, of our religious, moral and educational influences. Such so-called awareness is the result of our memory—memory as the 'me', the Dutchman, the Hindu, the Buddhist, the Catholic, or whatever it may be. It is the 'me'—my memories, my family, my property, my qualities—which is looking judging, evaluating. With that we are quite familiar, if we are at all alert. Now, can there be awareness without all that, without the self? Is it possible just to look without condemnation, just to observe the movement of the mind, one's own mind, without judging, without evaluating, without saying 'It is good', or 'It is bad'?

The awareness which springs from the self, which is the awareness of evaluation and judgement, always creates duality, the conflict of the opposites—that 'which is' and that 'which should be'. In that awareness there is judgement, there is fear, there is evaluation, condemnation, identification. That is but the awareness of the 'me', of the self, of the 'I' with all its traditions memories, and all the rest of it. Such awareness always creates conflict between the observer and the observed, between what I am and what I should be. Now, is it possible to be aware without this process of condemnation, judgement, evaluation? Is it possible to look at myself, whatever my thoughts are, and not condemn, not judge, not evaluate? I do not know if you have ever tried it. It is quite arduous—because all our training from childhood leads us to condemn or to approve. And in the process of condemnation and approval there is frustration, there is fear, there is a gnawing pain, anxiety, which is the very process of the 'me', the self.

So, knowing all that, can the mind, without effort, without trying not to condemn—because the moment it says 'I mustn't condemn', it is already caught in the process of condemnation—can the mind be aware without judgement? Can it just watch, with dispassion, and so observe the very thoughts and feelings themselves in the mirror of relationship—relationship with things, with people and with ideas? Such silent observation does not breed aloofness, an icy intellectualism—on the contrary. If I would understand something, obviously there must be no condemnation, there must be no comparison—surely, that is simple. But we think understanding comes through comparison, so we multiply comparisons. Our education is comparative, and our whole moral, religious structure is to compare and condemn.

So the awareness of which I am speaking is the awareness of the whole process of condemnation, and the ending of it. In that there is observation without any judgement—which is extremely difficult; it implies the cessation, the ending, of all terming, naming. When I am aware that I am greedy, acquisitive, angry, passionate, or what you will, is it not possible just to observe it, to be aware of it, without condemning?—which means, putting an end to the very naming of the feeling. For when I give a name, such as 'greed', that very naming is the process of condemning. To us, neurologically, the very word 'greed' is already a condemnation. To free the mind from all condemnation means putting an end to all naming. After all, the naming is the process of the thinker. It is the thinker separating himself from thought—which is a totally artificial process, it is unreal. There is only thinking, there is no thinker; there is only a state of experiencing, not the entity who experiences.

So this whole process of awareness, observation, is the process of meditation. It is, if I can put it differently, the willingness to invite thought. For most of us, thoughts come in without invitation—one thought after another; there is no end to thinking; the mind is a slave to every kind of vagrant thought. If you realize that, then you will see that there can be an invitation to thought—an inviting of thought and then a pursuing of every thought that arises. For most of us, thought comes uninvited; it comes any old way. To understand that process, and then to invite thought and pursue that thought through to the end, is the whole process which I have described as awareness; and in that there is no naming. Then you will see that the mind becomes extraordinarily quiet—-not through fatigue, not through discipline, not through any form of self-torture and control. Through awareness of its own activities the mind becomes astonishingly quiet, still, creative—without the action of any discipline, or any enforcement.

Then, in that stillness of mind, comes that which is true, without invitation. You cannot invite truth, it is the unknown. And in that silence there is no experiencer. Therefore that which is experienced is not stored, is not remembered as 'my experience of truth'. Then something which is timeless comes into being—that which cannot be measured by the one who has not experienced, or who merely remembers a past experience. Truth is something which comes from moment to moment. It is not to be cultivated, not to be gathered, stored up and held in memory. It comes only when there is an awareness in which there is no experiencer.

First Talk in London
25 June 1955

One of our problems, it seems to me, amongst so many others, is this dependence—dependence on people for our happiness, dependence on capacity, the dependence that leads the mind to cling to something. And the question is: Can the mind ever be totally free from all dependence? I think that is a fundamental question and one which we should be constantly asking ourselves.

Obviously, superficial dependence is not what we are talking about, but at the deeper level there is that psychological demand for some kind of security, for some method which will assure the mind of a state of permanency; there is the search for an idea, a relationship, that will be enduring. As this is one of our major problems, it seems to me it is very important to go into it rather deeply, and not respond superficially with an immediate reaction.

Why do we depend? Psychologically, inwardly, we depend on a belief, on a system, on a philosophy, we ask another for a mode of conduct, we seek teachers who will give us a way of life which will lead us to some hope, some happiness. So we are always, are we not, searching for some kind of dependence, security. Is it possible for the mind ever to free itself from this sense of dependence? Which does not mean that the mind must achieve independence, that is the only reaction to dependence. We are not talking of independence, of freedom from a particular state. If we can enquire, without the reaction of seeking freedom from a particular state of dependence, then we can go much more deeply into it. But if we are drawn away at a tangent in search of independence, we shall not understand this whole question of psychological dependence of which we are talking.

We know we depend—on our relationships with people, or on some idea, or on a system of thought. Why? We accept the necessity for dependence, we say it is inevitable. We have never questioned the whole issue at all, why each one of us seeks some kind of dependence. Is it not that we really, deep down, demand security, permanency? Being in a state of confusion, we want someone to get us out of that confusion. So we are always concerned with how to escape or avoid the state in which we are. In the process of avoiding that state, we are bound to create some kind of dependence, which becomes our authority. If we depend on another for our security, for our inward well-being, there arise out of that dependence innumerable problems, and then we try to solve those problems—the problems of attachment. But we never question, we never go into the problem of dependence itself. Perhaps if we can really intelligently, with full awareness, go into this problem. then we may find that dependence is not the issue at all—that it is only a way of escaping from a deeper fact.

May I suggest that those who are taking notes should refrain from doing so? Because these meetings will not be worthwhile if you are merely trying to remember what is said for afterwards. But if we can directly experience what is being said now, not afterwards, then it will have a definite significance, it will be a direct experience, and not an experience to be gathered later through your notes and thought over in memory. Also, if I may point it out, taking notes disturbs others around you.

As I was saying, why do we depend, and make dependence a problem? Actually, I do not think dependence is the problem; I think there is some other deeper factor that makes us depend. And if we can unravel that, then both dependence and the struggle for freedom will have very little significance; then all the problems which arise through dependence will wither away. So, what is the deeper issue? Is it that the mind abhors, fears, the idea of being alone? And does the mind know that state which it avoids? I depend on somebody, psychologically, inwardly, because of a state which I am trying to avoid but which I have never gone into, which I have never examined. So my dependence on a person—for love, for encouragement, for guidance—becomes immensely important, as do all the many problems that arise from it. Whereas, if I am capable of looking at the factor that is making me depend—on a person, on God, on prayer, on some capacity, on some formula or conclusion which I call a belief—then perhaps I can discover that such dependence is the result of an inward demand which I have never really looked at, never considered.

Can we, this evening, look at that factor?—the factor which the mind avoids, that sense of complete loneliness with which we are superficially familiar. What is it to be lonely? Can we discuss that now and keep to that issue, and not introduce any other problem?

I think this is really very important. Because so long as that loneliness is not really understood, felt, penetrated, dissolved—whatever word you may like to use—so long as that sense of loneliness remains, dependence is inevitable, and one can never be free, one can never find out for oneself that which is true, that which is religion. While I depend, there must be authority, there must be imitation, there must be various forms of compulsion, regimentation, and discipline to a certain pattern. So, can my mind find out what it is to be lonely, and go beyond it?—so that the mind is set totally free and therefore does not depend on beliefs, on gods, on systems, on prayers, or on anything else.

Surely, so long as we are seeking a result, an end, an ideal, that very urge to find creates dependence, from which arise the problems of envy, exclusion, isolation, and all the rest of it. So, can my mind know the loneliness in which it actually is, though I may cover it up with knowledge, with relationship, amusement, and various other forms of distraction? Can I really understand that loneliness? Because, is it not one of our major problems—this attachment and the struggle to be detached? Can we talk this over together, or is that too impossible?

So long as there is attachment, dependence, there must be exclusion. The dependence on nationality, identification with a particular group, with a particular race, with a particular person or belief, obviously separates. So it may be that the mind is constantly seeking exclusion, as a separate entity, and is avoiding a deeper issue which is actually separative—the self-enclosing process of its own thinking, which breeds loneliness. You know the feeling that one must identify oneself as being a Hindu, a Christian, belonging to a certain caste, group, race—you know the whole business. If we can, each of us, understand the deeper issue involved, then perhaps all influence which breeds dependence will come to an end, and the mind be wholly free.

Perhaps this may be too difficult a problem to discuss, in such a large group?

Question: Can you define the word 'alone', in contrast to 'loneliness'?

Krishnamurti: Please—we are surely not seeking definitions, are we? We are asking if each one of us is aware of this loneliness?—not now, perhaps, but we know of that state, and we know, do we not?, that we are escaping from this state through various means and so multiplying our problems. Now can I, through awareness, burn away the root of the problem?—so that it will never again arise, or if it does, I will know how to deal with it without causing further problems.

Question: Does that mean we have to break unsatisfactory bonds?

Krishnamurti: Surely, that is not what we are discussing, is it? I do not think we are following each other. And that is why I am hesitant as to whether it is possible to discuss this problem in so large a group.

We know, do we not?, that we are attached. We depend on people, on ideas. It is part of our nature, our being, to depend on somebody. And that dependence is called love. Now, I am asking myself, and perhaps you also are asking yourselves, whether it is possible to free the mind—psychologically, inwardly, from all dependence. Because I see that through dependence many, many problems arise—there is never an ending to them. Therefore I ask myself, is it possible to be so aware that the very awareness totally burns away this feeling of dependence on another, or on an idea, so that the mind is no longer exclusive, no longer isolated, because the demand for dependence has totally ceased?

For example, I depend on identification with a particular group; it satisfies me to call myself a Hindu or a Christian; to belong to a particular nationality is very satisfactory. In myself I feel dwarfed. I am a nobody, so to call myself somebody gives me satisfaction. That is a form of dependence at a very superficial level perhaps, but it breeds the poison of nationalism. And there are so many other deeper forms of dependence. Now, can I go beyond all that, so that the mind will never depend psychologically, so that it has no dependence at all, and does not seek any form of security? It will not seek security if I can understand this sense of extraordinary exclusion, of which I am aware, and which I call loneliness—this self-enclosing process of thinking which breeds isolation.

So the problem is not how to be detached, how to free oneself from people or ideas, but, can the mind stop this process of enclosing itself through its own activities, through its demands, through its urges? So long as there is the idea of the 'me', the 'I', there must be loneliness. The very essence, the ultimate self-enclosing process, is the discovery of this extraordinary sense of loneliness. Can I burn that away, so that the mind never seeks any form of security, never demands?

This can only be answered, not by me, but by each one of us. I can only describe, but the description becomes merely a hindrance if it is not actually experienced. But if it reveals the process of your own thinking, then that very description is an awareness of yourself and of your own state. Then, can I remain in that state? Can I no longer wander away from the fact of loneliness, but remain there, without any escape, without any avoidance? Seeing, understanding, that dependence is not the problem but loneliness is, can my mind remain without any movement in that state which I have called loneliness? It is extraordinarily difficult, because the mind can never be with a fact; it either translates it, interprets it, or does something about the fact; it never is with the fact.

Now, if the mind can remain with the fact, without giving any opinion about the fact, without translating, without condemning, without avoiding it, then, is the fact different from the mind? Is there a division between the fact and the mind, or is the mind itself the fact? For example, I am lonely. I am aware of that, I know what it means; it is one of the problems of our daily existence, of our existence altogether. And I want to tackle for myself this question of dependence, and see if the mind can be really free—not just speculatively or theoretically or philosophically, but actually be free of dependence. Because, if I depend on another for my love, it is not love. And I want to find out what that state is which we call love. In trying to find it out, obviously all sense of dependence, security in relationship, all sense of demand, desire for permanency, may go, and I may have to face something entirely different. So in enquiring, in going within myself, I may come upon this thing called loneliness. Now, can I remain with that? I mean, by 'remain', not interpreting it, not evaluating it, not condemning it, but just observing that state of loneliness without any withdrawal. Then, if my mind can remain with that state, is that state different from my mind? It may be that my mind itself is lonely, empty—and not that there is a state of emptiness which the mind observes.

My mind observes loneliness and avoids it, runs away from it. But if I do not run away from it, is there a division, is there a separation, is there an observer watching loneliness? Or, is there only a state of loneliness, my mind itself being empty, lonely?—not that there is an observer who knows that there is loneliness.

I think this is important to grasp—swiftly, not verbalizing too much. We say now 'I am envious, and I want to get rid of envy', so there is an observer and the observed; the observer wishes to get rid of that which he observes. But is the observer not the same as the observed? It is the mind itself that has created the envy, and so the mind cannot do anything about envy.

So my mind observes loneliness; the thinker is aware that he is lonely. But by remaining with it, being fully in contact—which is, not to run away from it, not to translate and all the rest of it—then, is there a difference between the observer and the observed? Or is there only one state, which is, the mind itself is lonely, empty? Not that the mind observes itself as being empty, but mind itself is empty. Then, can the mind, being aware that it itself is empty, and that whatever its endeavour, any movement away from that emptiness is merely an escape, a dependence—can the mind put away all dependence and be what it is, completely empty, completely lonely? And if it is in that state, is there not freedom from all dependence, from all attachment?

Please, this is a thing that must be gone into, not accepted because I am saying it. It has no meaning if you merely accept it. But if you are experiencing the thing as we are going along, then you will see that any movement on the part of the mind—movement being evaluation, condemnation, translation, and so on—is a distraction from the fact of 'what is', and so creates a conflict between itself and the observed.

This is really—to go further—a question of whether the mind can ever be without effort, without duality, without conflict, and therefore be free. The moment the mind is caught in conflict it is not free. When there is no effort to be, then there is freedom. So, can the mind be without effort—and therefore free?

Question: I am now able to accept problems on my own behalf. But how can I stop myself suffering on my children's behalf, when they are affected by the same problems?

Krishnamurti: Why do we depend on our children? And also, do we love our children? If it is love, then how can there be dependence, how can there be suffering? Our idea of love is that we suffer for others. Is it love that suffers? Or is it that I depend on my children, that through them I am seeking immortality, fulfilment, and all the rest of it? So I want my children to be something, and when they are not that, I suffer. The problem may not be the children at all, it may be me. Again we come back to the same thing—perhaps we do not know what it is to love. If we did love our children, we would stop all wars tomorrow, obviously. We would not condition our children. They would not be Englishmen, Hindus, Brahmins, and non-Brahmins; they would be children.

But we do not love, and therefore we depend on our children; through them we hope to fulfil ourselves. So when the child, through whom we are going to fulfil, does something which is not what we demand, then there is sorrow, then there is conflict.

Merely putting a question and waiting for an answer has very little meaning. But if we can observe for ourselves the process of attachment, the process of seeking fulfilment through another, which is dependence and which must inevitably create sorrow—if we can see that as a fact for ourselves, then there may be something else, perhaps love. Then that relationship will produce quite a different society, quite a different world.

Question: When one has reached the stage of a quiet mind, and has no immediate problem, what proceeds from that stillness?

Krishnamurti: Quite an extraordinary question, is it not? You have taken it for granted that you have reached that still mind, and you want to know what happens after it.

But to have a still mind is one of the most difficult things. Theoretically, it is the easiest, but factually, it is one of the most extraordinary states, which cannot be described. What happens you will discover when you come to it. But that coming to it is the problem, not what happens after.

You cannot come to that state. It is not a process. It is not something which you are going to achieve through a practice. It cannot be bought through time, through knowledge, through discipline, but only by understanding knowledge, by understanding the whole process of discipline, by understanding the total process of one's own thinking, and not trying to achieve a result. Then, perhaps, that quietness may come into being. What happens afterwards is indescribable, it has no word and it has no 'meaning'.

You see, every experience, so long as there is an experiencer, leaves a memory, a scar. And to that memory the mind clings, and it wants more, and so breeds time. But the state of stillness is timeless, therefore there is no experiencer to experience that stillness.

Please, this is really, if you wish to understand it, very important. So long as there is an experiencer who says, 'I must experience stillness', and knows the experience, then it is not stillness; it is a trick of the mind. When one says, 'I have experienced stillness', it is just an avoidance of confusion, of conflict—that is all. The stillness of which we are talking is something totally different. That is why it is very important to understand the thinker, the experiencer, the self that demands a state which it calls stillness. You may have a moment of stillness, but when you do, the mind clings to it, and lives in that stillness in memory. That is not stillness, that is merely a reaction. What we are talking of is something entirely different. It is a state in which there is no experiencer: and therefore such silence, quietness, is not an experience. If there is an entity who remembers that state, then there is an experiencer, therefore it is no longer that state.

This means, really, to die to every experience, with never a moment of gathering, accumulating. After all, it is this accumulation that brings about conflict, the desire to have more. A mind that is accumulating, greedy, can never die to everything it has accumulated. It is only the mind that has died to everything it has accumulated, even to its highest experience—only such a mind can know what that silence is. But that state cannot come about through discipline, because discipline implies the continuation of the experiencer, the strengthening of a particular intention towards a particular object, thereby giving the experiencer continuity.

If we see this thing very simply, very clearly, then we will find that silence of the mind of which we are talking. What happens after that is something that cannot be told, that cannot be described, because it has no 'meaning'—except in books and philosophy.

Question: If we have not experienced that complete stillness, how can we know that it exists?

Krishnamurti: Why do we want to know that it exists? It may not exist at all, it may be my illusion, a fancy. But one can see that so long as there is conflict, life is a misery. In understanding conflict, I will know what the other means.

It may be an illusion, an invention, a trick of the mind—
but in understanding the full significance of conflict I may
find something entirely different.

My mind is concerned with the conflict within itself
and without. Conflict inevitably arises so long as there is
an experiencer who is accumulating, who is gathering, and
therefore always thinking in terms of time, of the 'more'
and the 'less'. In understanding that, in being aware of
that, there may come a state which may be called silence—
give it any name you like. But the process is not the search
for silence, for stillness, but rather the understanding of
conflict, the understanding of myself in conflict.

I wonder if I have answered the question?—which is,
how do I know that there is silence? How do I recognize
it? You understand? So long as there is a process of recognition, there is no silence.

After all, the process of recognition is the process of
the conditioned mind. But in understanding the whole
content of the conditioned mind, then the mind itself becomes quiet, there is no observer to recognize that he is in
a state which he calls silence. Recognition of an experience
has ceased.

*Question: I would like to ask if you recognize the teaching of
the Buddha that right understanding will help to solve the inner problems of man, and that inner peace of the mind depends
entirely on self-discipline. Do you agree with the teachings of
Buddha?*

Krishnamurti: If one is enquiring to find out the truth of
anything, all authority must be set aside, surely. There is

neither the Buddha nor the Christ when one wishes to find what is true. Which means, really, the mind must be capable of being completely alone, and not dependent. The Buddha may be wrong, Christ may be wrong, and one may be wrong oneself. One must come to the state, surely, of not accepting any authority of any kind. That is the first thing—to dismantle the structure of authority. In dismantling the immense structure of tradition, that very process brings about an understanding. But merely to accept something because it has been said in a sacred book has very little meaning.

Surely, to find that which is beyond time, all the process of time must cease, must it not? The very process of search must come to an end. Because if I am seeking, then I depend—not only on another, but also on my own experience, for if I have learned something, I try to use that to guide myself. To find what is true, there must be no search of any kind—and that is the real stillness of the mind.

It is very difficult for a person who has been brought up in a particular culture, in a particular belief, with certain symbols of tremendous authority, to set aside all that and to think simply for himself and find out. He cannot think simply if he does not know himself, if there is no self-knowledge. And no one can give us self-knowledge—no teacher, no book, no philosophy, no discipline. The self is in constant movement; as it lives, it must be understood. And only through self-knowledge, through understanding the process of my own thinking, observed in the mirror of every reaction, do I find out that so long as there is any movement of the 'me', of the mind, towards anything— towards God, towards Truth, towards peace—then such a mind is not a quiet mind, it is still wanting to achieve, to grasp, to come to some state. If there is any form of authority, any compulsion, any imitation, the mind cannot understand. And to know that the mind imitates, to know that it is crippled by tradition, to be aware that it is pursuing its own experiences, its own projections—that demands a great deal of insight, a great deal of awareness, of self-knowledge.

Only then, with the whole content of the mind, the whole consciousness, unravelled and understood, is there a possibility of a state which may be called stillness—in which there is no experiencer, no recognition.

First Talk in Madanapalle
26 February 1956

I think most of us find life very dull. To earn a livelihood we have to do a certain job, and it becomes very monotonous; a routine is set going which we follow year after year almost till our death. Whether we are rich or poor, and though we may be very erudite, have a philosophical bent, our lives are for the most part rather shallow, empty. There is obviously an insufficiency in ourselves, and being aware of this emptiness, we try to enrich it through knowledge, or through some kind of social activity, or we escape through various kinds of amusement, or cling to a religious belief. Even if we have a certain capacity and are very efficient, our lives are still pretty dull, and to get away from this dullness, this weary monotony of life, we seek some form of religious enrichment, we try to capture that unworldly state of being which is not routine and which for the moment may be called otherness. In seeking that otherness we find there are many different systems, different ways or paths which are supposed to lead to it, and by disciplining ourselves, by practising a particular system of meditation, by performing some ritual or repeating certain phrases, we hope to achieve that state. Because our daily life is an endless round of sorrow and pleasure, a variety of experiences without much significance, or a meaningless repetition of the same experience, living for most of us is a monotonous routine; therefore the problem of enrichment, of capturing that otherness—call it God, Truth, bliss, or what you will—becomes very urgent, does it not? You may be well-off and well-married, you may have children, you may be able to think intelligently and sanely, but without that state of otherness, life becomes extraordinarily empty.

So, what is one to do? How is one to capture that state? Or is it not possible to capture it at all? As they are now, our minds are obviously very small, petty, limited, conditioned, and though a small mind may speculate about that otherness, its speculations will always be small. It may formulate an ideal state, conceive and describe that otherness, but its conception will still be within the limitations of the little mind, and I think that is where the clue lies—in seeing that the mind cannot possibly experience that otherness by living it, formulating it, or speculating about it. Surely, that is a tremendous realization: to see that, because it is limited, petty, narrow, superficial, any movement of the mind towards that extraordinary state is a hindrance. To realize that fact, not speculatively but actually, is the beginning of a different approach to the problem.

After all, our minds are the outcome of time, of many thousands of yesterdays; they are the result of experience based on the known, and such a mind is the continuity of the known. The mind of each one of us is the result of culture, of education, and however extensive its knowledge or its technical training, it is still the product of time; therefore it is limited, conditioned. With that mind we try to discover the unknowable, and to realize that such a mind can never discover the unknowable is really an extraordinary experience. To realize that, however cunning, however subtle, however erudite one's mind may be, it cannot possibly understand that otherness—this realization in itself brings about a certain factual comprehension, and I think it is the beginning of a way of looking at life which may open the door to that otherness.

To put the problem differently, the mind is ceaselessly active, chattering, planning; it is capable of extraordinary subtleties and inventions; and how can such a mind be quiet? One can see that any activity of the mind, any movement in any direction, is a reaction of the past; and how can such a mind be still? And if it is made still through discipline, such stillness is a state in which there is no enquiring, no searching, is it not? Therefore there is no openness to the unknown, to that state of otherness.

I don't know if you have thought about this problem at all, or have merely thought about it in terms of the traditional approach, which is to have an ideal and to move towards the ideal through a formula, through the practice of a certain discipline. Discipline invariably implies suppression and the conflict of duality, all of which is within the area of the mind, and we proceed along this line, hoping to capture that otherness; but we have never intelligently and sanely enquired whether the mind can ever capture it. We have had the hint that the mind must be still, but stillness has always been cultivated through discipline. That is, we have the ideal of a still mind, and we pursue it through control, through struggle, through effort.

Now, if you look at this whole process, you will see that it is all within the field of the known. Being aware of the monotony of its existence, realizing the weariness of its multiplying experiences, the mind is always trying to capture that otherness; but when one sees that the mind is the known, and that whatever movement it makes, it can never capture that otherness, which is the unknown, then our problem is, not how to capture the unknown, but whether the mind can free itself from the known. I think this problem must be considered by anyone who wants to find out if there is a possibility of the coming into being of that otherness, the unknown. So, how can the mind which is the result of the past, of the known, free itself from the known? I hope I am making myself clear.

As I said, the present mind, the conscious as well as the unconscious, is the outcome of the past, it is the accumulated result of racial, climatic, dietetic, traditional, and other influences. So the mind is conditioned—conditioned as a Christian, a Buddhist, a Hindu, or a communist— and it obviously projects what it considers to be the real. But whether its projection is that of the communist, who thinks he knows the future and wants to force all mankind into the pattern of his particular utopia, or that of the so-called religious man, who also thinks he knows the future and educates the child to think along his particular line, neither projection is the real. Without the real, life becomes very dull, as it is at present for most people; and our lives being dull, we become romantic, sentimental, about that otherness, the real.

Now, seeing this whole pattern of existence, without going into too many details, is it possible for the mind to free itself from the known—the known being the psychological accumulations of the past? There is also the known of everyday activity, but from this the mind obviously cannot be free, for if one forgot the way to one's house, or the knowledge which enables one to earn a livelihood, one would be bordering on insanity. But can the mind free itself from the psychological factors of the known, which give assurance through association and identification?

To enquire into this matter, we shall have to find out whether there is really a difference between the thinker and the thought, between the one who observes and the thing observed. At present there is a division between them, is there not? We think the 'I', the entity who experiences, is different from the experience, from the thought. There is a gap, a division between the thinker and the thought, and that is why we say, 'I must control thought.' But is the 'I', the thinker, different from thought? The thinker is always trying to control thought, mould it according to what he considers to be a good pattern, but is there a thinker if there is no thought? Obviously not. There is only thinking, which creates the thinker. You may put the thinker at any level, you may call him the Supreme, the Atman, or whatever you like, but he is still the result of thinking. The thinker has not created thought; it is thought that has created the thinker. Realizing its own impermanency, thought creates the thinker as a separate entity in order to give itself permanency—which is after all what we all want. You may say that the entity which you call the Atman, the soul, the thinker, is separate from thought, from experience; but you are only aware of a separate entity through thought, and also through your conditioning as a Hindu, a Christian, or whatever it is you happen to be. As long as this duality exists between the thinker and the thought, there must be conflict, effort, which implies will; and a mind that wills to free itself, that says, 'I must be free from the past', merely creates another pattern.

So the mind can free itself—and thereby, perhaps, that otherness can come into being—only when there is the cessation of effort as the 'I' desiring to achieve a result. But you see, all our life is based on effort: the effort to be good, the effort to discipline ourselves, the effort to achieve a result in this world, or in the next. Everything we do is based on striving, ambition, success, achievement; and so we think that the realization of God, or Truth, must also come about through effort. But such effort signifies the self-centred activity of achievement, does it not? It is not the abandonment of the self.

Now, if you are aware of this whole process of the mind, the conscious as well as the unconscious, if you really see and understand it, then you will find that the mind becomes extraordinarily quiet without any effort. The stillness which is brought about by discipline, control, suppression, is the stillness of death, but the stillness of which I am speaking comes about effortlessly when one understands this whole process of the mind. Then only is there a possibility of the coming into being of that otherness which may be called Truth, or God.

Question: Do you not concede that guidance is necessary? If, as you say, there must be no tradition and no authority, then everybody will have to start laying down a new foundation for himself. As the physical body has had a beginning, is there not also a beginning for our spiritual and mental bodies, and should they not grow from each stage to the next higher stage?

J. Krishnamurti

Just as our thought is kindled by listening to you, does it not need reawakening by getting into contact with the great minds of the past?

Krishnamurti: Sir, this is an age-old problem. We think that we need a guru, a teacher, to awaken our minds. Now, what is implied in all that? It implies the one who knows, and the other who does not. Let us proceed slowly, not in a prejudiced manner. The one who knows becomes the authority, and the one who does not know becomes the disciple; and the disciple is everlastingly following, hoping to overtake the other, to come up to the level of the master. Now, please follow this. When the guru says he knows, he ceases to be the guru; the man who says he knows, does not know. Please see why. Because Truth, Reality, or that otherness, has no fixed point, it obviously cannot be approached by a path, but must be discovered from moment to moment. If it has a fixed point, then that point is within the limits of time. To a fixed point there may be a path, as there is a path to your house; but to a thing that is living, that has no abode, that has neither a beginning nor an end, there can be no path.

Surely, a guru who says he will help you to realize can help you to realize only that which you already know, for what you realize, experience, must be recognizable, must it not? If you can recognize it, then you say, 'I have experienced', but what you can recognize is not that otherness. That otherness is not recognizable; it is not known; it is not something which you have experienced and are therefore able to recognize. That otherness is a thing that must be uncovered from moment to moment, and to discover it, the mind must be free. Sir, the mind must be free to discover anything, and a mind that is bound by tradition, whether ancient or modern, a mind that is burdened with belief, with dogma, with rituals, is obviously not free. To me, the idea that another can awaken you has no validity. This is not an opinion, it is a fact. If another awakens you, then you are under his influence, you are depending on him; therefore you are not free, and it is only the free mind that can find.

So the problem is this, is it not?—we want that otherness, and since we don't know how to get it, we invariably depend on someone whom we call the teacher, the guru, or on a book, or on our own experience. So dependence is created, and where there is dependence there is authority; therefore the mind becomes a slave to authority, to tradition, and such a mind is obviously not free. It is only the free mind that can find, and to rely on another for the awakening of your mind is like relying on a drug. Of course, you can take a drug that will make you see things very sharply, clearly. There are drugs that can momentarily make life seem much more vital, so that everything stands out brilliantly—the colours that you see every day, and pass by, become extraordinarily beautiful, and so on. That may be your 'awakening' of the mind, but then you will be depending on the drug, as now you depend on your guru, or on some sacred book; and the moment the mind becomes dependent, it is made dull. Out of dependence there is fear—fear of not achieving, of not gaining. When you depend on another, whether it be the Saviour or anyone else, it means that the mind is seeking success, a gratifying end. You may call it God, Truth, or what you like, but it is still a thing to be gained; so the mind is caught, it becomes a slave, and do what it will—sacrifice, discipline, torture itself—such a mind can never find that otherness.

So the problem is not who is the right teacher, but whether the mind can keep itself awake, and you will find it can keep itself awake only when all relationship is a mirror in which it sees itself as it is. But the mind cannot see itself as it is if there is condemnation or justification of that which it sees, or any form of identification. All these things make the mind dull, and being dull, we want to be awakened, so we look to somebody else to awaken us.

But by this very demand to be awakened, a dull mind is made still more dull, because it does not see the cause of its dullness. It is only when the mind sees and understands this whole process, and does not depend on the explanation of another, that it is able to free itself.

But how easily we are satisfied with words, with explanations! Very few of us break through the barrier of explanations, go beyond words, and find out for ourselves what is true. Capacity comes with application, does it not? But we don't apply ourselves, because we are satisfied with words, with speculations, with the traditional answers and explanations on which we have been brought up.

Question: In all religions, prayer is advocated as necessary. What do you say about prayer?

Krishnamurti: It is not a matter of what I say about prayer, for then it merely becomes one opinion against another, and opinion has no validity; but what we can do is to find out what the facts are.

What do we mean by prayer? One part of prayer is supplication, petition, demand. Being in trouble, in sorrow, and wanting to be comforted, you pray. You are confused, and you want clarity. Books don't satisfy you, the guru does not give you what you want, so you pray; that is, you either silently supplicate, or you verbally repeat certain phrases.

Now, if you keep on repeating certain words or phrases, you will find that the mind becomes very quiet. It is an obvious psychological fact that quietness of the superficial mind is induced by repetition. And then what happens? The unconscious may have an answer to the problem which is agitating the superficial mind. When the superficial mind becomes quiet, the unconscious is able to intimate its solution, and then we say, 'God has answered me.' It is really fantastic, when you come to think of it, for the petty little mind, being caught in sorrow which it has brought upon itself, to expect an answer from that otherness, the immeasurable, the unknown. But our petition is answered, we have found a solution, and we are satisfied. That is one form of prayer, is it not?

Now, do you ever pray when you are happy? When you are aware of the smiles and the tears of those about you, when you see the lovely skies, the mountains, the rich fields, and the swift movement of the birds, when there is joy and delight in your heart—do you indulge in what you call prayer? Obviously not. And yet, to see the beauty of the earth, to be cognizant of starvation and misery, to be aware of everything that is happening about us—surely, this is also a form of prayer. Perhaps this has much more significance, a far greater value, for it may sweep away the cobwebs of memory, of revenge, all the accumulated stupidities of the 'I'. But a mind that is preoccupied with itself and its designs, that is caught up in its beliefs, its dogmas, its fears and jealousies, its ambition, greed, envy—such a mind cannot possibly be aware of this extraordinary thing called life. It is bound by its own self-centred activity, and when such a mind prays, whether it be for a refrigerator, or to have its problems solved, it is still petty, even though it may receive an answer.

All this brings up the question of what is meditation, does it not? Obviously, there must be meditation. Meditation is an extraordinary thing, but most of us don't know what it means to meditate; we are only concerned with how to meditate, with practising a method or a system through which we hope to get something, to realize what we call peace, or God. We are never concerned to find out what is meditation, and who is the meditator, but if we begin to enquire into what is meditation, then perhaps we shall find out how to meditate. The enquiry into meditation is meditation. But to enquire into meditation, you cannot be tethered to any system, because then your enquiry is conditioned by the system. To really probe into this whole problem of what is meditation, all systems must go. Only a free mind can explore, and the very process of freeing the mind to explore is meditation.

Question: The thought of death is bearable to me only if I can believe in a future life. But you say that belief is an obstacle to understanding. Please help me to see the truth of this.

Krishnamurti: Belief in a future life is the result of one's desire for comfort. Whether or not there is a future life in reality can be found out only when the mind is not desirous of being comforted by a belief. If I am in sorrow because my son has died, and to overcome that sorrow I believe in reincarnation, in eternal life, or what you will, then belief becomes a necessity to me; and such a mind can obviously never find out what death is, because all it is concerned with is to have a hope, a comfort, a reassurance.

Now, whether or not there is continuity after death is quite a different problem. One sees that the body comes to an end; through constant use, the physical organism wears out. Then what is it that continues? It is the accumulated experience, the knowledge, the name, the memories, the identification of thought as the 'me'. But you are not satisfied with that; you say there must be another form of continuance as the permanent soul, the Atman. If there is this Atman which continues, it is the creation of thought, and the thought which has created the Atman is still part of time; therefore it is not spiritual. If you really go into this matter, you will see there is only thought identified as the 'me'—my house, my wife, my family, my virtue, my failure, my success, and all the rest of it—and you want that to continue. You say, 'I want to finish my book before I die', or, 'I want to perfect the qualities I have been trying to develop, and what is the point of my having struggled all these years to achieve something if in the end there is annihilation?' So the mind, which is the product of the known, wants to continue in the future, and because there is the uncertainty which we call death, we are frightened and want reassurance.

Now, I think the problem should be approached differently, which is to find out for oneself whether it is possible, while living, to experience that state of ending which we call death. This does not mean committing suicide, but it is to actually experience that astonishing state, that sacred moment of dying to everything of yesterday. After all, death is the unknown, and no amount of rationalization, no belief or disbelief, will ever bring about that extraordinary experience. To have that inward fullness of life, which includes death, the mind must free itself from the known. The known must cease for the unknown to be.

First Talk in Brussels
24 June 1956

One of our great difficulties is to know how to free ourselves from the complex problem of sorrow. Intellectually we try to grapple with it, but unfortunately the intellect has no solution to the problem. The best it can do is to find some verbal rationalization or invent a theory, or else it becomes cynical and bitter. But if we can very seriously examine the problem of suffering—not just verbally, but actually experience the whole process of it—then perhaps we shall discover its cause, and find out whether that discovery brings about the solution of it.

Obviously, the problem of sorrow is one of the fundamental issues in our life. Most of us have some kind of sorrow, secret or open, and we are always trying to find a way to go beyond it, to be free of it. But it seems to me that unless we begin to understand for ourselves the really deep workings of the mind, sorrow will inevitably continue.

Is sorrow a thing to be got rid of through rationalization, that is, by explaining the cause of sorrow? Superficially, we all know why we suffer. I am talking particularly of psychological suffering, not merely of physical pain. If I know why I suffer, in the sense that I recognize the cause of my sorrow, will that sorrow disappear? Must I not look for a deeper issue, rather than be satisfied with one of the innumerable explanations of what it is that brings about the state which we call sorrow? And how am I to seek out the deeper issue? Most of us are very easily satisfied by superficial responses, are we not? We quickly accept the satisfactory escapes from the deep issue of suffering.

Consciously or unconsciously, verbally or actually, we all know that we suffer, because we have in us the contradiction of desires, one desire trying to dominate another. These contradictory desires make for conflict, and conflict invariably leads to the state of mind which we call suffering. The whole complex of desire which creates conflict—this, it seems to me, is the source of all sorrow.

Most of us are caught up in this mass of contradictory desires, wishes, longings, hopes, fears, memories. That is, we are concerned with our achievements, our successes, our well-being, the fulfilment of our ambitions; we are concerned about ourselves. And I think this self-concern is the real source of our conflict and misery. Realizing this, we try to escape from our self-concern by throwing ourselves into various philanthropic activities, or by identifying ourselves with a particular reform, or we stupidly cling to some kind of religious belief, which is not religious at all. What we are essentially concerned with is how to escape from our suffering, how to resolve it.

So it seems to me very important, if we would free ourselves from sorrow, to go into this whole complex which we call desire, this bundle of memories which we call the 'me'. Is it possible to live in the world without this complex of desire, without this entity called the 'me', from which all suffering arises? I do not know if you have thought of this problem at all. When we suffer for various reasons, most of us try to find an answer, we try to escape by identifying ourselves with one thing or another, hoping it will alleviate our suffering. Yet the suffering goes on, either consciously or underground.

Now, can the mind free itself from suffering? This must be a problem to all of us who think about these things, because all of us suffer, acutely or superficially. Can there be an ending to sorrow, or is sorrow inevitable? If it is our human lot to suffer endlessly, then we must accept it and live with it. But I think merely to accept the state of sorrow would be foolish, because no man wants to be in that state.

So, is it possible to end sorrow? Surely, sorrow is the result, not only of ignorance—which is lack of self-knowledge—but also of this enormous effort that everyone is continually making to be something, to acquire something, or to reject something. Can we live in this world without any effort to be or become something, without trying to achieve, to reject, to acquire? That is what we are doing all the time, is it not? We are making effort. I am not saying that there must be no effort, but I am enquiring into the whole problem of effort. I can see in myself—and it must be obvious to most of us—that so long as I desire to be successful, for example, either in this world or psychologically, spiritually, I must make effort, I must exert myself to achieve; and it seems to me that suffering is inherent in the very nature of that effort.

Please do not brush this aside. It is easy to say 'One cannot live in this world without effort. Everything in nature struggles, and if we do not make effort there will be no life at all.' That is not what I am talking about. I am enquiring into the whole process of effort; I am not saying that we should reject or sustain effort, augment or decrease it. I am asking whether effort is necessary psychologically, and whether it does not produce the seed of sorrow.

When we make an effort, it is obviously with a motive—to achieve, to be, or to become something. Where there is effort there is the action of will, which is essentially desire—one desire opposing another, so there is a contradiction. To overcome this contradiction, we try in various ways to bring about an integration—which again involves effort. So our way of thinking, our whole way of living, is a process of ceaseless effort.

Now, this effort, surely, is centred in the 'me', the self, which is concerned with itself and its own activities. And can the mind free itself from this complex, from this bundle of desires, urges, compulsions, without effort, without a motive?

I hope I am making myself clear because this is a very complex problem. I know that my life is a series of desires; it is made up of many wants and frustrations, many hopes, longings and aspirations; there is the cultivation of virtue, the search for moral standing, trying to conform to an ideal, and so on; and through it all there is the urge to be free. All that is the 'me', the self, which is the source of sorrow.

Surely, any move I make in order to be free of sorrow, furthers sorrow, because that again involves effort. I think one must understand this fundamentally—that any effort to be or become something, to achieve success, and so on, produces sorrow. By making an effort to get rid of sorrow, I build a resistance against it, and that very resistance is a form of suppression which breeds further sorrow. If I see this, then what am I to do? How is the mind which is caught in sorrow to free itself from sorrow? Can it do anything? Because any action on its part has a motive behind it, and a motive invariably breeds conflict, which again begets sorrow.

This is the whole issue. I think I shall be happy if I make a success of my life, have plenty of things, position, power, money. So I struggle. And in the very process of struggling to achieve that which I want, there is conflict, there is pain, there is frustration; so sorrow is set going. Or, if I am not worldly-minded, I turn to so-called spiritual things. There also I try to achieve something—to realize God, Truth, and all the rest of it—I cultivate virtue, obey the sanctions of the church, follow yoga or some other system to the end that my mind may be at peace. So again there is a struggle, there is conflict, suppression, resistance—which seems to me utterly futile, without meaning.

So, what is the mind to do? I know the whole pattern of suffering, and the causes of suffering; I also know the ways of escape, and I see that escaping from suffering is no answer. One may escape momentarily, but suffering is still there, like a lingering poison. So, what is the mind to do?

How does the mind know anything? When I say 'I know the pattern of suffering', what do I mean by that? Is it merely intellectual knowledge, a verbal, rationalized understanding of this whole network of suffering? Or am I aware of it totally, inwardly? Do I know it merely as something which I have learned, which I have been taught, which I have read about and captured through a description? Or am I actually aware of suffering as a process taking place in myself, at every moment of my existence? Which is it? I think this is an important question.

How do I know that I suffer? Do I know it merely because I feel frustrated, or because I have lost someone—my son is dead? Or do I know with my whole being that suffering is the nature of all desire, of all becoming? And must I go through the process of every desire in order to find that out?

Surely, there must be suffering so long as one does not totally comprehend desire, which includes the action of will and involves contradiction, suppression, resistance, conflict. Whether we desire superficial things, or the deep, fundamental things, conflict is always involved. So, can we find out whether the mind is capable of being free from desire—from the whole psychological process of the desire to be something, to succeed, to become, to find God, to achieve? Can the mind understand all that and be free from it? Otherwise life is a process of continuous conflict, misery. You may find a panacea, a semi-permanent escape, but misery awaits you. You may throw yourself into some activity, take refuge in a belief, find various ways of forgetting yourself, but conflict is still there.

So, can the mind understand the process of desire? And is this understanding a matter of effort? Or does understanding come only when the mind sees the whole process of desire—sees it, experiences it, is totally aware of it, and knowing that it cannot do anything about it, becomes silent with regard to that problem?

I think this is the fundamental issue—not how to transcend, transform, or control desire, but to know the full significance of desire, and knowing it, to be completely motionless, silent, without any action with regard to it. Because, when the mind is confronted with an enormous problem like desire, any action on its part distorts that problem; any effort to grapple with it makes the problem petty, shallow. Whereas, if the mind can look at this enormous problem of desire without any movement, without any denial, without accepting or rejecting it, then I think we shall find that desire has quite a different significance, and that one can live in this world without contradiction, without struggle, without this everlasting effort to arrive, to achieve.

When the mind is thus able to look at the whole process of desire, you will find that it becomes astonishingly capable of experiencing without adding anything to itself. When the mind is no longer contaminated by desire and all the problems connected with it, then the mind itself is reality—not the mind as we know it, but a mind that is completely without the self, without desire.

Question: You talked yesterday of mediocrity. I realize my own mediocrity, but how am I to break through it?

Krishnamurti: It is the mediocre mind that demands a way to break through or achieve. Therefore when you say 'I am mediocre, how am I to break through it?', you do not realize the full significance of mediocrity. The mind that wants to change or improve itself will always remain mediocre, however great its effort. And that is what we all want, is it not? We all want to change from this to that. Being stupid, I want to become clever. The stupid man who is attempting to become clever will always remain stupid. But the man

who is aware that he is stupid, and realizes the full significance of stupidity, without wishing to change it—that very
realization puts an end to stupidity.

So, can the mind look at the fact of what it is without
trying to alter it? Can I see that I am arrogant, or stupid,
or vain—just realize the fact, and not wish to change it?
The desire to change it breeds mediocrity, because then
I look to someone to tell me what to do about it; I go to
lectures, read books, in order to find out how to change
what I am. So I am led away from facing the fact of what
I am, and being led away from the fact is the cultivation
of mediocrity.

Now, can I look at the fact of mediocrity without wishing to break through it? After all, the mind is mediocre—
it does not matter whose mind it is. The mind is mediocre,
bound by tradition, by the past; and when the mind tries
to improve itself, to break through its own limitations,
it remains the same mediocre mind, only it is seeking a
new sensation, that is, to experience the state of not being
mediocre.

So the problem is not how to break through mediocrity, for mediocrity is invariably the result of pursuing
tradition, whether that tradition has been established by
society, or cultivated by oneself. Any effort on the part of
the mind to break through mediocrity will be an activity of
mediocrity, therefore the result will still be mediocre.

This is the real issue. We do not see that the mind,
however cultivated, however clever, however erudite, is
essentially mediocre, and that however much it may try
to break through mediocrity, it is still mediocre. When
the mind sees the fact of its own mediocrity, not just the

superficial part, but the totality of it, with all that it involves, and does not try to do something about it, then you will find you are no longer concerned with mediocrity, or with attempting to change this into that. Then the very fact itself begins to operate.

That is, when the mind is aware of the fact of its own stupidity, mediocrity, and does not operate on that fact, then the fact begins to operate on the mind, and then you will see that the mind has undergone a fundamental change. But so long as the mind wants to change, whatever change it may bring about will be a continuation of that which it has been, only under a different cloak.

That is why it is very important to understand the whole process of thinking, and why self-knowledge is essential. But you cannot know yourself if you are merely accumulating knowledge about yourself, for then you know only that which you have accumulated—which is not to know the ways of your own self and its activities from moment to moment.

Question: How are we to put an end to man's cruelty towards animals in the form of vivisection, slaughter-houses, and so on?

Krishnamurti: I do not think we will put an end to it, because I do not think we know what it means to love. Why are we so concerned about animals? Not that we should not be—we must be. But why this concern about animals only? Are we not cruel to each other? Our whole social structure is based on violence, which erupts every so often into war. If you really loved your children, you would put a stop to war. But you do not love your children, so you sacrifice them to protect your property, to defend the State, or the church, or some other organization which demands of you certain things. As our society, of which we are a part, is based on acquisitive violence, we are invariably cruel to each other. The whole structure of competition, comparison, position, property, inheritance—violence is inherent in all that, and we accept it as inevitable; so we are cruel to each other, as we are cruel to animals.

The problem is not how to do away with slaughterhouses and be more kind to animals, but the fact that we have lost the art of love—not sensation, not emotionalism, but the feeling of being really kind, of being really gentle, compassionate. Do we know what it is to be really compassionate—not in order to get to heaven, but compassionate in the sense of not wanting anything for oneself?

Surely, that demands quite a different psychological education. We are trained from childhood to compete, to be cruel, to fit into society. So long as we are educated to fit into society, we will invariably be cruel because society is based on violence. If we loved our children, we would educate them entirely differently, so that there would be no more war, no nationalism, no rich and no poor, and the whole structure of this ugly society would be transformed.

But we are not interested in all that, which is a very complex and profound problem. We are only concerned with how to stop some aspect of cruelty. Not that we should not be concerned with stopping cruelty. The point is, we can found or join an organization for stopping cruelty, we can subscribe, write, work for it ceaselessly, we can become the secretary, the president, and all the rest of it, but that which is love will be missing. Whereas, if we can concern ourselves with finding out what it is to love without any attachment, without any demand, without the search for sensation—which is an immense problem—then perhaps we shall bring about a different relationship between human beings, and with the animals.

Question: What is death, and why is there such fear of it?

Krishnamurti: I think it would be worthwhile to go into this problem, not merely verbally, but actually. Why do we divide life and death? Is living separate from death? Or is death part of living? It may be that we do not know what living is, and that is why death seems such a terrible thing, something to be shunned, to be avoided, to be explained away.

Is not living part of dying? Am I living if I am constantly accumulating property, money, position, as well as knowledge and virtue, all of which I cherish and hold on to? I may call that living, but is it living? Is not that whole process merely a series of struggles, contradictions, miseries, frustrations? But we call it living, and so we want to know what death is.

We know that death is the end for all of us; the body, the physical organism, wears out and dies. Seeing this, the mind says 'I have lived, I have gathered, I have suffered, and what is to happen to me? What lies for me beyond death?' Not knowing what lies beyond, the mind is afraid of death, so it begins to invent ideas, theories—reincarnation, resurrection—or it goes back and lives in the past. If it believes in reincarnation, it tries to prove that belief through hypnosis, and so on.

That is essentially what we are all doing. Our life is overshadowed by this thing called death, and we want to know if there is any form of continuity. Or else we are so sick of life that we want to die, and we are horrified at the thought that there might be a beyond.

Now, what is the answer to all this? Why have we separated death from living, and why does the mind cling to continuity? Cannot the mind be aware of that which it calls death in the same way that it knows living? Can it not be aware of the whole significance of dying? We know what our life is—a process of gathering, enjoying, suffering, renouncing, searching, and constant anxiety. That is our existence, and in that there is a continuity. I know that I am alive because I am aware of suffering, of enjoyment; memory goes on, and my past experiences colour my future experiences. There is a sense of continuity, the momentum of a series of events linked by memory. I know this process, and I call it living. But do I know what death is? Can I ever know it? We are not asking what lies beyond, which is really not very important. But can one know or experience the meaning of that which is called death while actually living? While I am conscious, physically vigorous, while my mind is clear and capable of thinking without any sentimentality or emotionalism, can I directly experience that thing which I call death? I know what living is, and can I, in the same way, with the same vigour, the same potency, know the meaning of death? If I merely die at the last moment, through disease, or through some accident, I shall not know.

So the problem is not what lies beyond death, or how to avoid the fear of death. You cannot avoid the fear of death so long as the mind accumulates for itself a series of events and experiences linked by memory, because the ending of all that is what we actually fear.

Surely, that which has continuity is never creative. Only the mind which dies to everything from moment to moment really knows what it is to die. This is not emotionalism; it requires a great deal of insight, thought, enquiry. We can know death, as well as life, while living; while living we can enter the house of death, the unknown. But for the mind, which is the result of the known, to enter the unknown, there must be a cessation of all that it has known, of all the things it has gathered—not only consciously, but much more profoundly, in the unconscious. To wipe all that away is to die, and then we shall find there is no fear.

I am not offering this as a panacea for fear, but can we know and understand the full meaning of death? That is, can the mind be completely nothing, with no residue of the past? Whether that is possible or not is something we can enquire into, search out diligently, vigorously, work hard to find out. But if the mind merely clings to what it calls living—which is suffering, this whole process of accumulation—and tries to avoid the other, then it knows neither life nor death.

So the problem is to free the mind from the known, from all the things it has gathered, acquired, experienced, so that it is made innocent and can therefore understand that which is death, the unknowable.

Second Talk in Brussels
25 June 1956

I think it would be a waste of time and energy if we regarded these talks merely as an intellectual stimulation, or as an entertainment of new ideas. It would be like ploughing a field everlastingly, without ever sowing.

For those who are eager to find something much more significant than the weary routine of daily existence, who want to understand the greater significance of a life, it seems very difficult not to get side-tracked in their search because there are so many things in which the mind can lose itself—in work, in politics, in social activity, in the acquisition of the knowledge, or in various associations and organizations. These things apparently give a great deal of satisfaction, and when we are satisfied, our lives invariably become very superficial.

But there are some, I think, who are really serious, and who do not wish to be distracted from the central issue. They want to go to the very end of their search and discover for themselves if there is something more vital than mere reason and the logical explanation of things. Such people are not easily side-tracked. They have a certain spontaneous virtue, which is not the emptiness of cultivated virtue; they have a certain quietness, gentleness, and a sense of proportion; they lead a sane, balanced life, and do not accept the extremes. But unfortunately even they seem to find it very difficult to go beyond the everyday struggles, and the understanding of them, and discover for themselves if there is something really deeply significant.

Those of us who have thought about these things at all, and who are alert both to the recurrent problems in our personal lives, and to the crises that periodically come upon society, must be aware that the merely virtuous or good life is not enough, and that unless we can go beyond and discover something of greater significance—a wider vision, more fullness of life—then, however noble our efforts and endeavour, we shall always remain in this state of turmoil and ceaseless strife. The good life is obviously necessary, but surely that by itself is not religion. And is it possible to go beyond all that?

Some of us, I think, have seen the stupidity of dogmas, of beliefs, of organized religions, and have set them aside. We fully realize the importance of the good life, the balanced, sane, unexaggerated life—being content with little, being kindly, generous—yet somehow we do not seem to discover that vital something which brings about the truly religious life. One may be virtuous, very active in doing good, satisfied with little, unconcerned about oneself, but surely the truly religious life must mean something much more. Any respectable person, any good citizen, is all those things in one degree or another, but that is not religion. Belonging to a church, going to Sunday gatherings, reading an occasional book on religious matters, worshipping a symbol, dedicating one's life to a particular idea or ideal—surely, none of that is religion. Those are all man-made things; they are within the limits of time, of culture and civilization. And yet even those of us who have dropped all such things seem unable to go beyond.

What is the difficulty? Is it the gift of the few to go beyond? Can only a few understand, or realize, or experience Reality—which means that the many must depend on the few for help, for guidance? I think such an idea is utterly false. In this whole idea that only a few can realize, and the rest must follow, lie many forms of thoughtlessness, exploitation and cruelty. If once we accept it, our lives become very shallow, meaningless, trivial.

And most of us accept that idea very easily, do we not? We think that only the few can understand, or that there is only one Son of God, and the rest of us are just—whatever we are. We accept such an idea because in ourselves we are very lazy, or perhaps we do not have the capacity to penetrate. It may be mostly our lack of this capacity to penetrate, to go to the root of things, that is preventing deep understanding, this extraordinary sense of unity—which is not identification with the idea of unity. Most of us identify ourselves with something—with the family, with the country, with an idea, with a belief—hoping thereby to forget our petty little selves. But I am afraid that is no solution. The greater does contain the lesser, but when the lesser tries to identify itself with the greater, it is merely a pose and has no value.

So, is it possible for each one of us to have this capacity to go beyond routine virtue, goodness, sensitivity, compassion? These are essential in daily life, but can we not awaken the capacity to penetrate beyond them, beyond all the conscious movements of the mind, beyond all inclinations, hopes, aspirations, desires, so that the mind is no longer an instrument which creates and destroys, which is caught in its own projections, in its own ideas?

If we can sanely and diligently find out for ourselves how this capacity comes into being, without trying to cultivate it or wishing for it to happen, then I think we shall know what it is to lead a religious life. But this demands an extraordinary revolution in our thinking—which is the only real revolution. Any merely economic or social revolution only breeds the need of further reform, and that is an endless process. Real revolution is inward, and it comes into being without the mind seeking it. What the mind seeks and finds, however reasonable, however rational and intelligent, is never the final answer. For the mind is put together, and what it creates is also put together; therefore it can be undone. But the revolution of which I am speaking is the truly religious life, stripped of all the absurdities of organized religions throughout the world. It has nothing to do with priests, with symbols, with churches.

How is this revolution to take place? As we do not know, we say that we must have faith, or that grace must descend upon us. This may be so; grace may come. But the faith that is cultivated is only another creation of the mind, and therefore it can be destroyed. Whether there is grace or not is not our concern; a mind that seeks grace will never find it.

So, if you have thought at all about these matters, if you have meditated upon life, then you must have asked yourself whether this inward revolution can take place, and whether it is dependent upon a capacity that can be cultivated, as one cultivates the capacity for accountancy, or engineering, or chemistry. Those are cultivable capacities; they can be built up, and will produce certain results. But I am talking of a capacity which is not cultivable, something that you cannot go after, that you cannot pursue or search out in the dark places of the mind. And without that something, virtue becomes mere respectability—which is a terrible thing; without that something, all activity is contradictory, leading to further conflict and misery.

Now, being aware of our own ceaseless struggling within the field of self-conscious activity, our self-concern—taking all this multifarious action and contradiction into account—how are we to come to that other state? How is one to live in that moment which is eternity? All this is not mere sentiment or romanticism. Religion has nothing whatever to do with romanticism or sentimentality. It is a very hard thing—hard in the sense that one must work furiously to find out what is truly religious.

Perceiving all the contradiction and confusion that exists in the outward structure of society, and the psychological conflict that is perpetually going on within oneself, one realizes that all our endeavour to be loving or brotherly is actually a pose, a mask. However beautiful the mask may be, behind it there is nothing; so we develop a philosophy of cynicism or despair, or we cling to a belief in something mysterious beyond this ceaseless turmoil. Again, this is obviously not religion, and without the perfume of true religion, life has very little meaning. That is why we are everlastingly struggling to find something. We pursue the many gurus and teachers, haunt the various churches, practise this or that system of meditation, rejecting one and accepting another. And yet we never seem to cross the threshold; the mind seems incapable of going beyond itself.

So, what is it, I wonder, that brings the other into being? Or is it that we cannot do anything but go up to the threshold and remain there, not knowing what lies beyond? It may be that we have to come to the very edge of the precipice of everything we have known, so that there is the cessation of all endeavour, of all cultivation of virtue, and the mind is no longer seeking anything. I think that is all the conscious mind can do. Whatever else it does only creates another pattern, another habit. Must not the mind strip itself of all the things it has gathered, all its accumulations of experience and knowledge, so that it is in a state of innocency which is not cultivated?

Perhaps that is our difficulty. We hear that we must be innocent in order to find out, so we cultivate innocence. But can innocence ever be cultivated? Is it not like the cultivation of humility? Surely, a man who cultivates humility is never humble, any more than the man who practises non-violence ceases to be violent. So it may be that one must see the truth of this—that the mind which is put together, which is made up of many things, cannot do anything. To see this truth may be all that it can do. Probably there must be the capacity to see the truth in a flash—and I think that very perception will cleanse the mind of all the past in an instant.

The more serious, the more earnest we are, the greater danger there is of our trying to become or achieve something. Surely, only the man who is spontaneously humble, who has immense unconscious humility—only such a man is capable of understanding from moment to moment and

145

never accumulating what he has learned. So this great humility of not-knowing is essential, is it not?

But you see, we are all seeking success, we want a result. We say 'I have done all these things, and I have got nowhere, I have received nothing; I am still the same.' This despairing sense of desiring success, of wanting to arrive, to attain, to understand, emphasizes, does it not?, the separativity of the mind; there is always the conscious or unconscious endeavour to achieve a result, and therefore the mind is never empty, never free for a second from the movement of the past, of time.

So I think what is important is not to read more, discuss more, or to attend more talks, but rather to be conscious of the motives, the intentions, the deceptions of one's own mind—to be simply aware of all that, and leave it alone, not try to change it, not try to become something else, because the effort to become something else is like putting on another mask. That is why the danger is much greater for those of us who are earnest and deeply serious than it is for the flippant and the casual. Our very seriousness may prevent the understanding of things as they are.

It seems to me that what each one of us has to do is to capture the significance of the totality of our thinking. But much concern over detail, over the many conflicting thoughts and feelings, will not bring about an understanding of the whole. What is required is the sudden perception of the totality of the mind—which is not the outcome of asking how to see it, but of constantly looking, enquiring, searching. Then, I think, we shall find out for ourselves what is the truly religious life.

Question: What are your ideas about education?

Krishnamurti: I think mere ideas are no good at all, because one idea is as good as another, depending on whether the mind accepts or rejects it. But perhaps it would be worthwhile to find out what we mean by education. Let us see if we can think out together the whole significance of education, and not merely think in terms of my idea, or your idea, or the idea of some specialist.

Why do we educate our children at all? Is it to help the child to understand the whole significance of life, or merely to prepare him to earn a livelihood in a particular culture or society? Which is it that we want? Not what we should want, or what is desirable, but what is it that we as parents actually insist on? We want the child to conform, to be a respectable citizen in a corrupt society, in a society that is at war both within itself and with other societies, that is brutal, acquisitive, violent, greedy, with occasional spots of affection, tolerance and kindliness. That is what we actually want, is it not? If the child does not fit into society—whether it be communist, socialist, or capitalist—we are afraid of what will happen to him, so we begin to educate him to conform to the pattern of our own making. That is all we want where the child is concerned, and that is essentially what is taking place. And any revolt of the child against society, against the pattern of conformity, we call delinquency.

We want the children to conform; we want to control their minds, to shape their conduct, their way of living, so that they will fit into the pattern of society. That is what every parent wants, is it not? And that is exactly what is happening, whether it be in America or in Europe, in Russia or in India. The pattern may vary slightly, but they all want the child to conform.

Now, is that education? Or does education mean that the parents and the teachers themselves see the significance of the whole pattern, and are helping the child from the very beginning to be alert to all its influences? Seeing the full significance of the pattern, with its religious, social and economic influences, its influences of class, of family, of tradition—seeing the significance of all this for oneself and helping the child to understand and not be caught in it—that may be education. To educate the child may be to help him to be outside of society, so that he creates his own society. Since our society is not at all what it should be, why encourage the child to stay within its pattern?

At present we force the child to conform to a social pattern which we have established individually, as a family, and as the collective; and he unfortunately inherits, not only our property, but some of our psychological characteristics as well. So from the very beginning he is a slave to the environment.

Seeing all this, if we really love our children and are therefore deeply concerned about education, we will contrive from the very beginning to bring about an atmosphere which will encourage them to be free. A few real educators have thought about all this, but unfortunately very few parents ever think about it at all. We leave it to the experts—religion to the priest, psychology to the psychologist, and our children to the so-called teachers. Surely, the parent is also the educator; he is the teacher, and also the one who learns—not only the child.

So this is a very complex problem, and if we really wish to resolve it we must go into it most profoundly; and then, I think, we shall find out how to bring about the right kind of education.

Question: What is the meaning of existence? What is it all about?

Krishnamurti: This is a question that is constantly arising all over the world: What is the purpose of life? We are now asking it of ourselves, and I wonder why we ask it. Is it because life has very little significance for us, and we ask this question in the hope of being assured that it has a greater significance? Is it that we are so confused in ourselves that we do not know how to find the answer, which way to turn? I think that is most likely. Being confused in ourselves, we look, we ask; and in asking, in looking, we invent theories, we give a purpose or a meaning of life.

So what is important is not to define the purpose, the significance, the meaning of existence, but rather to find out why the mind asks this question. If we see something very clearly, we do not have to ask about it; so probably we are confused. We have been in the habit of accepting the things imposed upon us by authority; we have always followed authority without much thought, except the thoughts which authority encourage. Now, however, we have begun to reject authority, because we want to find things out for ourselves, and in trying to find things out for ourselves, we become very confused. That is why we again ask 'What is the purpose of life?' If someone tells you what is the purpose of life, and their answer is satisfactory, you may accept it as your authority and guide your life accordingly, but fundamentally you will still be confused. The question, then, is not what the purpose of life is, but whether the mind can clear itself of its own confusion. If it can and does, then you will never ask that other question.

But the difficulty for most of us is to realize that we are thoroughly confused. We think we are only superficially confused, and that there is a higher part of the mind which is not contaminated by confusion. To realize that the totality of the mind is confused is very difficult, because most of us have been educated to believe that there is a higher part of the mind which can direct, shape, and guide us; but surely this again is an invention of the mind.

To free oneself from confusion, one must first know that one is confused. To see that one is really confused is the beginning of clarification, is it not? But it requires deep perception and great honesty to see and to acknowledge to oneself that one is totally confused. When one knows that one is totally confused, one will not seek clarification, because any action on the part of a confused mind to find clarification will only add to the confusion. That is fairly obvious, is it not? If I am confused, I may read, or look, or ask, but my search, my asking, is the outcome of my confusion, and therefore it can only lead to further confusion. Whereas, the mind that is confused and really knows it is confused will have no movement of search, of asking, and in that very moment of being silently aware of its confusion, there is a beginning of clarification.

If you are really following this, you are bound to see the truth of it psychologically. But the difficulty is that we do not really know, we are not actually aware of how extraordinarily confused we are. The moment one fully realizes one's own confusion, one's thought becomes very tentative, hesitant, it is never assertive or dogmatic. Therefore the mind begins to enquire from a totally different point of view, and it is this new kind of enquiry alone that will clear up the confusion.

Question: Do you believe in God?

Krishnamurti: It is easy to ask questions, and it is very important to know how to ask a right question. In this particular question, the words 'believe' and 'God' seem to me so contradictory. A man who merely believes in God will never know what God is, because his belief is a form of conditioning—which again is very obvious. In Christianity you are taught from childhood to believe in God, so from the very beginning your mind is conditioned. In the communist countries, belief in God is called sheer nonsense— at which you are horrified. You want to convert them, and they want to convert you. They have conditioned their minds not to believe, and you call them godless, while you consider yourself God-fearing, or whatever it is. I do not see much difference between the two. You may go to church, pray, listen to sermons, or perform certain rituals and get some kind of stimulation out of it—but none of that, surely, is the experiencing of the unknown. And can the mind experience the unknown, whatever name one may give it? The name does not matter. That is the question— not whether one believes or does not believe in God.

One can see that any form of conditioning will never set the mind free, and that only the free mind can discover, experience. Experiencing is a very strange thing. The moment you know you are experiencing, there is the cessation of that experience. The moment I know I am happy, I am no longer happy. To experience this immeasurable Reality, the experiencer must come to an end. The experiencer is the result of the known, of many centuries of cultivated memory; he is an accumulation of the things he has experienced. So when he says, 'I must experience Reality', and is cognizant of that experience, then what he experiences is not Reality, but a projection of his own past, his own conditioning.

That is why it is very important to understand that the thinker and the thought, or the experiencer and the experience, are the same; they are not different. When there is an experiencer separate from the experience, then the experiencer is constantly pursuing further experience, but that experience is always a projection of himself.

So Reality, the timeless state, is not to be found through mere verbalization, or acceptance, or through the repetition of what one has heard—which is all folly. To really find out, one must go into this whole question of the experiencer. So long as there is the 'me' who wants to experience, there can be no experiencing of Reality. That is why the experiencer—the entity who is seeking God, who believes in God, who prays to God—must totally cease. Only then can that immeasurable Reality come into being.

First Talk in Hamburg
6 September 1956

I think, it is important, in listening to each other, to find out for oneself if what is being said is true; that is, to experience it directly, and not merely argue about whether what is said is true or false, which would be completely useless. And perhaps this evening we can find out if it is possible to set about the very complex process of forgetting oneself.

Many of us must have experienced, at one time or another, that state when the 'me', the self, with its aggressive demands, has completely ceased, and the mind is extraordinarily quiet, without any direct volition—that state wherein, perhaps, one may experience something that is without measure, something that it is impossible to put into words. There must have been these rare moments when the self, the 'me', with all its memories and travails, with all its anxieties and fears, has completely ceased. One is then a being without any motive, without any compulsion, and in that state one feels or is aware of an astonishing sense of immeasurable distance, of limitless space and being.

This must have happened to many of us. And I think it would be worthwhile if we could go into this question together and see whether it is possible to resolve the enclosing, limiting self, this restricting 'me' that worries, that has anxieties, fears, that is dominating and dominated, that has innumerable memories, that is cultivating virtue and trying in every way to become something, to be important. I do not know if you have noticed the constant effort that one is consciously or unconsciously making to express oneself, to be something, either socially, morally, or economically. This entails, does it not?, a great deal of striving; our whole life is based on the everlasting struggle to arrive, to achieve, to become. The more we struggle, the more significant and exaggerated the self becomes, with all its limitations, fears, ambitions, frustrations; and there must have been times when each one has asked himself whether it is not possible to be totally without the self.

After all, we do have rare moments when the sense of the self is not. I am not talking of the transmutation of the self to a higher level, but of the simple cessation of the 'me' with its anxieties, worries, fears—the absence of the self. One realizes that such a thing is possible, and then one sets about deliberately, consciously, to eliminate the self. After all, that is what organized religions try to do—to help each worshipper, each believer, to lose himself in something greater, and thereby perhaps to experience some higher state. If you are not a so-called religious person, then you identify yourself with the State, with the country, and try to lose yourself in that identification, which gives you the feeling of greatness, of being something much larger than the petty little self, and all the rest of it. Or, if we do not do that, we try to lose ourselves in social work of some kind, again with the same intention. We think that if we can forget ourselves, deny ourselves, put ourselves out of the way by dedicating our lives to something much greater and more vital than ourselves, we shall perhaps experience a bliss, a happiness, which is not merely a physical sensation. And if we do none of these things, we hope to stop thinking about ourselves through the cultivation of virtue, through discipline, through control, through constant practice.

Now, I do not know if you have thought about it, but all this implies, surely, a ceaseless effort to be or become something. And perhaps, in listening to what is being said, we can together go into this whole process and discover for ourselves whether it is possible to wipe away the sense of the 'me' without this fearful, restricting discipline, without this enormous effort to deny ourselves, this constant struggle to renounce our wants, our ambitions, in order to be something or to achieve some reality. I think in this lies the real issue. Because all effort implies motive, does it not? I make an effort to forget myself in something, in some ritual or ideology, because in thinking about myself I am unhappy. When I think about something else, I am more relaxed, my mind is quieter, I seem to feel better, I look at things differently. So I make an effort to forget myself. But behind my effort there is a motive, which is to escape from myself because I suffer, and that motive is essentially a part of the self. When I renounce this world and become a monk, or a very devout religious person, the motive is that I want to achieve something better, but that is still the process of the self, is it not? I may give up my name and just be a number in a religious order, but the motive is still there.

Now, is it possible to forget oneself without any motive? Because, we can see very well that any motive has within it the seed of the self, with its anxiety, ambition, frustration, its fear of not-being, and the immense urge to be secure. And can all that fall away easily, without any effort? Which means, really, can you and I, as individuals, live in this world without being identified with anything? After all, I identify myself with my country, with my religion, with my family, with my name, because without identification I am nothing. Without a position, without power, without prestige of one kind or another, I feel lost; and so I identify myself with my name, with my family, with my religion, I join some organization or become a monk—we all know the various types of identification that the mind clings to. But can we live in this world without any identification at all?

If we can think about this, if we can listen to what is being said, and at the same time be aware of our own intimations regarding the implications of identification, then I think we shall discover, if we are at all serious, that it is possible to live in this world without the nightmare of identification and the ceaseless struggle to achieve a result. Then, I think, knowledge has quite a different significance. At present we identify ourselves with our knowledge and use it as a means of self-expansion, just as we do with the nation, with a religion, or with some activity. Identification with the knowledge we have gained is another way of furthering the self, is it not? Through knowledge the 'me' continues its struggle to be something, and thereby perpetuates misery, pain.

If we can very humbly and simply see the implications of all this, be aware, without assuming anything, of how our minds operate and what our thinking is based on, then I think we shall realize the extraordinary contradiction that exists in this whole process of identification. After all, it is because I feel empty, lonely, miserable, that I identify myself with my country, and this identification gives me a sense of well-being, a feeling of power. Or, for the same reason, I identify myself with a hero, with a saint. But if I can go into this process of identification very deeply, then I will see that the whole movement of my thinking and all my activity, however noble, is essentially based on the continuance of myself in one form or another.

Now, if I once see that, if I realize it, feel it with my whole being, then religion has quite a different meaning. Then religion is no longer a process of identifying myself with God, but rather the coming into being of a state in which there is only that Reality, and not the 'me'. But this cannot be a mere verbal assertion, it is not just a phrase to be repeated.

That is why it is very important, it seems to me, to have self-knowledge, which means going very deeply into oneself without assuming anything, so that the mind has no deceptions, no illusions, so that it does not trick itself into visions and false states. Then, perhaps, it is possible for the enclosing process of the self to come to an end—but not through any form of compulsion or discipline because the more you discipline the self, the stronger the self becomes. What is important is to go into all this very deeply and patiently, without taking anything for granted, so that one begins to understand the ways, the purposes, the motives and directions of the mind. Then, I think, the mind comes to a state in which there is no identification at all, and therefore no effort to be something; then there is the cessation of the self, and I think that is the real.

Although we may swiftly, fleetingly experience this state, the difficulty for most of us is that the mind clings to the experience and wants more of it, and the very wanting of more is again the beginning of the self. That is why it is very important, for those of us who are really serious in these matters, to be inwardly aware of the process of our own thinking, to silently observe our motives, our emotional reactions, and not merely say 'I know myself very well'—for actually one does not. You may know your reactions and motives superficially, at the conscious level. But the self, the 'me', is a very complex affair, and to go into the totality of the self needs persistent and continuous enquiry without a motive, without an end in view, and such enquiry is surely a form of meditation.

That immense Reality cannot be found through any organization, through any church, through any book, through any person or teacher. One has to find it for oneself—which means that one has to be completely alone, uninfluenced. But we are all of us the result of so many influences, so many pressures, known and unknown; and that is why it is very important to understand these many pressures, influences, and be dissociated from them all, so that the mind becomes extraordinarily simple, clear. Then, perhaps, it will be possible to experience that which cannot be put into words.

Question: You said yesterday that authority is evil. Why is it evil?

Krishnamurti: Is not all following evil? Why do we follow authority of any kind? Why do we establish authority? Why do human beings accept authority—governmental, religious, every form of authority?

Authority does not come into being by itself; we create it. We create the tyrannical ruler, as well as the tyrannical priest with his gods, rituals and beliefs. Why? Why do we create authority and become followers? Obviously, because we all want to be secure, we want to be powerful in different ways and in varying degrees. All of us are seeking position, prestige, which the leader, the country, the government, the minister, is offering—so we follow. Or we create the image of authority in our own minds, and follow that image. The church is as tyrannical as the political leaders, and while we object to the tyranny of governments, most of us submit to the tyranny of the church, or of some religious teacher.

If we begin to examine the whole process of following, we will see, I think, that we follow, first of all, because we are confused, and we want somebody to tell us what to do. And being confused, we are bound to follow those who are also confused, however much they may assert that they are the messengers of God or the saviours of the State. We follow because we are confused, and as we choose leaders, both religious and political, out of our confusion, we inevitably create more confusion, more conflict, more misery.

That is why it is very important for us to understand the confusion in ourselves, and not look to another to help us to clear it up. For how can a man who is confused know what is wrong and choose what is right, what is true? First he must clear up his own confusion. And once he has cleared up his own confusion, there is no choice; he will not follow anybody.

So we follow because we want to be secure, whether economically, socially, or religiously. After all, the mind is always seeking security, it wants to be safe in this world, and also in the next world. All we are concerned with is to be secure, both with Mammon and with God. That is why we create the authority of the government, the dictator, and the authority of the church, the idol, the image. So long as we follow, we must create authority, and that authority becomes ultimately evil, because we have thoughtlessly given ourselves over to domination by another.

I think it is important to go deeply into this whole question and begin to understand why the mind insists on following. You follow, not only political and religious leaders, but also what you read in the newspapers, in magazines, in books; you seek the authority of the specialists, the authority of the written word. All this indicates, does it not?, that the mind is uncertain of itself. One is afraid to think apart from what has been said by the leaders, because one might lose one's job, be ostracized, excommunicated, or put into a concentration camp. We submit to authority because all of us have this inward demand to be safe, this urge to be secure. So long as we want to be secure—in our possessions, in our power, in our thoughts—we must have authority, we must be followers; and in that lies the seed of evil, for it invariably leads to the exploitation of man by man. He who would really find out what Truth is, what God is, can have no authority, whether of the book, of the government, of the image, or of the priest; he must be totally free of all that.

This is very difficult for most of us, because it means being insecure, standing completely alone, searching, groping, never being satisfied, never seeking success. But if we seriously experiment with it, then I think we shall find that there is no longer any question of creating or following authority, because something else begins to operate—which is not a mere verbal statement, but an actual fact. The man who is ceaselessly questioning, who has no authority, who does not follow any tradition, any book or teacher, becomes a light unto himself.

Question: Why do you put so much emphasis on self-knowledge? We know very well what we are.

Krishnamurti: I wonder if we do know what we are. We are, surely, everything that we have been taught; we are the totality of our past; we are a bundle of memories, are we not? When you say 'I belong to God', or 'The self is eternal', and all the rest of it—that is all part of your background, your conditioning. Similarly, when the communist says, 'There is no God', he also is reflecting his conditioning.

Merely to say 'Yes, I know myself very well' is just a superficial remark. But to realize, to actually experience that your whole being is nothing but a bundle of memories, that all your thinking, your reactions, are mechanical, is not at all easy. It means being aware, not only of the workings of the conscious mind, but also of the unconscious residue, the racial impressions, memories, the things that we have learned; it means discovering the whole field of the mind, the hidden as well as the visible, and that is extremely arduous. And if my mind is merely the residue of the past, if it is only a bundle of memories, impressions, shaped by so-called education and various other influences, then is there any part of me which is not all that? Because, if I am merely a repeating machine, as most of us are—repeating what we have learned, what we have gathered, passing on what has been told to us—then any thought arising within this conditioned field obviously can only lead to further conditioning, further misery and limitation.

So, can the mind, knowing its limitation, being aware of its conditioning, go beyond itself? That is the problem. Merely to assert that it can, or it cannot, would be silly. Surely it is fairly obvious that the whole mind is conditioned. We are all conditioned—by tradition, by family, by experience, through the process of time. If you believe in God, that belief is the outcome of a particular conditioning, just as is the disbelief of the man who says he does not believe in God. So belief and disbelief have very little importance. But what is important is to understand the whole field of thought, and to see if the mind can go beyond it all.

To go beyond, you must know yourself. The motives, the urges, the responses, the immense pressure of what people have taught you, the dreams, the inhibitions, the conscious and hidden compulsions—you must know them all. Only then I think is it possible to find out if the mind, which is now so mechanical, can discover something totally new, something which has never been corrupted by time.

Question: You say that true religion is neither belief, nor dogma, nor ceremonies. What then is true religion?

Krishnamurti: How are you going to find out? It is not for me just to answer, surely. How is the individual to find out what is true religion? We know what is generally called religion—dogma, belief, ceremonies, meditation, the practice of yoga, fasting, disciplining oneself, and so on. We all know the whole gamut of the so-called religious approach. But is that religion? And if I want to find out what is true religion, how am I to set about it?

First of all, I must obviously be free from all dogmas, must I not? And that is extraordinarily difficult. I may be free from the dogmas imposed upon me in childhood, but I may have created a dogma or belief of my own—which is equally pernicious. So I must also be free from that. And I can be free only when I have no motive, when there is no desire at all to be secure, either with God or in this world. Again, this is extremely difficult, because surreptitiously, deep down, the mind is always wanting a position of certainty. And there are all the images that have been imposed upon the mind: the saviours, the teachers, the doctrines, the superstitions—I must be free of all that. Then, perhaps, I shall find out what it is to be truly religious—which may be the greatest revolution, and I think it is. The only true revolution is not the economic revolution, or the revolution of the communists, but the deep religious revolution which comes about when the mind is no longer seeking shelter in any dogma or belief, in any church or saviour, in any teacher or sacred book. And I think such a revolution has immense significance in the world, for then the mind has no ideology, it is neither of the West nor of the East. Surely, this religious revolution is the only salvation.

To find out what is true religion requires not a mere one-day effort or one-day search and forgetfulness the next day, but constant questioning, a disturbing enquiry, so that you begin to discard everything. After all, this process of discarding is the highest form of thinking. The pursuit of positive thinking is not thinking at all, it is merely copying. But when there is enquiry without a motive, without the desire for a result, which is the negative approach—in that enquiry the mind goes beyond all traditional religions; and then, perhaps, one may find out for oneself what God is, what Truth is.

First Talk in New Delhi
31 October 1956

It seems to me that what is important is not the problem, but the mind that approaches the problem. We have many problems of every kind: the growth of tyranny, the multiplication of conflicts in the individual as well as in the collective life, and the utter lack of any directive purpose in life except that which is artificially created by society or by the individual himself. Our many problems seem to be increasing, they are not diminishing. The more civilization has progressed, the greater has become the complexity of the problems of living, and I think most of us are aware that the various ways of life which most people follow—the communist way of life, the so-called religious way of life, and the purely materialistic or progressive way of life, the life of many possessions—have not solved these problems. Seeing all this, those of us who are at all serious must have considered the question of how to bring about a change, not only in ourselves and in our relationship with particular individuals, but also in our relationship with the collective, with society. Our problems multiply, but as I said, I don't think the problem, whatever it be, is the real issue. The real issue, surely, is the mind that approaches the problem.

If my mind is incapable of dealing with a problem, and I act, the problem multiplies, does it not? That is a fairly obvious fact. And seeing that whatever it does with regard to the problem only multiplies the problem, what is the mind to do? Do you understand the issue? The problem—whether it be the problem of God, the problem of starvation, the problem of collective tyranny in the name of government, and so on—exists at different levels of our being, and we approach it hoping to solve it, which I think is a wrong approach altogether, because we are laying emphasis on the problem. It seems to me that the real problem is the mind itself, and not the problem which the mind has created and tries to solve. If the mind is petty, small, narrow, limited, however great and complex the problem may be, the mind approaches that problem in terms of its own pettiness. If I have a little mind and I think of God, the God of my thinking will be a little God, though I may clothe him with grandeur, beauty, wisdom, and all the rest of it.

It is the same with the problem of existence, the problem of bread, the problem of love, the problem of sex, the problem of relationship, the problem of death. These are all enormous problems, and we approach them with a small mind; we try to resolve them with a mind that is very limited. Though it has extraordinary capacities and is capable of invention, of subtle, cunning thought, the mind is still petty. It may be able to quote Marx, or the Gita, or some other religious book, but it is still a small mind, and a small mind confronted with a complex problem can only translate that problem in terms of itself, and therefore the problem, the misery increases. So the question is: Can the mind that is small, petty, be transformed into something which is not bound by its own limitations?

Are you following what I am talking about, or am I not making myself clear? Take, for example, the problem of love, which is very complex. Though I may be married, have children, unless there is that sense of beauty, the depth and clarity of love, life is very shallow, without much meaning, and I approach love with a very small mind. I want to know what it is, but I have all kinds of assumptions about it, I have already clothed it with my petty mind. So the problem is not how to understand what love is, but to free from its own pettiness the mind that approaches the problem, and the minds of most people are petty.

By a petty mind I mean a mind that is occupied. Do you understand? A mind that is occupied with God, with plans, with virtue, with how to carry out what certain authorities say about economics or religion; a mind that is occupied with itself, with its own development, with culture, with following a certain way of existence; a mind that is occupied with an identity, with a country, belief, or ideology—such a mind is a petty mind.

When you are occupied with something, what happens psychologically, inwardly? There is no space in your mind, is there? Have you ever watched your own mind in operation? If you have, you will know that it is everlastingly busy with itself. An ambitious man is concerned from morning till night, and during his sleep, with his successes and failures, with his frustrations, with his innumerable demands and the fulfilment of his ambition. He is like the so-called religious man who endlessly repeats a certain phrase, or is occupied with an ideal and with trying to conform to that ideal. So the mind that is occupied is a petty mind. If one really understands this, then quite a different process is at work.

After all, a mind that is vain, arrogant, full of the desire for power, and that tries to cultivate humility, is occupied with itself; therefore it is a petty mind. The mind that is trying to improve itself through the acquisition of knowledge, that is trying to become very clever, to be more powerful, to have a better job—such a mind is petty. It may occupy itself with God, with Truth, with the Atman, or with sitting in the seats of the mighty, but it is still a petty mind.

So what happens? Your mind is petty, occupied, it starts with certain conclusions, assumptions, it posits certain ideas, and with this occupied mind you try to solve the problem. When a small mind meets an enormous problem there is action, obviously, and that action does produce a result—the result being an increase of the problem; and if you observe, that is exactly what is happening in the world. The people in the big seats are occupied with themselves in the name of the country; like you and me, they want position, power, prestige. We are all in the same boat, and with petty little minds we are trying to solve the extraordinary problems of living, problems which demand an unoccupied mind. Life is a vital, moving thing, is it not? Therefore one must come to it afresh, with a mind that is not wholly occupied, that is capable of some space, some emptiness.

Now, what is the state of the mind that knows it is occupied and sees that occupation is petty? That is, when I realize that my mind is occupied, and that an occupied mind is a petty mind, what happens?

I don't think we see sufficiently clearly the truth that an occupied mind is a petty mind. Whether the mind is occupied with self-improvement, with God, with drink, with sexual passion, or the desire for power, it is all essentially the same, though sociologically these various occupations may have a difference. Occupation is occupation, and the mind that is occupied is petty because it is concerned with itself. If you see, if you actually experience the truth of that fact, surely your mind is no longer concerned with itself, with its own improvement, so there is a possibility for the mind that has been enclosed to remove its enclosure.

Just as an experiment, observe for yourself how your whole life is based on an assumption—that there is God or there is no God, that a certain pattern of living is better than other patterns, and so on. A mind which is occupied starts with an assumption, it approaches life with an idea, a conclusion. And can the mind approach a problem totally, removing all its conclusions, its previous experiences, which åre also a form of conclusion? After all, a challenge is always new, is it not? If the mind is incapable of responding adequately to challenge, there is a deterioration, a going back; and the mind cannot respond adequately if it is consciously or unconsciously occupied, occupation being based on some ideology or conclusion. If you realize the truth of this, you will find that the mind is no longer petty, because it is in a state of enquiry, in a state of healthy doubt—which is not to have doubts *about* something, because that again becomes an occupation. A mind that is truly enquiring is not accumulating. It is the accumulating mind that is petty, whether it is accumulating knowledge, or money, power, position. When you see the truth of that totally, there is real transformation of the mind, and it is such a mind that is capable of dealing with the many problems.

I am going to answer some questions, and as I have pointed out, the answer is not important. What is important is the problem, and the mind cannot give undivided attention to the problem if it is distracted by trying to find a solution to the problem. All solutions are based on desire, and the problem exists because of desire—desire for a hundred things. Without understanding the whole process of desire, merely to respond to the problem through one particular activity of desire, hoping it will produce the right answer, will not bring about the dissolution of the problem. So we are concerned, not with an answer, but with the problem itself.

Question: I entirely agree with you that it is necessary to uncondition one's mind. But how can a conditioned mind uncondition itself?

Krishnamurti: The questioner states that he agrees with what I have said. Before we go into the question of unconditioning the mind, let us find out what we mean by agreement. You can agree with an opinion, with an idea; you cannot agree with a fact. You and I may agree in the sense that we share an opinion about a fact, but an opinion held by many does not make truth. To understand there must be a living, vital scepticism, not acceptance or agreement. If you merely agree with me, you are agreeing with an opinion which you think I have. I have no opinions, so we are not in agreement. If you and I both see a poisonous snake, there is no question of agreement—we both stay away from it. When we say we agree, we are intellectually agreeing about an idea; but this enquiry into how to free the mind from conditioning does not demand an intellectual agreement. As long as the mind is conditioned as a Hindu, a communist, or what you will, it is incapable of thinking anew. That is not a matter of opinion. It is a fact. You don't have to agree.

So the question is: How can a mind which is conditioned, uncondition itself? You realize that your mind is conditioned as a Hindu, with all the various beliefs of Hinduism, or as a communist, a Christian, a Muslim, and so on. Your mind is conditioned, that is obvious. You believe in something, in the supernatural, in God, whereas another who has been brought up in a different social and psychological environment says there is no such thing, it is all rubbish. You are both conditioned, and your God is no more real than the no-God in which the other fellow believes.

So, whether you like it or not, your mind is conditioned, not partially, but all the way through. Don't say the Atman is unconditioned. You have been told that the Atman exists, otherwise you don't know anything about it, and when you think of the Atman, your thought is conditioning the Atman. This again is so obvious. It is like the man who believes in Masters. He has been told there are Masters, and through his own desire for security he longs to find them, so he has visions, which are psychologically very simple and immature.

Now, the question is this. I know that my mind is conditioned, and how am I to free my mind from conditioning when the entity that tries to free it is also conditioned? Do you understand the issue? When a conditioned mind realizes that it is conditioned and wishes to uncondition itself, that very wish is also conditioned; so what is the mind to do?

Are you following this? Please, sirs, don't merely listen to my words, but watch your own minds in operation. This is a very difficult issue to discuss with such a large group, and unless you pay real attention you will not find the answer. I am not going to give you the answer, so you have to observe your own minds very intently.

I know that my mind is conditioned as a Hindu, as a Buddhist, or whatever it is, and I see that any movement of the mind to uncondition itself is still conditioned. When the mind tries to uncondition itself, the maker of that effort is also conditioned, is he not? I hope I am explaining this.

Sirs, can you not take a pill and stop coughing? I can go on, but coughing and taking notes disturbs the others who are listening. So I will begin again.

Your mind is conditioned right through; there is no part of you which is unconditioned. That is a fact, whether you like it or not. You may say there is a part of you—the watcher, the super-soul, the Atman—which is not conditioned; but because you think about it, it is within the field of thought, therefore it is conditioned. You can invent lots of theories about it, but the fact is that your mind is conditioned right through, the conscious as well as the unconscious, and any effort it makes to free itself is also conditioned. So, what is the mind to do? Or rather, what is the state of the mind when it knows that it is conditioned and realizes that any effort it makes to uncondition itself is still conditioned? Am I making myself clear?

Now, when you say, 'I know I am conditioned', do you really know it, or is that merely a verbal statement? Do you know it with the same potency with which you see a cobra? When you see a snake and know it to be a cobra, there is immediate, unpremeditated action; and when you say, 'I know I am conditioned', has it the same vital significance as your perception of the cobra? Or is it merely a superficial acknowledgment of the fact, and not the realization of the fact? When I realize the fact that I am conditioned, there is immediate action. I don't have to make an effort to uncondition myself. The very fact that I am conditioned, and the realization of that fact, brings an immediate clarification. The difficulty lies in not realizing that you are conditioned—not realizing it in the sense of understanding all its implications, seeing that all thought, however subtle, however cunning, however sophisticated or philosophical, is conditioned.

All thinking is obviously based on memory, conscious or unconscious, and when the thinker says, 'I must free myself from conditioning', that very thinker, being the result of thought, is conditioned; and when you realize this, there is the cessation of all effort to change the conditioning. As long as you make an effort to change, you are still conditioned, because the maker of the effort is himself conditioned; therefore his effort will result in further conditioning, only in a different pattern. The mind that fully realizes this is in an unconditioned state, because it has seen the totality of conditioning, the truth or the falseness of it. Sirs, it is like seeing something true. The very perception of what is true is the liberating factor. But to see what is true demands total attention—not a forced attention, not the calculated, profitable attention of fear or gain. When you see the truth that whatever the conditioned mind does to free itself, it is still conditioned, there is the cessation of all such effort, and it is this perception of what is true that is the liberating factor.

Question: How can I experience God, which will give a meaning to my weary life? Without that experience, what is the purpose of living?

Krishnamurti: Can I understand life directly, or must I experience something which will give a meaning to life? Do you understand, sirs? To appreciate beauty, must I know what its purpose is? Must love have a cause? And if there is a cause to love, is it love? The questioner says he must have a certain experience that will give a meaning to life— which implies that for him life in itself is not important. So in seeking God, he is really escaping from life, escaping from sorrow, from beauty, from ugliness, from anger, pettiness, jealousy and the desire for power, from the extraordinary complexity of living. All that is life, and as he does not understand it, he says, 'I will find some greater thing which will give a meaning to life.'

Please listen to what I am saying, but not just at the verbal, intellectual level, because then it will have very little meaning. You can spin a lot of words about all this, read all the sacred books in the land, but it will be worthless because it is not related to your life, to your daily existence.

So, what is our living? What is this thing that we call our existence? Very simply, not philosophically, it is a series of experiences of pleasure and pain, and we want to avoid the pains while holding on to the pleasures. The pleasure of power, of being a big man in the big world, the pleasure of dominating one's little wife or husband, the pain, the frustration, fear and anxiety which come with ambition, the ugliness of playing up to the man of importance, and so on—all that goes to make up our daily living. That is, what we call living is a series of memories within the field of the known, and the known becomes a problem when the mind is not free of the known. Functioning within the field of the known—the known being knowledge, experience and the memory of that experience—the mind says, 'I must know God.' So, according to its tradition, according to its ideas, its conditioning, it projects an entity which it calls God, but that entity is the result of the known; it is still within the field of time.

So you can find out with clarity, with truth, with real experience whether there is God or not, only when the mind is totally free from the known. Surely, that something which may be called God or Truth must be totally new, unrecognizable, and a mind that approaches it through knowledge, through experience, through ideas and accumulated virtues, is trying to capture the unknown while living in the field of the known, which is an impossibility. All that the mind can do is to enquire whether it is possible to free itself from the known. To be free from the known is to be completely free from all the impressions of the past, from the whole weight of tradition. The mind itself is the product of the known, it is put together by time as the 'me' and the 'not-me', which is the conflict of duality. If the known totally ceases, consciously as well as unconsciously—and I say, not theoretically, that there is a possibility of its ceasing—then you will never ask if there is God, because such a mind is immeasurable in itself; like love, it is its own eternity.

Question: I have practised meditation most earnestly for twenty-five years, and I am still unable to go beyond a certain point. How am I to proceed further?

Krishnamurti: Before we enquire into how to proceed further, must we not find out what meditation is? When I ask, 'How am I to meditate?', am I not putting a wrong question? Such a question implies that I want to get somewhere, and I am willing to practise a method in order to get what I want. It is like taking an examination in order to get a job. Surely, the right question is to ask what meditation is, because right meditation gives perfume, depth, significance to life, and without it life has very little meaning. Do you understand, sirs? To know what is right meditation is much more important than earning a livelihood, getting married, having money, property, because without understanding, these things are all destroyed. So the understanding of the heart is the beginning of meditation.

I want to know what is meditation. I hope you will follow this, not just verbally, but in your own hearts, because without meditation you can know nothing of beauty, of love, or sorrow, of death and the whole expanse of life. The mind that says, 'I must learn a method in order to meditate', is a silly mind, because it has not understood what meditation is.

So, what is meditation? Is not that very enquiry the beginning of meditation? Do you understand, sirs? No? I will go on and you will see. Is meditation a process of concentration, forcing the mind to conform to a particular pattern? That is what most of you do who 'meditate'. You try to force your mind to focus on a certain idea, but other ideas creep in; you brush them away, but they creep in again. You go on playing this game for the next twenty years, and if at last you can manage to concentrate your mind on a chosen idea, you think you have learned how to meditate. But is that meditation? Let us see what is involved in concentration.

When a child is concentrating on a toy, what is happening? The attention of the child is being absorbed by the toy. He is not giving his attention to the toy, but the toy is very interesting and it absorbs his attention. That is exactly what is happening to you when you concentrate on the idea of the Master, on a picture, or when you repeat mantras, and all the rest of it. The toy is absorbing you, and you are merely a plaything of the toy. You thought you were the master of the toy, but the toy is the master.

Concentration also implies exclusiveness. You exclude in order to arrive at a particular result, like a boy trying to pass an examination. The boy wants a profitable result, so he forces himself to concentrate, he makes tremendous effort to get what he wants, which is based on his desire, on his conditioning. And does not this process of forcing the mind to concentrate, which involves suppression, exclusiveness, make the mind narrow? A mind that is made narrow, one-pointed, has extraordinary possibilities in the sense that it may achieve a great deal; but life is not one-pointed, it is an enormous thing to be comprehended, to be loved. It is not petty. Sirs, this is not rhetoric, this is not mere verbiage. When one feels something real, the expression of it may sound rhetorical, but it is not.

So, to concentrate is not to meditate, even though that is what most of you do, calling it meditation. And if concentration is not meditation, then what is? Surely, meditation is to understand every thought that comes into being, and not to dwell upon one particular thought; it is to invite all thoughts so that you understand the whole process of thinking. But what do you do now? You try to think of just one good thought, one good image, you repeat one good sentence which you have learnt from the Gita, the Bible, or what you will; therefore your mind becomes very narrow, limited, petty. Whereas, to be aware of every thought as it arises, and to understand the whole process of thinking, does not demand concentration. On the contrary. To understand the total process of thinking, the mind must be astonishingly alert, and then you will see that what you call thinking is based on a mind that is conditioned. So your enquiry is not how to control thought, but how to free the mind from conditioning. The effort to control thought is part of the process of concentration in which the concentrator tries to make his mind silent, peaceful, is it not? 'To have peace of mind'—that is a phrase which all of us use.

Now, what is peace of mind? How can the mind be quiet, have peace? Surely, not through discipline. The mind cannot be *made* still. A mind that is made still is a dead mind. To discover what it is to be still, one must enquire into the whole content of the mind—which means, really, finding out why the mind is seeking. Is the motive of search the desire for comfort, for permanency, for reward? If so, then such a mind may be still, but it will not find peace, because its stillness is forced, it is based on compulsion, fear, and such a mind is not a peaceful mind. We are still enquiring into the whole process of meditation.

People who 'meditate' and have visions of Christ, Krishna, Buddha, the Virgin, or whoever it be, think they are advancing, making marvellous progress, but after all, the vision is the projection of their own background. What they want to see, they see, and that is obviously not meditation. On the contrary, meditation is to free the mind from all conditioning, and this is not a process that comes into being at a particular moment of the day when you are sitting cross-legged in a room by yourself. It must go on when you are walking, when you are frightened, when you are getting into the bus; it means watching the manner of your speech when you are talking to your wife, to your boss, to your servant. All that is meditation.

So meditation is the understanding of the meditator. Without understanding the one who meditates, which is yourself, enquiry into how to meditate has very little value. The beginning of meditation is self-knowledge, and self-knowledge cannot be gathered from a book, nor is it to be had by listening to some professor of psychology, or to someone who interprets the Gita, or any of that rubbish. All interpreters are traitors because they are not original experiences, they are merely second-hand repeaters of something which they believe someone else has experienced and which they think is true. So beware of interpreters.

The mind which understands itself is a meditative mind. Self-knowledge is the beginning of meditation, and as you proceed deeply into it you will find that the mind becomes astonishingly quiet, unforced, completely still, without motion—which means there is no experiencer demanding experience. When there is only that state of stillness without any movement of the mind, then you will find that in that state something else takes place. But you cannot possibly find out intellectually what that state is; you cannot come to it through the description of another, including myself. All that you can do is to free the mind from its conditioning, from the traditions, the greed, and all the petty things with which it is now burdened. Then you will see that, without your seeking it, the mind is astonishingly quiet; and for such a mind, that which is immeasurable comes into being. You cannot go to the immeasurable, you cannot search it out, you cannot delve into the depths of it. You can delve only into the recesses of your own heart and mind. You cannot invite Truth, it must come to you; therefore don't seek it. Understand your own life and then Truth will come darkly, without any invitation; and then you will discover that there is immense beauty, a sensitivity to both the ugly and the beautiful.

First Talk in Madras
26 December 1956

I think it must be a matter of grave concern for most people to see how little they fundamentally change. What is needed is not a modified continuity of things as they are, because the immediate problems of war, the pressures and tremendous challenges that confront us every day, demand that we change in a totally different manner than before. The moralists, the politicians and reformers all urge some kind of change, and change is obviously essential, yet we don't seem to change. By change I do not mean throwing out one particular ideology or pattern of thought and taking up another, or leaving one religious group and joining another. To be caught in the movement of change, if you know what I mean, is not to have a residual point from which change takes place. That is, if I as a Hindu change to Buddhism or Christianity, I am merely changing from one residual thought to another, from one tradition to another, and that is obviously no change at all. So it seems to me very important to be caught in the movement of change, which I shall go into presently.

Most of us are aware that technologically the world is advancing with extraordinary rapidity but the human problems which technological progress brings cannot be adequately met by a mind that is merely functioning in a routine, or according to a pattern. You can see that technology will presently feed man—perhaps not tomorrow, but sooner or later it is going to happen. Through every form of force and compulsion, through legislation, propaganda, ideology, and so on, man is going to be clothed, fed and sheltered; but even though that is ultimately done, inwardly there will be very little change. You may all be well fed, clothed and sheltered, but the mind will remain about the same; it will be more capable of dealing with technological matters, with the machine, but inwardly there will be no compassion, no sense of goodness or the flowering of it. So it seems to me that the problem is not merely how to meet the challenge technologically, but to find out how the individual is to change—not just you and I, but how the majority of people are to change and be compassionate, or to change so that compassion is.

Can compassion, that sense of goodness, that feeling of the sacredness of life about which we were talking last time we met—can that feeling be brought into being through compulsion? Surely, when there is compulsion in any form, when there is propaganda or moralizing, there is no compassion, nor is there compassion when change is brought about merely through seeing the necessity of meeting the technological challenge in such a way that human beings will remain human beings and not become machines. So there must be a change without any causation. A change that is brought about through causation is not compassion, it is merely a thing of the market place. So that is one problem.

Another problem is: If I change, how will it affect society? Or am I not concerned with that at all? Because the vast majority of people are not interested in what we are talking about—nor are you if you listen out of curiosity or some kind of impulse, and pass by. The machines are progressing so rapidly that most human beings are merely pushed along and are not capable of meeting life with the enrichment of love, with compassion, with deep thought. And if I change, how will it affect society, which is my relationship with you? Society is not some extraordinary mythical entity, it is our relationship with each other, and if two or three of us change, how will it affect the rest of the world? Or is there a way of affecting the total mind of man?

That is, is there a process by which the individual who is changed can touch the unconscious of man? Do you understand the problem, sirs? It is not my problem, I am not foisting it on you. It is your problem, so you have to deal with it. Man is going to be fed, clothed and sheltered by technology and that is going to influence his thinking, because he will be safe, he will have everything he needs, and if he is not astonishingly alert, inwardly rich, he will become, not a mature human being, but a repeating machine, and his change will be under pressure, under compulsion of the whole technological process, which includes the use of propaganda to convince a man of certain ideas and condition his mind to think in a certain direction—which is already being done. Seeing all this, you must obviously think, 'How am I to change? And if I do change, if I do become an integrated human being—which I must, other-wise I am merely part of the propaganda machine with various forms of coercion and so on—will it bring about a change in the collective? Or is that an impossibility?'

Now, must the collective be transformed gradually? Do you understand? When we talk about gradualness, obviously it implies compulsion, slow conviction through propaganda, which is educating the individual to think in a certain direction—to be good, kind, gentle—but under pressure. Therefore the mind is like a machine that is being driven by steam, and such a mind is not good, it is not compassionate, it has no appreciation of something sacred. Its action is all the result of being told what to do.

I don't know if you have thought about all this, but if you have, it must be a tremendous problem to you. More and more people are becoming mere repeaters of tradition, whether communist, Hindu, or whatever tradition it is, and there is no human being who is thinking totally anew of his relationship to society. And if I am concerned with this issue, not verbally or intellectually—not saying that life is one, that we are all brothers, that we must go and preach brotherhood, because all that is mere wordplay—but if I am concerned with compassion, with love, with the real feeling of something sacred, then how is that feeling to be transmitted? Please follow this. If I transmit it through the microphone, through the machinery of propaganda, and thereby convince another, his heart will still be empty. The flame of ideology will operate and he will merely repeat, as you are all repeating, that we must be kind, good, free—all the nonsense that the politicians, the socialists, and the rest of them talk. So, seeing that any form of compulsion, however subtle, does not bring this beauty, this flowering of goodness, of compassion, what is the individual to do?

If the man of compassion is a freak, then obviously he has no value. You may just as well shut him up in a museum. But the action of a freak is not the action of a man who has really thought it all out deeply, who actually feels compassion, the sense of loving, and does not merely enunciate a lot of intellectual ideas; and has such a man no effect on society? If he has not, then the problem will go on as it is. There will be a few freaks, and they will be valueless except as a pattern for the collective, who will repeat what they have said and moralize everlastingly about it.

So, what is the relationship between the man who has this sense of compassion, and the man whose mind is entrenched in the collective, in the traditional? How are we to find the relationship between these two, not theoretically but actually? Do you understand, sirs? It is like a man who is hungry—he does not talk about the theory of economics, nor is he satisfied with books that describe the good qualities of food. He must eat. So, what is the relationship between the man who is enlightened, not in some mysterious, mystical way, but who is not greedy, not envious, who knows what it is to love, to be kind, to be gentle—what is the relationship between such a man and you who are caught in the collective? Can he influence you? Influence is not the word, surely, because if he influences you, then you are under his propagandistic compulsion, and therefore you have not the real flame; you have only the imitation of it. So, what is one to do?

Is there an action which will affect the collective non-thinker, so that he thinks totally anew? Will education do that? That is, can the student be helped to understand the whole variety of influences that exist about him so that does not conform to any influence, thereby bringing into being a new generation with a totally different approach to life? Because the old generation is on the way out; they are obviously not going to change. Most of you will sit here listening for the next twenty years and change only when it suits you. Instead of a *dhoti* you will put on trousers, or you will drink, or eat meat, and think you have changed marvellously. But I am not talking about such trivialities at all.

Is this change to be brought about by beginning with the young, with the child? But that means there must be a new kind of teacher. Don't just agree with me, sirs. See the whole significance of it. There must be a new kind of mind operating in the teacher so that he helps the child to grow, not in tradition, not as a communist, a socialist, or whatever it be, but in freedom. The student must be helped to be free at the very beginning and not ultimately, free to understand the pressures of his home, of his parents, the pressures of propaganda through newspapers, books, ideas, through the whole paraphernalia of compulsion—and he himself must be encouraged to see the importance of not influencing others. And where are such teachers? You nod your heads in agreement and say that it should be done, but where are the teachers? Which means that you are the teachers. The teachers are at home, not in the school, because nobody else is interested in all this. Governments are certainly not interested. On the contrary, they want you to remain within the pattern, because the moment you step out you become a danger to the present society. Therefore they push you back. So the problem actually devolves upon you and me, not upon the supposed teacher.

Now, can you change immediately, without any compulsion? Sirs, do please listen to this. If you don't change now you will never change. There is no change within the field of time. Change is outside the field of time because any change within that field is merely a modification of the pattern, or a revolt against a particular pattern in order to establish a new one. So I think the problem is not how the enlightened individual will affect society. I am using that word 'enlightened' in the simplest, most ordinary sense—to describe one who thinks clearly and sees the absurdity of all the nonsense that is going on, who has compassion, who loves, but not because it is profitable or good for the State. To ask what effect such a man has on the collective, or of what use he is to society, may be a wrong question altogether. I think it is, because if we put the question in that way, we are still thinking in terms of the collective, so let us put the question differently.

Has the man of enlightenment, the man who is inwardly free of religions, of beliefs, of dogmas, who belongs to no organization that brings in the past—has such a man any reality in this world which is bound to the wheel of tradition? Do you understand, sirs? How would you answer that question? To put it again differently, there is sorrow in the world, sorrow arising from various causes. There is not only physical pain, but this complex psychological process of engendering and sustaining sorrow, which is fairly obvious.

Now, is there freedom from sorrow? I say there is—but not because someone else has said it, which is merely the traditional way of thinking. I say there is an ending to sorrow. And what relation has the man for whom sorrow has ended, to the man of sorrow? Has he any relation at all? We may be trying to establish an impossible relationship between the man who is free of sorrow and the man who is caught in sorrow, and creating thereby a whole series of complex issues. Must not the man of sorrow step out of his world, and not look to the man who is free from sorrow? Which means that every human being must cease to depend psychologically, and is that possible?

Dependence in any form creates sorrow, does it not? In depending on fulfilment there is frustration. Whether a man seeks fulfilment as a governor, as a poet, as a writer, as a speaker, or tries to fulfil himself in God, it is all essentially the same, because in the shadow of fulfilment there is pain, frustration. And how are you and I to meet this problem? Do you understand, sirs? I may be free, but has that any value to you? If it has no value, what right have I to exist? And if it has value, then how will you meet such a man—not how he will meet you, but how will you meet him? He may want to meet you and go with you, not just one mile, but a hundred miles; but how will you meet him? And is it possible to change so fundamentally, so radically and deeply, that your whole thinking-feeling process is exploded, made innocent, fresh, new?

Sirs, there is no answer to this question. I am only pointing it out. It is for you to expose it, to bite into it, to be tortured by it. It is for you to work hard on it, because if you don't, your life is over, finished, gone; and your children, the coming generation, will also be finished. You always say that the coming generation will create the new world, which is nonsense, because you are conditioning that generation right off through your books and newspapers, through your leaders, politicians and organized religions—everything is forcing the child in a particular direction, while you eternally verbalize about nothing.

So this is your problem, and I don't think you are taking it seriously. It is not a thing as vital to you as making money, or going to the office and being caught in the routine of that astonishing boredom which you call your life. Whether you are a lawyer, a judge, a governor or the highest politician, your life for the most part is a dreadful routine that is boring and destructive in the extreme, and you are caught in it; and your children are also going to be caught in it unless you change fundamentally. This is not rhetorical, sirs, it is something that you have to think out, work out, sit together and solve. Because the world does demand human beings who are thinking anew, not in the same old groove, and who do not revolt against the old pattern only to create a new one.

I think you will find the answer in right relationship when you know what love is. Strangely, love has its own action, probably not at the recognizable level; but the man who is really compassionate has an action, a something which other men have not. It is those who are serious, who listen, who think, who work at this thing—it is such people who will bring about a different action in the world, not eventually but now. And I think the problem is: How is a human being to change so fundamentally in his way of thinking that his mind is totally unconditioned? If you give your thought to it as much as you do to your office, to your puja, and all the rest of the nonsense, you will find out.

Sirs, I am going to answer this one question—or rather, I am not going to answer it, but together we will take the journey into the problem. Because the problem holds the answer, the answer is not outside of the problem. If I am open to the problem I can see the beauty of it, all its intricacies, its extraordinary nuances and implications, and then the problem dissolves; but if I look at the problem with the intention of finding an answer, obviously I am not open to the problem.

Question: My son and others who have been abroad seem to have had the moral fibre knocked out of them. How does this happen, and what can we do to develop their character?

Krishnamurti: Why do we think only of those people who have been abroad? Has not the moral fibre of most people who are listening been knocked out of them? Seriously, sirs, do not laugh. It is a very complex problem. Let us explore it together. We want to develop character, at least that is what we say. The newspapers, the government, the moralists, the religious people—are they doing it? You think so? How does character develop? How does goodness flower? Does it flower within the frame of social compulsion, which is called moral? Or does goodness flower, does character come into being, only when there is freedom? Freedom does not mean freedom to do what you like. But that is what happens when they go abroad. All the usual pressures are taken off—the pressure of the family, of tradition, of the country, the fear of the father and the mother—and they let loose. But did they have character before they left, or were they merely under the thumb of their parents, of tradition or society? And as long as a human being is under the thumb of the family, of society, of tradition, of propaganda, and all the rest of it, has he character? Or is he merely a machine functioning repetitiously according to a moral code and therefore inwardly dead, empty? Do you understand, sirs? That is what is happening in India, though the vast majority of people have not gone abroad. Moral fibre is rapidly disintegrating. You ought to know that better than I do. So your problem is, is it not?, how to develop character and yet remain within the social pattern so as not to disrupt society. Because, though it may talk about character or morality, society does not want character. It wants people who will conform, who will toe the line of tradition.

So we see that character is not developed in a pattern. Character exists only where there is freedom—and freedom is not freedom to do what you like. But society does not allow freedom. I don't have to tell you. Watch yourself in dealing with your own children. You don't want them to have character, you want them to conform to tradition, to a pattern. To have character there must be freedom, for only in freedom is the flowering of goodness possible, and that is character, that is morality, not the so-called morality that merely conforms to a pattern.

Is it possible, then, to develop character and yet remain within society? Surely, society does not want character, it is not concerned with the flowering of goodness; society is concerned with the word 'goodness', but not with the flowering of it, which can take place only in freedom. So the two are incompatible, and the man who would develop character must free himself from society. After all, society is based on greed, envy, ambition; and cannot human beings free themselves from these things and then help society to break its own pattern?

Sirs, if you look at India you will see what is happening. Everything is breaking down because essentially there is no character, essentially you have not flowered in goodness. You have merely followed the pattern of a certain culture, trying to be moral within that framework, and when the pressure comes your moral fiber breaks because it has no substance, no inward reality; and then all the elders tell you to go back to the old ways, to the temple, to the Upanishads, to this and that, which means conformity. But that which conforms can never flower in goodness. There must be freedom, and freedom comes only when you understand the whole problem of envy, greed, ambition, and the desire for power. It is freedom from those things that allows the extraordinary thing called character to flower. Such a man has compassion, he knows what it is to love—not the man who merely repeats a lot of words about morality.

So the flowering of goodness does not lie within society, because society in itself is always corrupt. Only the man who understands the whole structure and process of society, and is freeing himself from it, has character, and he alone can flower in goodness.

First Talk in Colombo
23 January 1957

One of our greatest difficulties is that we do not like to be disturbed, especially when we are a people steeped in tradition, in the easy ways of life, and with a culture that has merely become repetitive. Perhaps you have noticed that we put up a great deal of resistance to anything that is new. We do not want to be disturbed, and if we are disturbed, we soon adjust ourselves to a new pattern and again settle down, only to be again shaken, disturbed and troubled. So we go on through life, always being driven from a pattern into which we have settled down. The mind objects most violently and defensively to any suggestion of a change from within. It is willing to be compelled by economic, scientific, or political forces to adjust itself to a new environment, but inwardly it remains the same. One can observe this process going on if one is at all aware of things about one and within oneself.

And religion, it seems to me, is the most disturbing state of mind. It is not something from which to get comfort, solace, an easy explanation of the sorrows, travails and tribulations of life; on the contrary, religion demands a mind that is extraordinarily alert, questioning, doubting, enquiring, that does not accept at all. The truth of religion is to be discovered individually, it can never be made universal. And yet, if you observe, you will see that religions throughout the world have become universal—universal in the sense that a large number of people follow them and adhere to their ideas, beliefs, dogmas, rituals; therefore they cease to be religion at all.

Religion, surely, is the search for Truth on the part of each one of us, and not merely the acceptance of what has been said by another—it does not matter who it is, whether the Buddha, the Christ, or any other. They may point out certain things, but merely to repeat what has been said by them is so immature; it is merely verbal and without much significance. To discover the Truth, that

Reality which is beyond the measure of thought, the mind must be disturbed, shaken out of its habits, its easy acceptance of a philosophy, system of thought. As the mind is made up of all our thoughts, feelings and activities, conscious as well as unconscious, it is our only instrument of enquiry, of search, of discovery, and to allow it to settle down and function in a groove seems to me a heinous crime. It is of the utmost importance that we should be disturbed—and we are being disturbed externally. The impact of the West on the East is a shock, a disturbing element. Outwardly, superficially, we are adjusting ourselves to it, and we think we are making progress inwardly; but if you observe you will see that inwardly we are not seeking at all.

Seeking has an extraordinary significance in the life of the individual. Most of us seek with a motive. When we seek with a motive, the motive dictates the end of the search; and when a motive dictates the end, is there a search at all? It seems to me that to seek the realization of what you already know or have formulated is not search. There is search only when you do not know, when there is no motive, no compulsion, no escape, and only then is there a possibility of discovering that which is Truth, Reality, God.

But most of us are seeking with a motive, are we not? If you observe your own way of life, your own manner of thinking and feeling, you will see that most of us are discontented with ourselves and our environment, and we want to direct this discontent along easy channels till we find contentment. A mind that is pursuing satisfaction easily finds a way of overcoming discontent, and such a mind is obviously incapable of discovering what is truth. Discontent is the only force that makes you move, enquire, search. But the moment you canalize it and try to find contentment or fulfilment through any means, obviously you go to sleep.

That is exactly what is happening in religious matters. We are no longer on a journey, individually seeking what is Truth. We are merely being driven by the collective, which means going to the temple, repeating certain phrases, explanations, and thinking that is religion. Surely, religion is something entirely different. It is a state of mind in which the enquirer is not urged by any motive and has no centre from which to start his enquiry. Truth is not to be found through the motive of wanting contentment, peace, something superior in order to be satisfied. I think it is very important to understand this. We have made religion, have we not?, into something which gives us satisfaction, an explanation for our troubles, a solace for our sorrows, for the things that we are, and we easily fit into a satisfying groove of thought, thinking we have solved the problem. There is no individual enquiry on our part, but merely a repetition, a theoretical and not an actual understanding of 'what is'.

To find out what is Truth we must be free of the collective, which means we must be truly individual—which we are not. I do not know if you have observed how little individual you are. Being an individual is not a matter of character or habit. After all, character is the meeting of the past with the present, is it not? Your character is the result of the past in response to the present, and that response of the past is still the collective.

To put it differently, are you an individual at all? You have a name, a form, a family; you may have a separate house and a personal bank account, but are you inwardly an individual? Or are you merely the collective acting in a certain approved, respectable manner? Observe yourself and you will see that you are not at all an individual. You are a Sinhalese, a Buddhist, a Christian, an Englishman, an Indian, or a communist, which means that you are the collective; and surely one must be free of the collective, consciously as well as unconsciously, in order to find out what is Truth.

To free the mind from the repetitive urge of the collective requires very hard work, and only a mind thus free is capable of discovering what is Truth. This actually does happen when you are vitally interested in something. You put aside all the imaginations, ideas and struggles of the past, and you push forward to enquire. But in religious matters you do not. There you are conservative, you are the collective, you think in terms of the mass, of what you have been told about nirvana, samadhi, moksha, heaven, or what you will. There is no individual endeavour to discover wholly for yourself. I think such individual endeavour is very important, especially in the present world crisis, because it is only this individual search that will release the creative and open the door to Reality. As long as we are not real individuals, as long as we are merely the reaction of the past, as most of us are, life remains a series of repetitive responses without much significance. But if in our search we endeavour as individuals to find out what is Truth, then a totally new energy, a totally different kind of creation comes into being.

I do not know if you have ever experimented with yourself by watching your own mind and seeing how it accumulates memory. From memory you act, from knowledge there is action. Knowledge is, after all, experience, and this experience dictates future experience. So you will find that experience does not liberate at all; on the contrary, experience strengthens the past. A mind that would liberate itself from the past must understand this whole process of accumulating knowledge through experience, which conditions the mind. The centre from which you think, the 'me', the self, the ego, is a bundle of memories, and you are nothing else but that. You may think you are the Atman, the soul, but you are still cultivating memory, and that memory projects the coming experience, which further conditions the mind. So experience strengthens the 'me', the self, which is in essence memory—'my house', 'my qualities', 'my character', 'my race', 'my knowledge', and the whole structure which is built around that centre. In seeking Reality through experience, the mind only

J. Krishnamurti

further conditions itself and does not liberate itself from that centre.

Now, is it possible for the mind not to accumulate knowledge around the centre, and so be capable of discovering truth from moment to moment? Because it is only the truth discovered from moment to moment that is really important, not the truth which you have already experienced and which, having become a memory, creates the urge to further experience.

There are two kinds of knowledge—there is the factual knowledge of how to build a bridge, all the scientific information that has accumulated through the centuries, and there is knowledge as psychological memory. These two forms of knowledge are not clearly defined. One operates through the other. But it is psychological memory of which the 'me', the self is made up, and is it possible for the mind to be free of that memory? Is it possible for the mind not to think in terms of accumulation, in terms of gathering experience, but to move without that centre? Can we live in this world without the operation of the self, which is a bundle of psychological memories? You will find, if you really enquire into it deeply, that such a thing is possible, and then you can use factual knowledge without creating the havoc which is being created now. Then factual knowledge does not breed antagonism between man and man.

At present there is antagonism, there is hate, separation, anxiety, war, and all the rest of it, because psychologically you are using factual knowledge for self-aggrandizement, for a separative existence. One can see very well in the world that religions divide people—religions being ideas, belief, dogma, ritual, not the feeling of love, of compassion.

198

Such religions separate people, just as nationalism does. What is separating us, then, is not factual knowledge, but the knowledge upon which we depend psychologically for our emotional comfort, for our inward security.

So a mind that would find Reality, God, or what name you will, must be free of this bundle of memories which is identified as the 'me'. And it is really not so very difficult. This bundle is made up of ambition, greed, envy, the desire to be secure, and if one puts one's mind to the task and works hard, surely one can liberate the mind from this bundle. One can live in this world without ambition, without envy, without hate. We think it is impossible because we have never tried it. It is only the mind that is free from hate, from envy, from separative conclusions, beliefs—it is only such a mind that is capable of discovering that Reality which is love, compassion.

Question: What is understanding? Is it awareness? Is it right thinking? If understanding does not come about through the functioning of the mind, then what is the function of the mind?

Krishnamurti: Sir, there are several things involved in this question. First of all, what is thinking?—not right thinking or wrong thinking. Surely, what we call thinking is the response of memory to any challenge. That is, when I ask you a question, you respond quickly if you are familiar with the answer, or hesitantly, with an interval of time, if you are not. The mind looks into the records of memory within itself, and having found the answer, replies to the question; or, not finding the answer in the records of memory, it says 'I don't know.'

So thinking is the response of memory, obviously; it is not a very complex thing. You think as a Buddhist, a Sinhalese, a Christian, or a Hindu, because your background is that of a particular culture, race, or religion. If you do not belong to any of these groups, and you are a communist, for example, again you respond according to that particular pattern. This process of response according to a certain background is what you call thinking.

You have discovered, then, that there is no freedom in thinking, because your thinking is dictated by your background. Thinking as you know it now originates from knowledge, which is memory; it is mechanical because it is the response to challenge of a conditioned mind. There is creativeness, a perception of the new, only when there is no response of memory. In mathematics you may proceed step by step from the known to the known, but if you would go much further and discover something new, the known must for the time being be put in abeyance.

So the functioning of the mind is at present a mechanical response of memory, conscious as well as unconscious. The unconscious is a vast storehouse of accumulated tradition, of racial inheritance, and it is that background which responds to challenge. I think that is fairly obvious.

Now, is there right thinking and wrong thinking? Or is there only freedom from what we call thinking—from which follows right action? Do you understand, sirs? Being brought up in India, Europe, or America, I think in terms of my particular conditioning, according to the way I have been educated. My background tells me what to think, and it also tells me what is right thinking and what is wrong thinking. If I were brought up as a communist, then for me right thinking would be that which is anti-religious and anti-clerical, according to my communistic background; any other manner of thinking would be a deviation, and therefore to be liquidated. And is a mind that responds according to its background, which it calls thinking, capable of right action? Or is there right action only when the mind is free from the conditioning whose response it calls thinking? Do you understand, sirs? I hope I am making myself clear.

Most of us do not even ask what is right thinking. We want to know what is right thought, because right thinking might be very disturbing, it might demand enquiry, and we do not want to enquire. We want to be told what is right thought, and we are told what is right thought by organized religions, by social morality, by philosophies, and by our own experience. We proceed along that line until we are no longer satisfied with the pattern of right thought, and then we ask, 'What is right thinking?'—which means that the mind is a little more active, a little more willing to enquire, to be disturbed. Thinking is fluid, whereas right thought implies a static state, and most of us function in static states.

Now, if we really want to enquire into what is right thinking, we must first find out, not what is right thinking, but what is thinking; and we have seen that what we call thinking is a process of response from the background, from that centre of accumulated memory which is identified as the 'me'. And I say, is there right thinking in that field at all? Or is there right thinking, right response, right action only when the mind is free from the background?

The questioner wants to know what is understanding. Surely, understanding is this whole process of uncovering the ways of the mind, which is what we have been doing just now. Understanding implies, does it not?, a state of mind that is really enquiring, and you cannot enquire if you start with a conclusion, an assumption, a wish.

Then what is the function of the mind? The mind now functions fragmentarily, in departments, in parts; it does not function as a totality because it is now the instrument of desire, and desire can never be total, whole. Desire is always fragmentary, contradictory. You can easily find out the truth of all this if you observe these things in yourself.

As we know it now, the mind is an instrument of sensation, of gratification of desire, and desire is always fragmentary; there can never be total desire. Such a mind, with all its self-contradictory desires, can never be integrated. You cannot put hate and love together, you cannot integrate envy and goodness, you cannot harmonize the opposites. That is what most of us are trying to do, but it is an impossibility. So, what is the true function of the mind? Is it not to free itself from the contradictions of desire and be the instrument of an action which is not the mere response of memory?

I am afraid all this sounds rather difficult, but if you really observe yourself, you will find that it is not. I am only describing what actually takes place if you do not suppress, sublimate, or find a substitute for desire, but really understand it. You can understand desire only when there is no condemnation, no comparison. If I want to understand you, for example, I must not condemn, I must not justify, I must not compare you with somebody else—I must simply observe you. Similarly, if it would understand desire, the mind must watch itself without condemnation, without any sense of comparison, which only creates the conflict of duality.

So we see what understanding is. We see that there can be no right thinking, which is right action, as long as the mind is conditioned. There is right action only when the mind is free from conditioning. It is not a matter of right thinking, and then right action. Thinking and action are separate only as long as desire functions as memory, as the pursuit of success; but when there is freedom from that bundle of memories which is identified as the 'me', then there is action which is outside the social pattern. But that is much more complicated, and we shall leave it for the moment.

We see, then, that the function of the mind is to understand, and it cannot understand if it condemns, if it thinks segmentally, in parts. The mind will think in fragments, in compartments, as long as there is desire, whether it be the desire for God or for a car, because desire in itself is contradictory, and any one desire is always in opposition to other desires.

So there can be understanding only when the mind, through self-knowledge, discovers the ways of its own operation. And to discover the ways of the mind's operation there must be awareness; you must watch it as you would watch a child whom you love. You do not condemn or judge the child, you do not compare him with somebody else; you watch in order to understand him. Similarly, you must be aware of the operation of your own mind, see its subtleties, its recesses, its extraordinary depth. Then you will find, if you pursue it further, that the mind becomes astonishingly quiet, very still, and a still mind is capable of receiving that which is Truth.

Question: According to the theory of karma, in which many of us believe, our actions and circumstances in this life are largely governed by what we did in our past lives. Do you deny that we are governed by our karma? What about our duties and responsibilities?

Krishnamurti: Sir, again, this is a very complex question and it needs thinking out to the very end.

It is not a matter of what you believe. You believe that you are the result of the past, that previous lives have conditioned your present circumstances, and there are others who do not believe in all that. They have been brought up to believe that we live only one life and are conditioned only by our present environment. So let us for the moment put aside what you believe or do not believe, and let us find out what we mean by karma, which is much more important, because if you really understand what karma is, then you will find it is not a thing which dictates your present action. We shall go into it and you will see.

Now, what do we mean by karma? The word itself, as you know, means to act, to do. You never act without a cause, or without a motive, or without I being compelled by circumstances. You act either under the influence of the past, of a thousand yesterdays, or because you are pushed in a particular direction by the pressure of immediate circumstances. That is, there is a cause and an effect. Please follow this a little bit. For example, you have come here to listen to me. The cause is that you want to listen, and the effect of listening you will find out, if you are really interested. But the point is: there is a cause and there is an effect.

Now, is the cause ever fixed, and the effect already determined? Do you understand, sirs? In the case of an acorn, a seed, there is a fixed cause and a fixed effect. An acorn can never become a palm tree, it will always produce an oak. We think in the same way about karma, do we not? Having done something yesterday, which is the cause, I think the effect of that action is predetermined, fixed. But is it? Is the cause fixed? And is the effect fixed? Does not the effect of a cause become in its turn the cause of still another effect—do you understand? I do not want to take more examples, because examples do not really clarify the issue, but tend to confuse it. So we must think this out clearly without using examples.

We know that action has a cause. I am ambitious, therefore I do something. There is a cause and there is an effect. Now, does not the effect become the cause of a future action? Surely, there is never a fixed cause, nor a fixed effect. Each effect, undergoing innumerable influences and being transformed by them, becomes the cause of still another effect. So there is never a fixed cause and a fixed effect, but a chain of cause-effect-cause.

Sirs, this is so obvious. You did something yesterday which had its origin in a previous cause, and which will lead to certain consequences tomorrow; but in the meantime the consequences, being subject to innumerable pressures, influences, have undergone a change. You think that a given cause will produce a fixed effect, but the effect is never exactly the same, because something has happened between the two.

So there is a continuous chain of cause becoming effect, and effect becoming cause. If you think in terms of 'I was that in the past, I am this today, and I shall be such-and-such in the next life', it is too immature, utterly silly, because that way of thinking is not fluid, it has no living, vital quality. That is decay, deterioration, death. But if you think about the matter deeply, it is really marvellous, because then you will see that this chain of cause-effect becoming another cause can be broken at any time, and that the mind can be free of karma. Through understanding the whole process of the mind which is conditioned by the past, you will see for yourself that the effect of the past in the present or in the future is never fixed, never absolute, final. To think that it is final is degradation, ignorance, darkness. Whereas, if you see the significance of cause-effect becoming again the cause, then because that whole process is for you a living, moving thing, you can break it at any time; therefore you can be free of the past. You no longer need be a Christian, a Buddhist, a Hindu, with all the conditioning that goes with it; you can immediately transform yourself.

Sirs, don't you know that with one stroke you can cut away envy? Haven't you ever tried to break antagonism on the spot? I know it is very comforting to sit back and say, 'Well, it is karma that has made me antagonistic to you.' It gives a great sense of satisfaction to say that, the pleasure of continuing hate. But if you perceive the whole significance of karma, then you will see that the chain of cause-becoming-effect-becoming-cause can be snapped.

Therefore the mind can be astonishingly and vitally free from the past in the immediate.

But that requires hard work; it requires a great deal of attention, a great deal of enquiry, penetration, self-knowledge. And most of us are indolent, we are so easily satisfied by a belief in karma. Good God! What does it matter whether you believe or not believe? It is what you are now that matters, not what you did in the past and the effects of that in the present. And what are you now? You should know that better than I do. What you are now is obviously the result of the past, the result of innumerable influences, compulsions, the result of food, climate, contact with the West, and so on. Under the pressure of all that, the mind becomes lazy, indolent, easily satisfied by words. Such a mind may talk about Truth, God, it may believe in nirvana, and all the rest of it; but that belief has no value at all, any more than has the communist, the Catholic, or any other belief.

The mind can be transformed only when it understands the whole process of itself and the motives, the causations of that process. In that understanding there are immense possibilities for the mind, because it opens the door to an astonishing creativity, which is not the writing of a few poems, or the putting of some colours on a canvas, but that state which is Reality, God, Truth. And for that you need have no ideals. On the contrary, ideals prevent immediate understanding. We are fed on illusions, on things that have no value, and we easily succumb to authority, to religious as well as political tyranny; and how can such a mind discover that which is eternal, that which is beyond the projections of itself? I say it is possible to break this continuity of karma, but only when you understand the operations of karma, which is not static, predetermined, but a living, moving thing; and in breaking itself away from the past, the mind will know what Truth or God is.

Second Talk in Colombo
27 January 1957

As I have been pointing out during these talks here, it is surely very important, especially when the world is in such a grave crisis, that we should understand the true significance of religion because religion, it seems to me, is the only basic solution to all the problems of our existence. I do not mean the religions of dogma, of organized belief, which only condition the mind. To me, they are not religion at all. They are like any other propagandistic organization which merely shapes the mind according to a particular pattern of thinking.

To enquire into the whole question of what is true religion, one must first understand what behaviour is. To me, behaviour is righteousness. But most of us spend our energy and our thought in arguing over what kind of belief we should hold concerning reincarnation and the various other problems involved in religion; we do not start with the fundamental issue. The foundation of right enquiry is surely behaviour, which is righteousness, and righteousness is not merely the cultivation of virtue. A man who cultivates virtue ceases to be virtuous; a man who practises humility is no longer humble. The cultivation of humility is arrogance. Similarly, cultivated virtue only leads to respectability. We must have virtue, because virtue is essential to all real enquiry, but not the cultivated virtue which is a self-centred activity. What is important is to meet the whole movement of that virtue which is not self-centred and which, if we pursue it deeply, not only at the conscious but also at the unconscious level, does lead to that which is beyond the measure of the mind. This is true religious enquiry, and I think it is very important to understand it.

Most of us are involved in some form of organized belief, such as Buddhism, Hinduism, Christianity, communism, and so on; and when we are caught in the net of these organizations, whether political or so-called spiritual, we are more concerned, are we not, with what we believe than with how we live our life. What matters, surely, is not to find out what is the ideal way of living, but rather to discover for ourselves the pattern of behaviour in which the mind is caught and to see the true significance of such behaviour.

Righteousness has nothing whatever to do with organized conduct because organized conduct, which is social morality, has produced this great confusion and chaos in the world. Society accepts envy, greed, ambition, cruelty, the ruthless pursuit of one's own fulfilment; it admits and justifies the possibility of killing on a large scale. The soldier who kills more than the others in battle is a hero in the eyes of society, and when a society professing a particular religion sanctions killing on a vast and inhuman scale, then obviously the religion which it professes has failed.

To understand righteousness it is necessary to step out of the pattern of society. By society I do not mean the organized means of communication, of supplying food, clothing, shelter, and so on, but the whole psychological or moral issue which is involved in society. A person who seeks to enquire into what is true religion obviously cannot belong to a society which accepts greed, envy, the pursuit of personal ambition, the search for power, fame, and all the rest of it. To belong to a society based on cruelty and the pursuits of self-interest, and still be religious, is obviously impossible. Yet organized religions throughout the world have condoned such a society. Organized religions do not insist that you step out of greed, envy, ruthlessness. They are far more concerned with what you believe, with ritual, organization, property, and all the rest of the confusion, paraphernalia, and rigmarole that exist in and around every organized religion.

So a man who would enquire into what is true religion must lay the foundation of righteousness by being without envy, without ambition, without the greed for power. This is an actual possibility, I am not being idealistic. Ideals and actuality are incompatible. A man who pursues the ideal of non-violence is indulging in violence. He is concerned, not with ceasing to be violent, but with ultimately arriving at a state which he calls non-violence. Being violent, the mind has an ideal of non-violence which is over there in the distance; it will take time to achieve that state, and in the meantime the mind can continue to be violent. Such a mind is not concerned with getting rid of violence, but with slowly trying to become non-violent. The two states are entirely different, and I think it is very important to understand this fact. The ending of a quality such as violence or greed is not a matter of time, and it does not come about through ideals; it has to be done immediately, not

211

through time. We get caught up in the gradualism of ideals when we are concerned with time.

Please do not jump to conclusions or say, 'Without ideals I shall be lost', but rather listen to what is being said. I know all the arguments, all the justifications of ideals. Just listen, if you kindly will, without a conclusion, and try to understand what the speaker is talking about; do not block your understanding by saying 'I must have ideals.'

Ideals have existed for centuries. Various religious teachers have talked of ideals, but they may all be wrong and probably are. To adhere to an ideal is obviously to postpone freeing the mind from violence, greed, envy, ambition and the desire for power. If one is concerned, as one should be, with righteousness, which is the foundation upon which rests all true enquiry into what religion is, then one must investigate the possibility of ridding the mind of violence, of greed, of envy, of acquisitiveness, not at some time in the distant future, but now. It is entirely possible for the mind to be free immediately of these and all the related qualities that society has imposed on us— or rather, that we have cultivated in our relationship with each other which is society.

Righteousness of behaviour is not something to be gained, to be arrived at, but it must be understood from moment to moment in the actuality of daily living. That is why it is important to have self-knowledge, to know how you think, how you feel, how you act, how you respond to another. All that indicates the manner of your approach to life, and therein lies the foundation of righteousness, not in some utopia, ideal or organized belief. The actual foundation must be laid in our daily living. But most of us are not concerned with that; we are concerned with the label which we call religion.

If you and I as individuals really put our minds to this, we shall see that change does not come about through ideals, through time, through pressure and convenience, or through any form of political activity, but only through being deeply concerned with bringing about a radical transformation in ourselves. Then we shall discover that it is possible to free the mind from violence, greed, and all the rest of it, not in time, but outside of time, because virtue or righteousness is not an end in itself. If virtue is an end in itself, it becomes a self-centred activity leading to mere respectability, and a mind that is merely respectable is imitative; it conforms to a pattern and is therefore not free.

Virtue is merely a matter of putting the mind in order, like putting a house in order, and nothing more than that. When the mind is in order, when it has clarity and is without confusion, without conflict, then it is possible to go further. But for a man who is seeking power, who is burning inwardly with ambition, greed, envy, cruelty, and all the rest of it—for such a man to talk about religion and God is errant nonsense; it has no meaning. His God is only the God of respectability.

That is why it is important to lay the foundation of righteousness, which is to step out of the present society. Stepping out of society does not mean becoming a hermit, a monk, or a sannyasi, but being without greed, without envy, without violence, without the desire for position and power. The moment you are without those things you are out of time, out of the society which is made up of them.

So the real revolution is religious, it is this stepping out of the present society, not remaining within the field of society and trying to modify it. Most revolutions are concerned with the modification of society, but to me that is not revolution at all; it is merely the perpetuation of the past in another form. The religious revolution is the only revolution, which is individually to step out of this complex society based on envy, greed, power, anger, violence, and brutality in the relationship between human beings.

It is only when the mind is free from violence, and from all this business of trying to cultivate virtue, that it is capable of enquiring into what is Truth, what is God— if there is God. It does not assume anything. When the mind is capable of such enquiry, that enquiry is devotion. Devotion is not attachment to some idol, to some picture, person, or symbol. But when the mind has freed itself from envy and greed, when it has put its own house in order, which is virtue, and is therefore capable of enquiring to find out what is true and whether there is something beyond the measure of the mind—then that enquiry, that perseverance is true devotion, without which there is irreverence and disrespect.

So the man who would be religious cannot belong to any organized belief, which only conditions the mind, but must be concerned with behaviour, which is righteousness—his own behaviour, not that of others. Most of us are so eager to reform others and so little concerned with the transformation of ourselves. What matters is not how others behave—your friend, your wife, or your husband— but how you behave.

If you consider this matter really seriously, you will find that education comes to have quite a different significance. What we call education now is merely a process of being trained to earn a livelihood as a lawyer, a doctor, a soldier, a businessman, a scientist, or what you will, and that is all most of us are concerned with. Such education is obviously very superficial, and so our lives are equally superficial. But if we understand this enquiry into what is true religion, into what is Reality, God, then we shall help the children, the coming generation, to grow in freedom so that they do not become machines in the routine of an office, or mere bread-winners, but are able to throw off the tyranny of organized belief, the tyranny of governments, and thereby to reshape the world. Then the whole structure, not only of our education, but of our culture, of our behaviour, of our relationship, will be entirely different. Again, this is not an ideal, a thing to be vaguely hoped for in the future.

So it seems to me very important that those of us who are serious—and I hope there are some who are serious—should be concerned with the understanding of ourselves. This is not a self-centred activity. It becomes a self-centred activity only when you are concerned with the understanding of yourself in order to arrive somewhere—in order to achieve freedom, to find God, not to be jealous, and so on. If you are concerned with God, or with sex, or with the attainment of power, your mind is occupied; and an occupied mind is obviously self-centred, though it may be occupied with God. You have to understand the whole process of self-knowledge, that is, you have to know yourself; and you cannot know yourself if you are not aware, observant, conscious of your words, of your gestures, of your manner of speech in relationship with another. To be aware in your relationship with another is to observe the way you talk to women, the way you talk to your wife, to your children, to the bus conductor, to the policeman; it is to see how respectful you are to the governor, and how contemptuous you are of the servant. To be aware is to be conscious of the operation of your own mind, but you cannot be aware if you condemn what you discover.

You will find that out of this self-knowledge comes a well-ordered mind—which is being virtuous, not becoming virtuous. Such a mind is capable of stillness because it is no longer in contradiction with itself, it is no longer driven or driven by desire. To be still requires a great deal of energy, and energy is depleted when the mind is self-contradictory, when it is not aware of its own operation, which means there is no self-knowledge. There is the depletion of energy as long as desire pulls in different directions, but such depletion of energy ceases when there is total self-knowledge. Then you will find that the mind, being full of energy, is capable of being completely still, and a still mind can receive that which is eternal.

Many questions have been sent in—questions about sex, about organized belief, about what kind of education the serious parent should give to his children, and so on. It is obviously impossible to answer all of them, because each question is very complex and cannot just be answered 'yes' or 'no'. Life has no 'yes' or 'no' answers. However, during these talks, representative questions have been dealt with, and if you care to go into what has already been said, I think you will find the answer to your particular question.

Books have been printed, and you may be interested in them—or you may not. That is your affair. But if you have sufficiently paid attention to what has been said, I think you will answer your questions for yourself. To find the right solution to a problem, no effort is required. Effort denies the understanding of the problem. Whereas, if you are really serious about enquiring into the problem, then you will find that the problem resolves itself.

Question: Religions have prescribed certain practices in meditation for one's spiritual growth. What practice do you advocate? Can right meditation be helpful in one's daily life?

Krishnamurti: Meditation is a very complex and serious problem, and I shall go into it step by step. Without meditation, life is merely a matter of environment, of circumstances, of pressures and influences, and therefore has very little significance. Without meditation, there is no perfume to life. Without meditation, there is no compassion, no love, and life is then merely a thing of sensation. And without meditation, the mind is not capable of finding out what is true.

Before we ask how to meditate, or what practice is necessary in order to meditate, must we not first find out what meditation is? And the very enquiry into what is meditation is meditation. Please listen to what I am saying, if you will, because this is very important. As I said, a mind that is incapable of meditation is incapable of understanding life. It is because we do not know what meditation is that our life is so stupid, superficial, made up of mere achievements, failures, successes, misery.

So, to find out what is meditation, is meditation; and this evening you and I are going to enquire into it together. To ask how to meditate when you do not know what meditation is, is too immature. How can you practise what you do not know? The books, the priests, the teachers will tell you what meditation is—and they may all be mistaken, because they are all interpreters. An interpreter is a traitor. Please listen, sirs, don't laugh it off. An interpreter is a traitor because he is interpreting according to his conditioning. Truth does not want any interpretation. There can be no interpreter of what is true, because it is you who have to find out what is true. We are now going to find out together the truth about meditation, but if you do not follow step by step, giving your whole attention to it, you will not understand what meditation is. I am not saying this dogmatically, but you will have to see the truth of it for yourself.

Prayer which is a supplication, a petition, either conscious or unconscious, is not meditation, even though such prayer may be answered. The mechanism by which prayer is answered is something which we won't go into now, because it is too complex and would require another half-hour to explain. But you can see that prayer which is a supplication, a petition, a demand, a begging, is not meditation because you are asking something for yourself or for somebody else.

Then you will find also that the process of controlling the mind is not meditation. Please listen to this, don't throw it out and say 'What nonsense!' We are enquiring.

Now, what is the way of concentration in so-called meditation? You try to fix your mind on an idea, on a thought, on a sentence, on a picture or an idol made by the hand or by the mind, but other thoughts constantly creep in. You spend your time fighting them off, till after years of practice in controlling the mind you are able to suppress all ideas except one, and you think you have achieved something. What you have achieved is the technique of suppressing, sublimating, or substituting one idea for another, one desire for another, but in that process is involved conflict; there is a division between the maker of effort and the object he hopes to achieve through effort. This effort to control the mind in order to achieve a result—peace, bliss, nirvana, or whatever it   be—is self-centred activity, and nothing more; therefore it is not meditation. This does not mean that in meditation the mind is allowed to wander as it likes. Let us go into this slowly.

We see the truth that a mind which is merely concerned with control, with discipline, with suppressing its own thoughts, is making itself narrow; it is an exclusive mind, and such a mind is incapable of understanding what is meditation. A mind that suppresses part of itself and concentrates on the idea of peace, on an image made by the hand or by the mind, is obviously afraid of its own desires, its own ambitions, its own feelings of envy, greed, and so on, and in suppressing them, such a mind is not meditating; though it may repeat a thousand mantras, or sit silent and alone in some dark forest or mountain cave, it is incapable of understanding meditation.

So, having discovered that control is not meditation, you begin to ask yourself what are these jumbling thoughts that precipitate themselves one on top of another, that wander all over the place like monkeys, or flutter after each other like butterflies. There is now no question of controlling them, because you see that you are the various thoughts and contradictory desires which are endlessly pursuing each other. These thoughts, these contradictions, these desires are part of you; you are not different from them, any more than the qualities of the diamond are different from the diamond itself. Remove the qualities of the diamond, and there is no diamond; remove the qualities, the thoughts of the mind, and there is no mind. So meditation is obviously not a matter of control.

But if you do not control your thoughts, then what? Then you begin to enquire into your thoughts. Do you understand, sirs? The mind is no longer suppressing thought, but enquiring into the motive, the background of its thought, and you will find that this enquiry into its own thought has an extraordinary effect on the mind. Then the mind ceases to manufacture thought. Please do understand this. When you begin to enquire into the whole process of thinking without suppressing, condemning, or justifying anything, without trying to concentrate on one thought by excluding all other thoughts, then you will find that the mind is no longer manufacturing thought. Please do listen. The mind manufactures thought through sensation, through memory, through the object which it wants to achieve; but the moment it begins to enquire into the process of thinking, it ceases to produce thought, because then the mind is beginning to free itself from that whole process. In this free movement of the mind as it enquires into its own pursuits and sorrows, the mind begins to understand itself, and that understanding comes from self-knowledge.

So you have seen that prayer—which involves conditioning, demand, petition, fear, and so on—is not meditation. Nor is there meditation when one part of the mind which you call the lower self is dominated by another part of the mind which you call the higher self, or the Atman. This contradiction in the mind is caused by the fact that one desire is controlling another, and that is obviously not meditation. Nor is it meditation to sit in front of a picture and repeat *japams*, mantras. What happens when you sit quietly and repeat certain phrases? Your mind becomes hypnotized, does it not? Your mind gradually goes to sleep, and you think that you have attained bliss, a marvellous peace. It is only in your daily life that you can find out what meditation is, not in the repetition of certain words and phrases.

Now, if praying, chanting, sitting in front of a picture, controlling thought, is not meditation, then what is meditation? The mind has moved away from the false, because it has seen the truth in the false. Do you understand, sirs? The mind has seen the truth that control is false, and this truth has liberated it from the desire to control. Therefore the mind is free to enquire into the process of thinking, which leads to self-knowledge. That is, the mind begins to understand itself when it is just watching its own operation without condemnation, judgement, or evaluation, and then you will find that the mind becomes very quiet, it is not made quiet. Generally you try to make the mind quiet; all your religious books, your priests, tell you to train the mind to be quiet, to practise quietness. The mind that has practised quietness, that has trained itself to be still, is like a monkey that has learnt a trick. You cannot have stillness through desire. You have to understand desire, not escape from or suppress it. Because desire is always contradictory, you have to understand it; and in the process of understanding desire, you will find that the mind becomes completely still—the totality of the mind, not just the superficial layer which is occupied with your daily living. Do you understand, sirs? To have ambition, envy, greed, the desire for power, and yet talk about meditation, is to be in a state of illusion. These two are incompatible, they don't go together.

It is only when there is self-knowledge, which is to have an understanding of your daily living, your daily relationships, that the mind becomes quiet without being forced or disciplined to be quiet. Then you will find that the mind is completely still—the totality of it, the unconscious as well as the conscious. The unconscious, which is the sum total of all your traditions, your memories, your motives, your ambitions, your greed, is far more conservative than the conscious mind, far more effective in its desires and pursuits; and it can be understood only through self-knowledge. When through self-knowledge the mind is completely still, in that stillness you will find there is no experiencer to experience, because the experiencer and the experienced are the same. To realize this requires a great deal of attention, enquiry, discovery. The observer and the observed, the watcher and the watched are one, they are not two separate entities. The thinker is not different from the thought; the two are essentially the same, though for various reasons—convenience, security, permanency, and so on—thought has made the thinker separate and permanent.

So, if you have followed this enquiry into what is meditation, and have understood the whole process of thinking, you will find that the mind is completely still. In that total stillness of the mind, there is no watcher, no observer, and therefore no experiencer at all; there is no entity who is gathering experience, which is the activity of a self-centred mind. Don't say, 'That is samadhi'—which is all nonsense, because you have only read of it in some book and have not discovered it for yourself. There is a vast difference between the word and the thing. The word is not the thing; the word 'door' is not the door.

So, to meditate is to purge the mind of its self-centred activity. And if you have come this far in meditation, you will find there is silence, a total emptiness. The mind is uncontaminated by society, it is no longer subject to any influence, to the pressure of any desire. It is completely alone, and being alone, untouched, it is innocent. Therefore there is a possibility for that which is timeless, eternal, to come into being.

This whole process is meditation.

First Talk in Poona
21 September 1958

I should think one of our great problems must be to know what is freedom, and the need to understand this problem must be fairly immense and continuous since there is so much propaganda, from so many specialists, so many and various forms of outward and inward compulsion, and all the chaotic, contradictory persuasions, influences and impressions. I am sure we must have asked ourselves the question: What is freedom? As you and I know, everywhere in the world authoritarianism is spreading, not only at the political, social and economic levels but also at the so-called spiritual level. Everywhere there is a compelling environmental influence; newspapers tell us what to think, and there are so many five-, ten- or fifteen-year plans. Then there are these specialists at the economic, scientific and bureaucratic levels; there are all the traditions of everyday activity, what we must do and what we must not do; then there is the whole influence of the so-called sacred books; and there is the cinema, the radio, the newspaper—everything in the world is trying to tell us what to do, what to think, and what we must not think. I do not know if you have noticed how increasingly difficult it has become to think for oneself.

We have become such experts in quoting what other people say, or have said, and in the midst of this authoritarian welter where is the freedom? And what do we mean by freedom? Is there such a thing? I am using that word 'freedom' in its most simple sense in which is included liberation, the mind that is liberated, free. I want, if I may, to go into that this evening.

First, I think we must realize that our minds are really not free. Everything we see, every thought we have, shapes our mind; whatever you think now, whatever you have thought in the past and whatever you are going to think in the future—it all shapes the mind. You think what you have been told either by the religious person, or the politician, by the teacher in your school, or by books and newspapers. Everything about you influences what you think. What you eat, what you look at, what you listen to, your wife, your husband, your child, your neighbour— everything is shaping the mind. I think that is fairly obvious. Even when you think that there is a God or that there is no God, that also is the influence of tradition. So our mind is the field in which there are many contradictory influences which are in battle one against the other.

Do please listen to all this because, as I have been saying, unless we directly experience for ourselves, your coming to a talk of this kind has no value at all. Please believe me that unless you experience what is being said, not merely follow the description but be aware, be cognizant, know the ways of your own thinking and thereby experience, these talks will have no meaning whatsoever. After all, I am only describing what is actually taking place in one's life, in one's environment, so that we can be aware of it and see if we can break through it, and what the implications of breaking through are. Because obviously we are now slaves, either the Hindu slave, the Catholic slave, the Russian slave, or slaves of one kind or another. We are all slaves to certain forms of thought, and in the midst of all this we ask if we can be free and talk about the anatomy of freedom and authority, and so on.

I think it must be fairly obvious to most of us that what we think is conditioned. Whatever your thought—however noble and wide or however limited and petty—it is conditioned, and if you further that thought there can be no freedom of thought. Thought itself is conditioned, because thought is the reaction of memory, and memory is the residue of all your experiences, which in turn are the result of your conditioning. So if one realizes that all thinking, at whatever level, is conditioned then we will see that thinking is not the means of breaking through this limitation—which does not mean that we must go into some blank or speculative silence. Actually the fact is, is it not?, that every thought, every feeling, every action is conformative, conditioned, influenced. For instance, a saint comes along and by his rhetoric, gestures, looks, by quoting this and that to you, influences you. And we want to be influenced and are afraid to move away from every form of influence and see if we can go deeply and discover if there is a state of being which is not the result of influence.

Why are we influenced? In politics, as you know, it is the job of the politician to influence us; and every book, every teacher, every guru—the more powerful, the more eloquent the better we like it—imposes his thought, his way of life, his manner of conduct, upon us. So life is a battle of ideas, a battle of influences, and your mind is the field of the battle. The politician wants your mind; the guru wants your mind; the saint says, 'Do this and not that', and he also wants your mind; and every tradition, every form of habit or custom, influences, shapes, guides, controls your mind. I think that is fairly obvious. It would be absurd to deny it. The fact is so.

You know, sirs, if I may deviate a little, I think it is essential to appreciate beauty. The beauty of the sky, the beauty of the sun upon the hill, the beauty of a smile, a face, a gesture, the beauty of the moonlight on the water, of the fading clouds, the song of the bird—it is essential to look at it, to feel it, to be with it, and I think this is the very first requirement for a man who would seek Truth. Most of us are so unconcerned with this extraordinary universe about us; we never even see the waving of the leaf in the wind; we never watch a blade of grass, touch it with our hand and know the quality of its being. This is not just being poetic, so please do not go off into a speculative emotional state. I say it is essential to have that deep feeling for life and not be caught in intellectual ramifications, discussions, passing examinations, quoting, and brushing something new aside by saying it has already been said. Intellect is not the way. Intellect will not solve our problems; the intellect will not give us that nourishment which is imperishable. The intellect can reason, discuss, analyse, come to a conclusion from inferences and so on, but intellect is limited for intellect is the result of our conditioning. But sensitivity is not. Sensitivity has no conditioning; it takes you right out of the field of fears and anxieties. The mind that is not sensitive to everything about it—to the mountain, the telegraph pole, the lamp, the voice, the smile, everything—is incapable of finding what is true.

But we spend our days and years in cultivating the intellect, in arguing, discussing, fighting, struggling to be something, and so on. And yet this extraordinarily wonderful world, this earth that is so rich—not the Bombay earth, the Punjab earth, the Russian earth or the American earth—this earth is ours, yours and mine, and that is not sentimental nonsense, it is a fact. But unfortunately we have divided it up through our pettiness, through our provincialism. And we know why we have done it—for our security, for better jobs and more jobs. That is the political game that is being played throughout the world, and so we forget to be human beings, to live happily on this earth which is ours and to make something of it. And it is because we do not have that feeling for beauty which is not sentimental, which is not corrupting, which is not sexual, but a sense of caring, it is because we have lost that feeling—or perhaps we have never had it—that we are fighting, battling with each other over words, and have no immediate understanding of anything. Look what you are doing in India—breaking up the land into sections, fighting and butchering, and this is happening the world over, and for what? To have better jobs, more jobs, more power? And so in this battle we lose that quality of mind which can see things freely, happily, and without envy. We do not know how to see somebody happy, driving a luxurious car, and to look at him and be happy with him; nor do we know how to sympathize with the very, very poor. We are envious of the man with the car, and we avoid the man who has nothing. So there is no love, and without that quality of love which is really the very essence of beauty, do what you will—go on all the pilgrimages in the world, go to every temple, cultivate all the virtues you can think of—you will get nowhere at all. Please believe me, you will not have it, that sense of beauty and love even if you sit cross-legged for meditation, holding your breath for the next ten thousand years. You laugh but you do not see the tragedy of it. We are not in that sensitive state of mind which receives, which sees immediately something which is true. You know a sensitive mind is a defenseless mind, it is a vulnerable mind, and the mind must be vulnerable for truth to enter—the truth that you have no sympathy, the truth that you are envious.

So it is essential to have this sense of beauty, for the feeling of beauty is the feeling of love. As I said, this is a slight digression but I think it has significance in relation to what we are talking about. We are saying that a mind that is influenced, shaped, authority-bound, obviously can never be free, and whatever it thinks, however lofty its ideals, however subtle and deep, it is still conditioned. I think it is very important to understand that the mind, through time, through experience, through the many thousands of yesterdays, is shaped, conditioned and that thought is not the way out. Which does not mean that you must be thoughtless; on the contrary. When you are capable of understanding very profoundly, very deeply, extensively, widely, subtly, then only will you fully recognize how petty thinking is, how small thought is. Then there is a breaking down of the wall of that conditioning.

So, can we not see that fact—that all thought is conditioned? Whether it is the thought of the communist, capitalist, Hindu, Buddhist, or the person who is speaking, thinking is conditioned. And obviously the mind is the result of time, the result of the reactions of a thousand years and of yesterday, of a second ago and ten years ago; the mind is the result of the period in which you have learnt and suffered and of all the influences of the past and present. Now, such a mind, obviously, cannot be free, and yet that is what we are seeking, is it not? You know even in Russia, in all the totalitarian countries where everything is controlled, there is this search for freedom. That search is there in the beginning for all of us when we are young, for then we are revolutionary, we are discontented, we want to know, we are curious, we are struggling; but soon that discontent is canalized into various channels, and there it dies slowly. So there is always within us the demand, the urge, to be free, and we never understand it, we never go into it, we have never searched out that deep instinctual demand. Being discontented when young, being dissatisfied with things as they are, with the stupidities of traditional values, we gradually, as we grow older, fall into the old patterns which society has established, and we get lost. It is very difficult to keep the pure discontent, the discontent which says, 'This is not enough; there must be something else.' We all know that feeling, the feeling of otherness which we soon translate as God, or nirvana, and we read a book about it and get lost. But this feeling of otherness, the search, the enquiry for it, that, I think, is the beginning of the real urge to be free from all these political, religious and traditional influences, and to break through this wall. Let us enquire into it.

Surely, there are several kinds of freedom. There is political freedom; there is the freedom which knowledge gives, when you know how to do things, the know-how; the freedom of a wealthy man who can go round the world; the freedom of capacity, to be able to write, to express oneself, to think clearly. Then there is the freedom from something: freedom from oppression, freedom from envy, freedom from tradition, from ambition, and so on. And then there is the freedom which is gained, we hope, at the end—at the end of the discipline, at the end of acquiring virtue, at the end of effort—the ultimate freedom we hope to get through doing certain things. So the freedom that capacity gives, the freedom from something and the freedom we are supposed to gain at the end of a virtuous life—those are types of freedom we all know. Now are not those various freedoms merely reactions? When you say, 'I want to be free from anger', that is merely a reaction; it is not freedom from anger. And the freedom which you think that you will get at the end of a virtuous life, by struggle, by discipline— that is also a reaction to what has been. Please, sirs, follow this carefully, because I am going to say something somewhat difficult in the sense that you are not accustomed to it. There is a sense of freedom which is not from anything, which has no cause, but which is a state of being free. You see, the freedom that we know is always brought about by will, is it not? I will be free, I will learn a technique, I will become a specialist, I will study, and that will give me freedom. So we use will as a means of achieving freedom, do we not? I do not want to be poor and therefore I exercise my capacity, my will, everything to get rich. Or I am vain and I exercise will, not to be vain. So we think we shall get freedom through the exercise of will. But will does not bring freedom, on the contrary, as I will show you.

What is will? I will be, I must not be, I am going to struggle to become something, I am going to learn—all these are forms of exercising will. Now what is this will, and how is it formed? Obviously, through desire. Our many desires, with their frustrations, compulsions and fulfilments, form as it were the threads of a cord, a rope. That is will, is it not? Your many contradictory desires together become a very strong and powerful rope with which you try to climb to success, to freedom. Now, will desire give freedom, or is the very desire for freedom the denial of it? Please watch yourselves, sirs, watch your own desires, your own ambition, your own will. And if one has no will and is merely being driven, that also is a part of will—the will to resist and go with the tide. Through that weight of desire, through that rope, we hope to climb to God, to bliss, or whatever it is.

So I am asking you whether your will is a liberating factor? Is freedom come by through will? Or is freedom something entirely different, which has nothing to do with reaction, which cannot be achieved through capacity, through thought, experience, discipline or constant conformity? That is what all the books say, do they not? Conform to the pattern and you will be free in the end; do all these things, obey, and ultimately there will be freedom. To me all that is sheer nonsense because freedom is at the beginning, not at the end, as I will show you.

To see something true is possible, is it not? You can see that the sky is blue—thousands of people have said so— but you can see that it is so for yourself. You can see for yourself, if you are at all sensitive, the movement of a leaf. From the very beginning there is the capacity to perceive that which is true, instinctively, not through any form of compulsion, adjustment, conformity. Now, sirs, I will show you another truth.

I say that a leader, a follower, a virtuous man does not know love. I say that to you. You who are leaders, you who are followers, who are struggling to be virtuous—I say you do not know love. Do not argue with me for a moment; do not say, 'Prove it to me.' I will reason with you, show you, but first, please listen to what I have to say, without being defensive, aggressive, approving or denying. I say that a leader, a follower, or a man who is trying to be virtuous, such an individual does not know what love is. If you really listen to that statement not with an aggressive or a submissive mind, then you will see the actual truth of it. If you do not see the truth of it, it is because you do not want to, or you are so supremely contented with your leadership, your following, or your so-called virtues that you deny everything else. But if you are at all sensitive, enquiring, open as when looking out of a window, then you must see the truth of it, you are bound to. Now I will give you the reasons because you are all fairly reasonable, intellectual people and you can be convinced. But you will never actually know the truth through intellect or reason. You will be convinced through reason, but being convinced is not the perception of what is true. There is a vast difference between the two. A man who is convinced of something is incapable of seeing what is true. A man who is convinced can be unconvinced, and convinced again in a different way. But a man who sees that which is true, is not 'convinced'; he sees that it just is true.

Now as I said, a leader who says, 'I know the way, I know all about life, I have experienced the ultimate Reality,

I have the goods', obviously is very concerned about himself and his visions and about transmitting his visions to the poor listener; a leader wants to lead people to something which he thinks is right. So the leader, whether it is the political, the social, the religious leader or whether it is your wife or husband, such a one has no love. He may talk about love, he may offer to show you the way of love, he may do all the things that love is supposed to do, but the actual feeling of love is not there—because he is a leader. If there is love you cease to be a leader, for love exercises no authority. And the same applies to the follower. The moment you follow, you are accepting authority, are you not?—the authority which gives you security, a safe corner in heaven or a safe corner in this world. When you follow, seeking security for yourself, your family, your race, your nation, that following indicates that you want to be safe, and a man who seeks safety knows no quality of love. And so also with the virtuous man. The man who cultivates humility surely is not virtuous. Humility is not a thing to be cultivated.

So I am trying to show you that a mind that is sensitive, enquiring, a mind that is really listening can perceive the truth of something immediately. But truth cannot be 'applied'. If you see the truth, it operates without your conscious effort, of its own accord.

So discontent is the beginning of freedom, and so long as you are trying to manipulate discontent, to accept authority in order that this discontent shall disappear, enter into safe channels, then you are already losing that pristine sense of real feeling. Most of us are discontented, are we not?, either with our jobs, our relationships or whatever we are doing. You want something to happen, to change, to move, to break through. You do not know what it is. There is a constant searching, enquiring, especially when one is young, open, sensitive. Later on, as you become old, you settle down in your habits, your job, because your family is safe, your wife will not run away. So this extraordinary flame disappears and you become respectable, petty and thoughtless.

So, as I have been pointing out, freedom from something is not freedom. You are trying to be free from anger; I do not say you must not be free from anger, but I say that that is not freedom. I may be rid of greed, pettiness, envy, or a dozen other things and yet not be free. Freedom is a quality of the mind. That quality does not come about through very careful, respectable searchings and enquiries, through very careful analysis or putting ideas together. That is why it is important to see the truth that the freedom we are constantly demanding is always from something, such as freedom from sorrow. Not that there is no freedom from sorrow, but the demand to be free from it is merely a reaction and therefore does not free you from sorrow. Am I making myself clear? I am in sorrow for various reasons, and I say I must be free. The urge to be free of sorrow is born out of pain. I suffer, because of my husband, or my son, or something else, I do not like that state I am in and I want to get away from it. That desire for freedom is a reaction; it is not freedom. It is just another desirable state I want in opposition to 'what is'. The man who can travel around the world because he has plenty of money is not necessarily free, nor is the man who is clever or efficient, for his wanting to be free is again merely a reaction. So, can I not see that freedom, liberation, cannot be learnt or acquired or sought after through any reaction? Therefore I must understand the reaction, and I must also understand that freedom does not come through any effort of will. Will and freedom are contradictory, as thought and freedom are contradictory. Thought cannot produce freedom because thought is conditioned. Economically you can, perhaps, arrange the world so that man can be more comfortable, have more food, clothing and shelter, and you may think that is freedom. Those are necessary and essential things, but that is not the totality of freedom. Freedom is a state and quality of mind. And it is that quality we are enquiring into. Without that quality, do what you will, cultivate all the virtues in the world, you will not have that freedom.

So, how is that sense of otherness, that quality of mind to come about? You cannot cultivate it because the moment you use your brain you are using thought, which is limited. Whether it is the thought of the Buddha or anyone else, all thought is limited. So our enquiry must be negative; we must come to that freedom obliquely, not directly. Do you understand, sirs? Am I giving some indication, or none at all? That freedom is not to be sought after aggressively, is not to be cultivated by denials, disciplines, by checking yourself, torturing yourself, by doing various exercises and all the rest of it. It must come without your knowing, like virtue. Cultivated virtue is not virtue; the virtue which is true virtue is not self-conscious. Surely, a man who has cultivated humility, who, because of his conceit, vanity, arrogance has made himself humble, such a man has no true sense of humility. Humility is a state in which the mind is not conscious of its own quality, as a flower which has fragrance is not conscious of its own perfume. So this freedom cannot be got through any form of discipline, nor can a mind which is undisciplined understand it. You use discipline to produce a result, but freedom is not a result. If it is a result, it is no longer free because it has been produced.

So, how is the mind, which is full of multitudinous influences, compulsions, various forms of contradictory desires, the product of time, how is that mind to have the quality of freedom? You understand, sirs? We know that all the things that I have been talking about are not freedom. They are all manufactured by the mind under various stresses, compulsions and influences. So, if I can approach it negatively, in the very awareness that all this is not freedom, then the mind is already disciplined—but not disciplined to achieve a result. Let us go into that briefly.

The mind says, 'I must discipline myself in order to achieve a result.' That is fairly obvious. But such discipline does not bring freedom. It brings a result because you have a motive, a cause which produces the result, but that result is never freedom, it is only a reaction. That is fairly clear. Now, if I begin to understand the operations of that kind of discipline, then, in the very process of understanding, enquiring, going into it, my mind is truly disciplined. I do not know if you can see what I mean, quickly. The exercise of will to produce a result is called discipline; whereas, the understanding of the whole significance of will, of discipline, and of what we call result, demands a mind that is extraordinarily clear and 'disciplined', not by the will but through negative understanding.

So, negatively, I have understood the whole problem of what is not freedom. I have examined it, I have searched my heart and my mind, the recesses of my being, to understand what freedom means, and I see that none of these things we have described is freedom because they are all based on desire, compulsion, will, on what I will get at the end, and they are all reactions. I see factually that they are not freedom. Therefore, because I have understood those things, my mind is open to find out or receive that which is free.

So my mind has a quality which is not that of a disciplined mind seeking a result, nor that of the undisciplined mind which wanders about, but it has understood, negatively, both 'what is' and 'what should be', and so can perceive, can understand that freedom which is not from something, that freedom which is not a result. Sirs, this requires a great deal of enquiry. If you just repeat that there is a freedom which is not the freedom from something, it has no meaning. So please do not say it. Or if you say, 'I want to get that other freedom', you are also on the wrong track, for you cannot. The universe cannot enter into the petty mind; the immeasurable cannot come to a mind that knows measurement. So our whole enquiry is how to break through the measurement—which does not mean I must go off to an ashram, become neurotic, devotional, and all that nonsense.

And here, if I may say so, what is important is the teaching and not the teacher. The person who speaks here at the moment is not important; throw him overboard. What is important is what is being said. So the mind only knows the measurable, the compass of itself, the frontiers, ambitions, hopes, desperation, misery, sorrows and joys. Such a mind cannot invite freedom. All that it can do is to be aware of itself and not condemn what it sees; not condemn the ugly or cling to the beautiful, but see 'what is'. The mere perception of 'what is' is the beginning of the breaking down of the measurement of the mind, of its frontiers, its patterns. Just to see things as they are. Then you will find that the mind can come to that freedom involuntarily, without knowing. This transformation in the mind itself is the true revolution. All other revolutions are reactions, even though they use the word 'freedom' and promise utopia, the heavens, everything. There is only true revolution in the quality of the mind.

First Talk in Madras
26 October 1958

I think it would be good if we could—you and I—quietly by ourselves, as two human beings together, talk over our problems. I think we should get much further if we had that feeling than by thinking of this as an audience being addressed by a speaker. That is, if you and I could go into some corner, a quiet room and explore our problems, I think we would get very much further, but unfortunately that is not possible. There are too many people and time is very limited. So one resorts to a large audience, and invariably one has to generalize, and in the process of generalization the particularities, the details have to be omitted, naturally. But for most of us the generalities seem to have very little significance and the particular problem, the particular issue, the particular conflict, seems all-important. One forgets the wider, deeper issues because one is forcibly faced with one's own little everyday problems.

So in discussing, in talking together, I think we must bear in mind both these issues, not only the general but also the particular. The wider and deeper issues escape most of us, but without understanding these, the approach to the little problems, the petty trivialities, the everyday conflict, will have very little meaning. I think we must see this very clearly right at the beginning—that if one would solve the everyday problems of existence, whatever they may be, one must first see the wider issues and then come to the detail. After all, the great painter, the great poet is one who sees the whole—who sees all the heavens, the blue skies, the radiant sunset, the tree, the fleeting bird—all at one glance; with one sweep he sees the whole thing. With the artist, the poet, there is an immediate, a direct communion with this whole marvellous world of beauty. Then he begins to paint, to write, to sculpt; he works it out in detail. If you and I could do the same, then we should be able to approach our problems—however contradictory, however conflicting, however disturbing—much more liberally, more wisely, with greater depth and colour, feeling. This is not mere romantic verbalization but actually it is so, and that is what I would like to talk about now and every time we get together. We must capture the whole and not be carried away by the detail, however pressing, immediate, anxious it may be. I think that is where the revolution begins. Please bear in mind that I am not talking as to a large audience but that I am talking, if I may respectfully say so, to you, to each one. And I hope we can understand that first principle of the immediate and the fundamental issue.

After all, we have many problems, not only the individual, personal problems but also the collective problems, as starvation, war, peace, and the terrible politicians. I am using the word 'terrible' in the verbal sense and I am not condemning them. They are superficial people who talk of these problems as though they can solve the whole thing in a nutshell. And our own personal problems are the problems of relationship, of our job, of fulfilment and frustration, of fear, love, beauty, sex, and so on.

Now, what happens with most of us is that we try to solve these problems separately, each one by itself. That is, I have a problem of fear and I try to solve it. But I will never be able to solve it by itself because it is related to a very, very complex issue, to a wider field, and without understanding the deeper problem, merely to tackle the particular trouble—one corner of the field instead of the whole—only creates more problems. I hope I am making this point clear. If we can establish that—you and I as two people in communication with each other—then I think we shall have resolved a great deal because, after all, understanding is that, is it not? What does it mean, to understand something? It means, does it not?, to grasp the significance of the thing totally. Otherwise there is no understanding, there is only intellection, merely a verbalization, the play of the mind. Without understanding the totality of your being, merely to take one layer of that being and try to solve it separately, in a watertight compartment unrelated to the totality, only leads to further complications, further misery. If we can really understand that, really feel the truth of it, then we shall be able to find out how to tackle our individual, immediate problems.

After all, sirs, it is like this. You never see the sky if you are looking through a window; you only see part of the sky, obviously. You must go outside to see the whole vast horizon, the limitless sky. But most of us view the sky through the window, and from such a narrow, limited outlook we think we can solve not only one particular problem but all our problems. That is the curse of society, of all organizations. But if you can have that feeling of the necessity of the comprehension of the whole—whatever that whole is, and we will go into that—then the mind has already a different outlook, a different capacity.

If that is very clearly established between you and me, as two individuals, not as a listener and a talker, not as a guru and a disciple—all that nonsense is wiped away, at least so far as I am concerned—then we can proceed. So what is the issue, the wide, profound issue? If I can see the totality of it then I will be able to tackle the detail. Now I may put it into words, but the word is not the thing. The word 'sky' is not the sky, is it? The word 'door' is not the door. We must be very clear to differentiate between the word and the fact, the word and the thing itself. The word 'freedom' is not the state of freedom, and the word 'mind' is not the actual thing, which is really totally indescribable. So again, if you are very clear that the word is not the thing, then we can proceed with our communication. Because I want to convey something to you and you want to understand, but if you merely hold on to the words and not to the significance then there is a barrier in communication.

So, what is that thing which, being understood, being explored, having its significance fully grasped, will help us to unravel and resolve the detail? Surely, it is the mind, is it not? Now, when I use that word 'mind', each one of you will interpret it differently according to your education, your culture, your conditioning. When I use the word 'mind', obviously you must have a reaction to that word and that reaction depends upon your reading, your environmental influences, how much or how little you have thought about it, and so on. So, what is the mind? If I can understand the workings of that extraordinary thing called the mind, the totality of it, the feeling, the nature, the amazing capacity of it, its profundity, width and quality, then whatever its reaction—which is merely the product of its culture, environment, education, reading, and so on—I can tackle it. So, what we are going to do, if we can, is to explore this thing called the mind. But you cannot explore it, obviously, if you already have an idea about it. If you say, 'the mind is Atman', it is finished. You have stopped all exploration, investigation, enquiry. Or if you are a communist and say that the mind is merely the result of some influence, then also you are incapable of examining. It is very important to understand that if you approach a problem with a mind already made up, you have stopped investigating the problem and therefore prevented the understanding of the problem. The socialist, the capitalist, the communist who approaches the problem of starvation does so with a system, a theory, and so what happens? He is incapable of making a further examination of the problem. Life does not stop. It is a movement, and if you approach it with a static mind you cannot touch it. Again this is fairly clear, is it not?, so let us proceed.

When I use the word 'mind' I look at it without any conclusion; therefore I am capable of examining it, or rather, the mind, having no conclusion about itself, is capable of looking at itself. A mind that starts to think from a conclusion is not really thinking. It is asking an enormous thing, is it not?, for the mind to examine a problem without any conclusion. I do not know if you see this—that with most of us thinking starts from a conclusion, a conclusion that there is God or no God, reincarnation or no reincarnation, that the communist system will save the world, or the capitalist. We start from one conclusion and go to another, and this process of moving from conclusion to conclusion we call thinking; and if you observe it, it is not thinking at all. Thinking implies a constant moving, a constant examination, a constant awareness of the movement of thought, not a fixed point from which to go to another fixed point.

So we are going to find out what this extraordinary thing called the mind is, because that is the problem and nothing else. It is the mind that creates the problem; it is the thought, the conditioned mind, the mind that is petty, narrow, bigoted, which has created beliefs, ideas and knowledge and which is crippled by its own concepts, vanities, greeds, ambitions and frustrations. So it is the mind which has to be understood, and that mind is the 'me', that mind is the self—not some higher self. The mind invents the higher self and then says it is only a tool for the higher. Such thinking is absurd, immature. It is the mind which invents all these avenues of escape and then proceeds from there to assert.

So we are going to find out what the mind is. Now, you cannot find out from my description. I am going to talk about it, but if you merely recognize it through the description then you are not knowing the state of your own mind. I hope you understand this. Now, I say the state of the mind is beauty, and that without knowing beauty, without the full comprehension of the feeling of beauty, without having beauty, you will never understand the mind. I have made that statement and you have heard it. Then what happens? Your mind says, 'What is beauty?', does it not? Then you begin to argue with yourself, to find words so that through a definition you may feel the beauty. So you depend on words to evoke a feeling, is that not so? I am enquiring what this extraordinary mind is, which is the product of time, the product of many thousands of years. Do not jump to the idea of reincarnation. The mind is the product of many yesterdays, is it not? It is the result of a thousand influences, it is the result of tradition, it is the result of habit, it is put together by various cultures. It knows despair and hope. It knows the past, it is the present and it creates the future. It has accumulated knowledge, the sciences of technology, of physics, of medicine and countless other pursuits; it is capable of extraordinary invention. It is also capable of enquiring beyond itself, of searching for freedom and breaking through its conditioning. It is all these things and much more. And if the mind is not aware of itself, of the extraordinary complexities, merely concentrating on any detail, on one particularity, will destroy the totality.

Please, I hope you are listening with care, because if you do not listen rightly you will go away and say, 'What on earth has he been talking about?' But if you listen rightly, which is an art, you will already have discovered what an extraordinary thing the mind is. It is not a matter of finding it out afterwards, but in the very course of listening you are discovering this mind. There is all the difference between being told what an astounding thing the mind is and making the discovery for yourself. The two states are entirely different. When you say, 'I know hunger', you have directly experienced it, but the man who has never experienced hunger can also say, 'I know hunger.' The two states of 'knowing' are entirely different; the one is direct experience and the other is descriptive knowledge.

So, can you experience directly the quality of this amazingly complex mind—the vastness of it, the immensity of it? It is not limited to a particularity, as the mind of a lawyer, prime minister or cook, but it is everything— the lawyer, the prime minister, the cook, the painter, the man who is frightened, jealous, anxious, ambitious, frustrated—it is all that. And it is the mind that is creating the problem, according to the environmental influences. Because of overpopulation in this country, because of the caste system, because of starvation and the rest of the business, the problem of employment has become immediate, important. And so the mind, this complex thing, because of pressure, because of the immediate demand, responds only at a certain level and hopes to solve the problem at that level. And the man who is not concerned with the immediate, immense problem of starvation, of war, escapes into some other form of immediate problem. But what is required is to investigate this whole totality of the mind. And to do that, what is essential is freedom, not authority. I think it is really very important to understand this, because it is authority which is destroying this unfortunate country. Do not say, 'Are not the other countries being destroyed too?' They are. But you and I are concerned for the moment with what is here, and this country is idolatrous. There is, here, the worship of authority, and the worship of success, the big man. Look at the way you treat your cook and the way you treat the man who is successful, the cabinet-minister, the man who has knowledge, the saint, and all the rest of it. So you worship authority and therefore you are never free. Freedom is the first demand, not the last demand of a mind which says, 'I must find out, I must look, I must enquire.' For the mind to investigate itself, to investigate the problems of its own making, to investigate that which is beyond its own limitations, it must be free at the beginning not at the end. Now, if you really feel that, if you see the necessity of it, there is an immediate revolution. Revolution is not the doing what you like, because you imagine you are free, but revolution is the seeing the necessity that the mind must be free. Then it is capable of adjustment through freedom, not through slavery, not from authority. Am I making myself clear?

Let us look at it again. Because of overpopulation, over-organization, and common communication, because of the fear of losing a job, of not being up to the mark and because of all the pressures of modern civilization with its amazing technology, and the threat of war, hate and all that, naturally the mind is confused and so it seeks an authority—the authority of a Hitler, of the prime minister, the guru, the book, or the commissar. That is what you are doing and therefore you are authority-bound, idolatrous. You may not worship a statue, a thing made by the hand, but you worship the man who is successful, who knows much or has much. All that indicates an idolatrous mind which is essentially the mind crippled by an example, by the hero. The hero means the authority, and a mind that worships authority is incapable of understanding.

Now, let us look at this extraordinary field of the mind, look at what it is capable of. The sputniks or the rockets— it is all the mind. It is the mind that slaughters, kills thousands because of its dogmas, as the churches and dictators have done. It is the mind that is afraid. It is the mind that says, 'I must know if there is a God or not.' And to understand this mind you must begin with freedom. But it is extremely difficult to be free because the mind which wants to be clear is at the same time afraid to be free. After all, most people want to be secure, secure in their relationships, secure in their jobs, secure in their ideas, in their professions, in their specialties, in their beliefs. Watch your own mind and see what is happening—you want to be secure and yet you know you must be free. So there is a contradiction going on. The mind which says there must be peace and yet creates and supports war is schizophrenic, in contradiction. In this country you talk about peace, non-violence and yet you are preparing for war. There is the mind that is peaceful and the mind that is violent, and so in the mind there is conflict.

So the first thing for all enquiry, for all new life, for all understanding and comprehension is freedom. But you do not demand freedom, you demand security. And the moment you want physical security you plan to create it—which means you establish various forms of authority, dictatorship, control, while at the same time you want freedom. So the conflict begins within the mind. But a mind which is aware of its conflict must find out which is of primary importance—freedom or security. After all, is there such a thing as security at all? You may want it, but is there such a thing? Events are showing that there is no such thing as security. Yet the mind clings to the idea. If the mind demands freedom first then security will follow, but if you seek security first you will never have freedom and so you will always have different forms of conflict, misery and sorrow. Surely, all this is obvious.

So to understand the quality of the mind and its immensity, there must be freedom—freedom from all conditioning, from all conclusions—because it is only such a mind that is a young mind. And it is only the young mind that can move freely, investigate, be innocent.

Then, it seems to me, beyond freedom is the sense of appreciation of beauty. So few of us are aware of the things about us. The beauty of the night, the beauty of a face, of a smile, the beauty of the river and of the cloud radiant at sunset, the beauty of moonlight on water; we are so little aware of this extraordinary beauty because we are so insensitive. To be free, sensitivity is essential. But you cannot be free if you are crowded with knowledge. No mind is sensitive if it is burdened with knowledge.

And I think the other thing beyond freedom is—to use a word which unfortunately is connected with such absurd sentiment and wishy-washyness—love. Love has nothing to do with sentiment. Love is hard, in the sense that it is crystal clear and what is clear can be hard. Love is not what you think of as love. That merely becomes a sentiment.

If we could understand, feel our way into this, we should see that freedom, beauty and love are the very essentials for discovery—not knowledge, not experience, not belief, not belonging to any organization. Not being anything is the beginning of freedom. So, if you are capable of feeling, of going into this you will find, as you become aware, that you are not free, that you are bound to very many different things and that at the same time the mind hopes to be free. And you can see that the two are contradictory. So the mind has to investigate why it clings to anything. All this implies hard work. It is much more arduous than going to an office, than any physical labour, than all the sciences put together. Because the humble, intelligent mind is concerned with itself without being self-centred; therefore it has to be extraordinarily alert, aware, and that means real hard work every day, every hour, every minute. And because we are not willing to do that, we have dictatorships, politicians, gurus, presidents of societies, and all the rest of the rubbish. This demands insistent work because freedom does not come easily. Everything impedes—your wife, your husband, your son, your neighbour, your Gods, your religions, your tradition. All these impede you but you have created them because you want security. And the mind that is seeking security can never find it. If you have watched a little in the world, you know there is no such thing as security. The wife dies, the husband dies, the son runs away—something happens. Life is not static, though we would like to make it so. No relationship is static because all life is movement. That is a thing to be grasped, the truth to be seen, felt, not something to be argued about. Then you will see, as you begin to investigate, that it is really a process of meditation. But do not be mesmerized by that word. To be aware of every thought, to know from what source it springs and what is its intention—that is meditation. And to know the whole content of one thought reveals the whole process of the mind.

Now, if you can move from freedom, then you will discover the most extraordinary things of the mind, and then you will find that the mind itself is the total Reality. It is not that there is a Reality to which the mind goes, but the mind itself, that extraordinary thing when there is no contradiction within itself, when there is no anxiety, no fear, no desire to be successful—then that mind itself is that which is eternal, unnameable. But to speculate about the eternal without understanding the whole process of the mind is just childish play. It is an immature game which scholars—whom you worship—play. So it would be good if you and I could really go into this, without any dramatic heroism, without any spectacular rubbish, but as two human beings interested in solving the problems we have, which are also the problems of the world. The personal problem is not different from the world problem. So if you and I can go into it with humility, knowing our states, tentatively enquiring, then you will find that without your asking, without your inviting, there is That which is not controllable, which is not nameable, to which there is no path. Then only, as you begin to enquire, you will see how extraordinarily easily you will be able to solve your problems, including the problem of starvation which is so enormous. But you cannot tackle it if you have not understood the mind. So please, till we meet next time do watch your mind, go into it, not merely when you have nothing to do, but from the moment you get up to the moment you go to bed, from the moment you wake up until you go back to sleep. Watch as you talk to your servant, to your boss, your wife, your children, as you see the bus conductor, the bus driver, watch as you look at the moon, the leaf, the sky. Then you will begin to find out what an extraordinary richness there is—a richness not in knowledge but in the nature of the mind itself. It is in the mind, also, that there is ignorance. The dispelling of ignorance is all-important, not the acquisition of knowledge. Because the dispelling of ignorance is negative while knowledge is positive. And a man who is capable of thinking negatively has the highest capacity for thinking. The mind which can dispel ignorance and not accumulate knowledge—such a mind is an innocent mind, and only the innocent mind can discover that which is beyond measure.

Second Talk in Madras
12 November 1958

I think almost all serious people must have thought a great deal about the necessity of bringing about a radical change in the quality of the mind. We see, as things are in the world, that there is no fundamental alteration or change in the human mind. Of course, through pressure, economic and social, through various forms of religious fear, through new inventions and so on, there is change, but this change is always peripheral, on the outside, and obviously such change does not bring about a deep, radical change in the quality of the mind. You must have noticed that society always follows a pattern, certain formulas, in the same way as every individual follows certain concepts, ideals, always moving within the pattern. You must have noticed it not only in yourself and in society but in all our relationships, and you must have wondered how to bring about a deep, lasting, integrated change, so that the interaction between the outer and the inner does not bring about corruption. I do not mean anything mysterious by the 'inner'. It is the inner quality of the mind that I am talking about, not inward things which the mind imagines and speculates about. All society, all human existence is a matter of this interrelationship between the outer and the inner which is constantly fluctuating and always modifying. And if I may, I would like to talk about the possibility of a radical change because I think it is very important. After all, we are social entities and we must live by action. Life is action. One cannot just sit and speculate; neither can one merely carry on with the corruption because, as we know, it only breeds contradiction within ourselves and everlasting torture and struggle.

So how is the mind to change? How is there to be a radical change in the total consciousness, not only on the upper levels of the mind but also at the deeper levels, and not along a set pattern? Following a pattern is not a change at all; it is merely a modified continuity of what has been. How is one to really change the quality, the substance of one's consciousness, totally? I do not know if you have thought about it, or are you merely concerned with outward changes which are brought about by every form of social and economic revolution, every new invention? If we are concerned with a total change of consciousness, of the quality of the mind, then I think we must think negatively because negative thinking is the highest form of thinking, not the so-called positive thinking. The positive is merely the pursuit of a formula, a conclusion, and all such thinking is limited, conditioned.

I hope you are listening rather than just hearing because I want to go into something rather difficult, if I can, and I hope we shall be able to proceed with it together. But if you are merely hearing and not listening, then you will be caught at the verbal level and words then become oversignificant. Words are only the means of communicating something. So I hope you are going to listen without any desire to understand mere ideas. I have no ideas because I think they are the most stupid things; they have no substance, no reality, they are just words. So I hope you are listening in the sense of trying to see the problem—just to see it, not to struggle to understand it or resolve it, but to see this extraordinary complex problem which we have—the problem of bringing about a total change in consciousness, in the mind.

As I was saying, negative thinking is the highest form of thinking. We never think negatively; we think only positively. That is, we think from a conclusion to a conclusion, from a pattern to a pattern, from a system to a system—that I must be this; I must acquire some virtue, follow this or that path, do certain disciplines. The positive thinking is always in the grooves of our own conditioned thinking—I hope you are watching your own mind, your own thought—and that way only leads to further limitation of the mind, to narrowness of the mind, to pettiness of action; it always strengthens the self-centred activity. Negative thinking is something entirely different, but it is not the opposite of positive thinking. If I can understand the limitations of positive thinking, which invariably leads to self-centred activity, if I can understand not only verbally, intellectually but as the whole process of human thinking, then there is a new awakening in negative thinking.

Most of us are attached to something—to property, to a person, an idea, a belief, an experience—are we not? You are attached to your family, your good name, your profession, your guru, to this and that. Now, this attachment invariably breeds suffering and conflict because the thing to which you are attached is constantly changing, obviously.

But you do not want the change; you want to hold on to it permanently. So, being aware that attachment breeds sorrow, grief, pain, you try to cultivate detachment. Obviously, both attachment and the cultivation of detachment are positive ways of thinking. Detachment is not the negation of attachment, it is merely attachment continued under a different verbal garb. The mental process is entirely the same, if you have ever noticed it. For instance, I am attached to my wife. In that there is pain, struggle, jealousy, frustration, and to escape from all that, I say, 'I must be detached, I must love in an impersonal manner'—whatever that may mean—'I must love without limitation', and I try to cultivate detachment. But the centre of my activity in attachment or detachment is exactly the same thing. So our thinking which we call positive is a conflict of the opposites or an endeavour to escape into a synthesis which again creates an opposite. Take communism—it is the antithesis of capitalism, and eventually through struggle the communists hope to create a synthesis, but because it is born of the conflict of opposites that synthesis is going to create another antithesis. And this process is what we call positive thinking, not only outwardly, socially, but inwardly also.

Now, if one understands the total process of all this, not only intellectually but actually, then we will see that a new way of thinking comes into being. It is a negative process unrelated to the positive. The positive way of thinking leads to immaturity, to a mind that is conditioned, shaped, and that is exactly what is happening with all of us. When you say you want to be happy, you want Truth, God, to create a different world, it is always in terms of

J. Krishnamurti

the positive—which is to follow a system that will produce the desired result, and the result is always the known and it becomes again the cause. Cause and effect are not two different things. The effect of today will be the cause of tomorrow. There is no cause, isolated, which produces an effect; they are interrelated. There is no such thing as a law of cause and effect, which means that there is really no such thing as what we call karma. To us, karma means a result with a previous cause, but in the interval between the effect and the cause there has been time. In that time there has been a tremendous lot of change and therefore the effect is never the same. And the effect is going to produce another cause which will never be merely the result of the effect. Do not say, 'I do not believe in karma'; that is not the point at all. Karma means, very simply, action and the result, with its further cause. Sow a mango seed and it is bound to produce a mango tree—but the human mind is not like that. The human mind is capable of transformation within itself, immediate comprehension, which is a breaking away from the cause, always.

So negative thinking is not thinking in terms of patterns because patterns imply a cause which will produce a result which the mind can manipulate, control and change. With that process we are all very familiar. What I am trying to convey is a negative thinking which has no causation. This may all sound too absurd, but we will go into it and you will see. We will approach it differently.

Most of us are discontented, are we not? We are discontented with our job, with our wife, husband, children, neighbours, society or whatever it is. I want position, I want money, I want love. We know all this. Now, discontent with something is positive, but discontent, in itself, is negative. I will explain. When we are discontented, what is actually taking place? If I am discontented with my job, with myself, what is happening? I want to find contentment, through this or through that. So the discontent is canalized until it finds something which will be satisfactory, and then it fades away. That is what we call positive action—to find something which will make us happy. But without the flame of real discontent—not discontent with something—life has no meaning.

You may have a marvellous job, an extraordinary brain, get degrees and be able to discuss, quote, but your discontent has merely taken the shape of cleverness, and there you are completely sterile. You started with discontent, and at school perhaps you were very good, but as you grew, that discontent became stratified into cleverness or into some form of technique, and there you are satisfied because you feel you have capacity and can function. That again is positive thinking. Whereas negative thinking is just to be in a state of discontent, and such a mind is a very disturbed mind. It is not satisfied and it is not seeking satisfaction because it sees that satisfaction leads only to that positive action which we all seek. To find a way to be satisfied everlastingly means to be dead. And that is what you want; you call it peace of mind and say, 'For God's sake, give me some corner in this universe where I can die peacefully.' So the positive action leads always to death. If you can see that, then you will see that a negative way of thinking is taking place. Therefore the negative way of thinking never starts with a conclusion, because one sees where conclusions lead.

So the negative way of thinking is the maintenance, the sustenance of the quality that is discontent—discontent in itself, not with something. Please do not get caught at the verbal level but see the significance of this. But we must understand that positive thinking is conditioned thinking and that there is no change in that; there is modification but no radical transformation. Radical transformation is only in the negative thinking, as we saw in relation to attachment and to discontent. This positive thinking leads only to a dull mind, an insensitive mind, a mind that is not capable of reception, a mind that thinks only in terms of its own security—either the security of the individual or of the family, group or race, which you can observe very clearly in world politics.

After all, this earth is ours, yours and mine. This earth which is so marvellous, so beautiful, so rich, is ours to live on happily, without all this fragmentation, without being broken up into different fields called England, Germany, Russia, India. Yet we are battling to keep up the separation. Nobody thinks of this whole world as ours, nobody says, 'Let us do something together about it.' Instead, we have this fragmentary way of thinking which we call positive, or we pursue some idea of internationalism, which is equally silly. If I can see that, then there is a different approach, a different feeling of the mind, whether it be the Russian or the German or whatever mind it is. Then there is no such thing as the nonsense of patriotism; there is the love of the earth—not your earth and my earth, you cultivating your little field and I cultivating mine, and quarrelling over it, but it is our earth.

Now, when we see that this positive way of thinking is destructive, then the negative way comes into being. To think negatively there must be sensitivity—sensitivity both to the beautiful and to the ugly. The man who is pursuing what he calls the beautiful and avoiding the ugly is not sensitive. The man who pursues virtue without understanding that which is not virtuous, merely avoiding it, is invariably insensitive. Please think this out with me, feel it out and you will see. So appreciation of the beauty of a tree, a leaf, the reflection on still waters, is not sensitivity if you are not also aware of the squalor, the dirt, the way you eat, the way you talk, the way you think, the way of your behaviour.

Under this tree it is very beautiful, very quiet, there is lovely shade and light, and just outside there is that filthy village with all the squalor and dirt and the unfortunate human beings who live there, but you are not aware of it. So we are always wanting beauty, Truth and God, and avoiding the other, and that pursuit is the positive and leads to insensitivity, if we are not aware of the other. And the positive way of erecting buildings for dances, having special schools for dancing, all that business becomes a personal racket, satisfying to the mind that is only thinking positively. Creation is not positive, ever. Creation is the state of mind in which there is no positive action as we know it.

So, radical transformation takes place in the mind only when there is this negative thinking. As I said the other day, the thinking that we know of is always in words or symbols. I do not know if you have noticed that there is thinking without words but that thinking is still the result of the positive word. I will explain. You always think in words, symbols, do you not? Please look. The word, the symbol, becomes very important to thought. It is the basis of all our thinking; there is association through memory and the memory is a picture, a word, and from that we proceed to think, again in symbols, words. That is all we know, and also if you are very alert, aware, you can see that there is thinking without the word, without the symbol. I am not going to give an example because then you will get lost, so please capture the significance, for negative thinking is not related to thought-with-the-word. Unless you see this you will not see what follows. I am thinking aloud; I have not worked it out at home and then come here to speak it out. So please see this, not merely verbally or speculatively but actually experience that thought functions in words, in symbols and also that thought functions without the word and the symbol. Both these are positive ways of thinking because they are still in the realm of the opposites. Let me put it differently.

You must have watched your mind, how vagrant it is, how it wanders all over the place, one thought pursuing another. When you try to examine one thought, another comes in. So the mind is full of this movement, the agitation of thought. The mind is always occupied with thought. Thought is the instrument of the mind, so the mind is never still. Do not at once say, 'How am I to make the mind still?' That is all too immature, stupid, because it means again a positive following of some pattern. So, realizing the incessant activity of the thought-producing mechanism, through memory, through association, being aware of that, cannot the mind empty itself of this mecha-nism? Do not ask how, just listen, because understanding is instantaneous; it is not a process which will ultimately get you a mind emptied of thought. If you see the posi-tive, destructive way—of the mind's activity of produc-ing thought and being controlled by it and then trying to empty the mind—if you can see the falseness or the truth of it, then you will also see that the mind can empty itself of itself, of its limitations, of its ego-centricity, of its self-centred activities. Please go with me a little.

The mind is perpetually active, producing and control-ling thought. It realizes that, and says, 'I must be quiet', but that generally means quiet through control, which is again positive, destructive, and limiting. But you can see if you go a little further that the mind can be emptied of thought, can free itself from the past, not be burdened by the past. It does not mean that memories are not there, but they do not shape or control the mind. Now all that is still positive thinking. If you see the falseness of it, the mind will invariably go further, which is, the mind then is not the slave of thought but it can think what it wants. I do not know how to put this. As I said, I am thinking aloud with you and you will have to excuse me if I try different ways of putting it.

I do not know if you have ever tried to think with-out being a slave to thought. With most of us the mind is a slave to thought—it pursues thought, contradictory thought, and all the rest of it. If you perceive that and empty the mind, it can then think, freed from thoughts associated with memory; and if you go further into it, you will see that the mind which is free—not in the sense of the opposite of slavery, but free in itself—then that mind, emptied of memory, can think in a negative way. Then you will see that the mind, being completely empty of systems, formulas, speculations, thoughts associated with memory, experiences and so on, can perceive that there is a state in which there is action in this world, not from fullness but from emptiness.

You see, we are acting now with full minds, overcrowded minds, minds that are incessantly active: in contradiction, struggling, adjusting, ambitious, envious, jealous, brutal or gentle and so on. You follow? We are acting on that level. The mind, being full, acts. That action can never produce a new mind, a new quality of mind, a fresh mind, an innocent mind—and it is only such an innocent, fresh mind that can create, that is in a state of creation. The mind sees that, and if the mind can empty itself, then the action that is born out of emptiness is the true positive action, not the other. That is the only true, positive, creative action, because it is born out of emptiness. If you have done any painting, written a poem, a song, you will find the deep feeling comes out of nothingness. But a mind that is crowded can never feel that nothingness and can therefore never be sensitive.

One sees that there can be a radical change in the quality of the mind, which is absolutely necessary now because the present society is a dead society, reforming itself through various forms of anesthesia and pumping activity into itself. If you as an individual are to change fundamentally, radically, deeply—and therefore change society—then this whole thing that I have described must take place. Then beauty has quite a different significance, as has ugliness, because beauty is not the opposite of the ugly. An ugly face can be beautiful. But such beauty is not conceived by the mind that has avoided ugliness.

So, if you have really listened and do not try to do anything about it—because whatever you do will be so-called positive and therefore destructive—then it is enough. It is to see something lovely and leave it alone, not try to capture it, not take it home and smother it by thought.

If you have seen for yourself, not through my persuasiveness, not through my words, my influence, if you have felt the beauty, the extraordinary quality of the mind that is empty, then from that emptiness there is a new birth.

It is this new birth which is needed, not the going back to *Mahabharata, Ramayana,* Marx or Engels, or revivalism. The mind that is really creative is the empty mind, not the blank mind or the mind that merely wishes to be creative. It is only the empty mind that can understand this whole thing—the extraordinary process of thought and thought emptying itself of its own impetus. Then you will see that there is a radical, deep change which is not brought about by influence, circumstances, culture or society. It is that mind which will create a new society. And the moment it creates a new society, that society is already in corruption. All societies are in corruption because that which is created is ever dying. Therefore, recognizing that no society, no tradition, no knowledge is permanent, we can see that the mind which is empty is creative, is in a state of creation.

First Talk in Bombay
28 December 1958

This will be the last talk and I wonder—not what each one has got out of listening, but—to what depth, to what extent each one has really gone into himself and discovered something for himself. It is not merely a matter of what has been said or what will be said, but rather whether each one, out of his own earnest endeavour, has uncovered the extraordinarily complicated process of the mind, how far each one of us has discovered the ways of consciousness, how deeply one has experienced for oneself the things we have been talking over. It seems to me that the mere repetition of words or of what you have read only puts the mind to rest, it makes the mind sluggish. An earnest mind is not one that merely repeats, either from the sacred religious books or from the latest equally sacred books on Marx, on capitalism, socialism, or psychology. Mere repetition does not open the door to direct experience. To speak from direct experience from direct understanding and direct knowledge is quite a different thing, for then there is an authenticity, a depth to what one has thought and felt. One who merely repeats from memory or from what he has learnt, heard or read surely is not a serious person. Nor is he serious who indulges in theoretical, abstract thinking. An earnest man, surely, is he who goes within himself, observes things about his own sorrow and misery, is sensitive to starvation, degradation, wars and injustice, and from the observation of the external begins to enquire within. Such a man is an earnest man, not he who is merely satisfied with explanations, who is everlastingly quoting, theorizing or seeking a purpose of life. The man who seeks a purpose of life merely wants a significance for his own living, and the significance he gives will depend upon his own conditioning. But the mind which, through the observation of everyday incidents and relationships, everyday activities and challenges, begins to enquire, goes more and more within itself and uncovers the hidden. Because after all, that is where the essential fundamental change has to take place. Though innumerable outward changes are obviously necessary—putting an end to wars, and so on—the only radical change is within.

So one of our major problems is: What makes one change? What makes the mind which is traditional, conditioned, in sorrow, jealous, envious, ambitious, what makes such a mind drop all those things and be fresh, new, clear? If you change because of pressure—pressure of new inventions, of legislation, of revolution, of family, and so on—surely such a change, which has a direction, is no change at all, is it? That kind of change is merely an adjustment, a conformity to laws or to a pattern of existence, and, if you have noticed it within yourself, change through compulsion, through anxiety, is the continuity of what has been before, modified, is it not? I think it is very important to understand what it is that makes a man change totally.

Technological knowledge obviously does not bring about an inward transformation; it may alter our point of view but it does not bring about that inward transformation in which there is no struggle but in which there is an enlightened, active intelligence.

I wonder if you have ever asked yourself what it is that makes you change? Of course, if the doctor tells you that if you continue to smoke cigarettes it will give you lung cancer, through fear you may abstain from smoking. The pressure of fear or the promise of reward may make you stop a certain activity, but is that a real change? If through pressure, through fear you change, modify, adjust, that is not transformation, it is merely the continuation of what has been in a different form. So, what will make you really transform yourself? I think such transformation comes not through any endeavour, any struggle, any pressure of reward or punishment, but it comes about instantaneously, immediately, spontaneously, when there is a comprehension, a perceiving of the whole. I am going into it, but as I have been saying, mere listening to the words will not help you to learn about what is being said. One has to see the totality of human existence, not only a section; one has to see and feel the whole depth of existence, of life, and when there is such a comprehension, in that state there is a total change, a total transformation. Now, we change only in fragments—controlling jealousy or envy, giving up smoking or eating too much, joining this group or that group to bring about some reform—but they are all segments, fragments, unrelated to the whole. Such activity, unrelated to the perception of the whole, obviously must lead to various forms of maladjustment, contradiction and strain. So our problem is really how to see, how to comprehend and feel the totality of life, be with it and from there act wholly, not fragmentarily.

Let me put it differently. I do not know if you have noticed it in yourself, but most of us are in a state of contradiction, are we not? You think one thing and do another, you feel something and deny it the next minute—not only as an individual but as a race, a group. You say you must have peace and talk about non-violence, and all the time you are inwardly violent and you have the police, the army, the bombers, the navy, and all the rest of it. So there is contradiction in us and outside of us. And the greater the contradiction the greater is the tension, until the tension ultimately leads to neurotic action and therefore an unbalanced mind. As most of us are in a state of self-contradiction, we live perpetually in tension and strain, and from that tension there is unbalanced activity. And if one realizes this tension of contradiction, then one tries to bring about an integration between two opposites, between hate and love for instance, and one only produces something which is non-recognizable, which you call non-violence and all that stuff. But the problem is to see the central fact that the mind is in contradiction within itself and not try to obliterate the contradiction by giving strength to one of the opposites.

So, when you see that the mind is in a state of self-contradiction and know the stress and the tension of it—the pain, sorrow, misery and struggle—when you comprehend, perceive, understand the whole process of the mind in a state of contradiction, then such a total understanding brings about quite a different state and quite a different activity. After all, if you perceive the whole, vast sky merely through a narrow window, your vision is obviously unrelated to the wide heavens. Similarly, action born of self-contradiction is very limited, giving rise only to pain and sorrow.

I wish I could make it clear, this feeling of the whole. To feel the quality of India, the quality of the whole world—not as a Parsi, Hindu, Muslim, not as a socialist, communist or congressman, not as a Russian, Englishman, German or American—but to feel the total suffering of man, his frustrations, his contradictions, his miserable, narrow existence, his aspirations—to have such a feeling, such a perception is to bring about the total transformation of the mind.

Let me put it differently. Governments, societies, every form of pressure and propaganda say you must change. But there is a constant resistance to change and so there is a conflict between the actual and the ideal. The actual and the ideal are contradictions, and we spend our lives from childhood to the grave struggling between the two, never coming to the end of something, never coming to the end of attachment but always pursuing detachment. In attachment there is pain, and so we cultivate detachment. Then the problem arises of how to detach oneself, and this brings in the practising of a system which, if you think about it, is all so silly. Whereas if you can understand the whole process of attachment and the whole process of detachment, what is implied in both, then you will never be either attached or detached, there is a totally different state, a real transformation of the mind. After all, you are attached only to dead things because you cannot be attached to a whole thing, a living thing, like living waters, can you? You are attached to your picture of your wife, your husband, and the picture is only the memory. You are attached to the memory of certain experiences, pleasures, pains, which means you are attached to the past, not to the living present, not to the woman or man who is at present endeavouring, struggling. Attachment is obviously to dying things and to the dead; you are attached to your house; the house is not a living thing, but you give life to it from your desire to be secure, which is a desire of the dead. Attachment is invariably not to the living, not to the present but to the past, which is of the dead. And without understanding that, we are trying to become detached, and what does it mean? Detachment from what? Not from the living thing because you have never held it; but you are trying to be detached from a memory, from what you think, which gives you pain. You do not radically change. So you are caught between attachment and detachment. Whereas if you really go within yourself very profoundly and find out what the root cause of your attachment is, you will find that it is obviously the desire to be comfortable, to be safe, and so on; then you would also understand the whole process of the cultivation of detachment and the implications of detachment. The understanding of both, completely, is the process of self-knowledge. If you go into it very deeply as a means of uncovering your own comprehension, then you will find that there is the intelligence which will respond; then you will see that there is not a change, but transformation.

Looking at this world with all its anxieties, its wars, its slow decay, surely most serious people want earnestly to find a means, a way by which the mind is not a mechanical entity but is ever new, fresh, young. But you cannot have such a fresh mind if you are everlastingly in conflict. Hitherto you have accepted conflict as the way of life, have you not?, but when you begin to understand the total process of the way of struggle, then you will see that there is actual transformation, and that the mind is no longer caught in the wheel of struggle.

Let me put the problem differently, sirs. Being simple is essential, but simplicity for most of us is merely expressed in outward things. You think you are simple, saintly and virtuous if you have only a few things, only a loincloth. A loincloth is not a symbol of simplicity of mind, nor does it indicate the understanding of the extensive richness, the liveliness, the beauty of life. But you have reduced all that to the loincloth level, and that is not simplicity. And a mind that is burdened with knowledge, with erudition, with information is not a simple mind; the electronic computers now can quote you almost anything—it is merely a mechanical response. And a mind that is constantly groping, wanting, searching, burning out desire and at the same time desirous, is not a simple mind. Please listen to all this, sirs, learn about it as I am talking, because if you really follow this, you will see that what will come out of this is true simplicity. But first you must see what is not simplicity, and obviously the man who is caught in ritual, perpetually repeating, calling on the name of God, and doing so-called good, is not a simple man. Then what is simplicity? The simple mind is the mind that transforms itself, the simple mind is the result of transformation. The mind that says, 'I must be simple', is a stupid mind, but the

mind that is aware of the extensiveness of its own deceptions, its own anxieties, its own illusions, aspirations and
all the turmoil of desires, such a mind is simple. Being
totally aware of all that—as one is aware of a tree or the
heavens—there comes this extraordinary simplicity. I am
using the word 'simplicity' to denote innocence, clarity, a
mind which has abandoned itself. A mind that is calculating, becoming virtuous, a mind that has got an end in view
which it is everlastingly trying to pursue—such a mind is
not abandoning itself. It is only out of total self-abandonment that simplicity comes, and to be completely aware
of the extensiveness of the illusions, fancies, myths, urges
and demands of the mind, is self-knowledge. It is the full
understanding of existence as it is and not as it should be.
But that beauty of simplicity does not come into being if
there is no self-abandonment, and abandonment means,
surely, the dropping away of all conditioning, as a dead leaf
falls away from a tree; and you cannot die to something if
you are not passionate. To die means the feeling of coming
to a point or state beyond which there is nothing; a state of
mind in which, with all the cunning tricks and speculation,
do what you will, you can proceed no further. In that state
there is neither despair nor hope, and the whole question
of search has come to an end. A total death has come into
being; and if you do not die, totally, to the past, how can
you learn? How can you learn, sirs, if you are always carry-
ing the burden of yesterday?

I do not know if you have ever enquired into yourself
as to how to be free of the yesterday, the thousand yesterdays, the thousands of experiences and reactions and
all the turmoil of restless time? How is one to be free of

all that so that the mind becomes extraordinarily quiet, simple, innocent? Such a state is only possible if you understand the totality of your existence—what you do, what you think, how you are absorbed in your daily activities, your job, the way you speak to your wife, your husband, the way you treat your so-called inferiors, the way you educate your children, and so on. If you regard your attitude in all that as merely a temporary reaction, something which can be got over, adjusted, then you have not understood the totality of life. And I say that in the understanding of the totality of oneself there is a transformation which is immediate and which has nothing to do with the restlessness of time. You may take time in the investigation, but the transformation is immediate. Do not confuse the process of time and transformation. There is time in the sense that there is a gap between what I am saying and your listening. The vibration of the word takes time to reach your ear, and the nervous response as well as the brain response takes a split second. Though it may take time for it to travel to your brain, once you understand all of what is being said, there is a complete break from the past. Revolution is not from the outside, but from within, and that revolution is not a gradual process, not a matter of time.

So transformation of the individual can take place only when there is a total comprehension of the ways of the mind, which is meditation. To understand oneself is a process in which there is no condemnation, no justification but just seeing what one is, just observing without judging, without checking, controlling or adjusting. The perception of what one is, without any evaluation, leads the mind to an extraordinary depth, and it is only at that depth that there is transformation; and naturally action from that depth of understanding is totally different from the action of adjustment.

So I hope you, as an individual, have listened to these talks not merely to gather information, to be intellectually amused, excited, or emotionally stirred, but have learnt about yourself in the process and therefore freed yourself. Because from the beginning of these talks until now we have been speaking about the actual, everyday, state of the mind, and if you disregard it and say you are only interested in God, in what happens after death, then you will find that your God and your 'after death' are only a set of speculative ideas which have no validity at all. To find what God is, if there is a God, you must come to it with a full being, with freshness, not with a mind that is decayed, burdened with its own experiences, broken and dwindled by discipline and burnt up with desires. A mind that is really passionate—and passion implies intensity and fullness—only such a mind can receive that which is immeasurable. That immeasurable cannot be found except as you dig deeper and deeper within yourself. Your repetition that there is the eternal is child's talk, and your seeking the eternal has no meaning either, for it is unknowable, inconceivable to the mind. The mind has to understand itself, to break the foundation of its learning, the frontiers of its own recognition, and that is the process of self-knowledge. What you need now is an inward revolution, a totally new approach to life, not new systems, new schools, new philosophies. Then, from this transformation, you will see that mind, as time, ceases. After all, time is as the sea which is never still, never calm, everlastingly in motion, everlastingly restless, and our minds, based on time, are caught up in its movement.

So, only when you have totally understood yourself, the conscious as well as the unconscious, only then is there a quietness, a motionlessness which is creation. And that stillness is action, true action. Only, we never touch it, we never know it because we are wasting our energy, our time, our sorrow, our endeavour, on things superficial.

So the earnest man is he who through self-knowledge breaks down the walls of time and brings about a motionless state of mind. Then there is a benediction which comes into being without invitation; then there is a Reality, a goodness which comes without your asking. If you crave it you will not get it, if you seek it you will not find it. It is only when the mind has understood itself totally, comprehended itself widely so that it is without any barrier and is dead to everything it has known—then only Reality comes into being.

First Talk in Madras
6 December 1959

I think it would be profitable and worthwhile to find out for ourselves why the mind is so restless. It is as restless as the sea, never stable, never quiet; though outwardly it may be still, inwardly it is full of ripples, full of grooves and every kind of disturbance. I think it is essential to go into this question rather deeply, and not merely ask how to quiet the mind. There is no way to quiet the mind. Of course, one can take pills, tranquillizers, or follow blindly some system; one can drug the mind with prayers, with repetitions, but a drugged mind is no mind at all. So it seems to me of the utmost importance to go deeply into this question of why the mind is everlastingly seeking something, and having found it, is not satisfied, but moves on to something else—an unceasing movement from satisfaction to disappointment, from fulfilment to pain and frustration. We must all be aware of this endless cycle of pleasure and sorrow. Everything is passing, impermanent; we live in a constant state of flight, and there is no place where one can be quiet, especially inwardly, because every recess of the mind is disturbed. There is no untrodden region in the mind. Consciously or unconsciously we have tried in various ways to bring quietness, stillness, a state of peace to the mind; and having got it, we have soon lost it again. You must be aware of this endless search, which is going on in your own mind.

So I would like to suggest that—with hesitance, without dogmatism, without quoting, or coming to conclusions—we try to probe into this restless activity of our minds. And I think we shall have to begin by asking ourselves why we seek at all, why we enquire, why there is this longing to arrive, to achieve, to become something. After all, you are probably here a little bit out of curiosity, but even more, I hope, out of the desire to seek, to find out. What is it that you are seeking? And why do you seek? If we can go deeply into this question by asking ourselves why we are seeking—if we can, as it were, open the door by means of that question, then I think we may perhaps have a glimpse into something which is not illusory, and which does not have the transient quality of that which is merely pleasurable or gratifying.

Why is it, and what is it, you are seeking? I wonder if you have ever put that question to yourselves? You know, a challenge is always new, because it is something that demands your attention. You have to respond; there is no turning your back on it, and either you respond totally, completely, or partially, inadequately. The incapacity to respond totally to a challenge creates conflict. The world in its present state is a constant challenge to each one of us, and when we do not respond with the fullness, with all the depth and beauty of the challenge itself, then inevitably there is turmoil, anxiety, fear, sorrow. In the same way, this question—what are you seeking, and why do you seek?— is a challenge, and if you do not respond with your whole being but treat it merely as an intellectual problem, which is to respond partially, then obviously you will never find a total answer. Your response to the challenge is partial, inadequate, when you merely make statements, or think in terms of definite conclusions to which you have come. The challenge is always new, and you have to respond to it anew—not in your habitual, customary way. If we can put this question to ourselves as though we are considering it for the first time, then our response will be entirely different from the superficial response of the intellect.

What is it that you are seeking, and why do you seek it? Does not this very seeking instigate restlessness? If there were no seeking, would you stagnate? Or would there then be a totally different kind of search? But before we go into the more complex aspects of our enquiry, it seems to me important to find out what you and I, as individual human beings, are seeking. Obviously, the superficial answer is always to say, 'I am seeking happiness, fulfilment.' But in seeking happiness, in seeking fulfilment, we never stop to ask ourselves if there is such a thing as fulfilment. We long for fulfilment, or satisfaction, and we go after it, without looking to see if there is any reality behind the word. In pursuing fulfilment, its expression varies from day to day, from year to year. Growing weary of the more worldly satisfactions, we seek happiness in good conduct, in social service, in being brotherly, in loving one's neighbour. But sooner or later this movement towards fulfilment through good conduct also comes to an end, and we turn in still another direction. We try to find happiness through intellectual pursuits, through reason, logic, or we become emotional, sentimental, romantic. We give to the word 'happiness' different connotations at different times. We translate it in terms of what we call peace, God, Truth; we think of it as a heavenly abode where we shall be completely fulfilled, never disturbed, and so on. That is what most of us want, is it not? That is why you read the Shastras, the Bible, the Koran, or other religious books—in the hope of bringing quietness to the restless mind. Probably that is why you are here.

Seeking implies an object, an end in view, does it not? There can be no search for what is unknown. You can only seek something which you have known and lost, or which you have heard of and want to gain. You cannot seek that which you do not know. In a peculiar way, you already know what happiness is. You have tasted the flavour of it, the past has given you the sensation, the pleasure, the beauty of it, so you already know its quality, its nature, and that memory you project. But what you have known is not 'what is'; your projection is not what you really want. What you have tasted is not sufficient, you want something more, more, more, and so your life is an everlasting struggle.

I hope you are listening to what is being said, not as to a lecture, but as though you were looking at a film of yourself struggling, groping, searching, longing. You are sorrowful, anxious, fearful, caught up in tremendous hope and despair, in the extremes of contradiction, and from this tension there is action. That is all you know. You seek fulfilment outwardly, in the house, in the family, in going to the office, in becoming a rich man, or the chief inspector, or a famous judge, or the prime minister—you know the whole business of climbing the ladder of success and achievement. You climb that ladder till you are old, and then you seek God. You collect money, honours, position, prestige, and when you have reached a certain age, you turn to poor old God. God does not want such a man, sirs. God wants a complete human being who is not a slave. He does not want a dehydrated human being, but one who is active, who knows love, who has a deep sense of joy.

But unfortunately, in our search for happiness, fulfilment, there is an endless struggle going on. Outwardly we do everything possible to assure ourselves of that happiness, but outward things fail. The house, the property, the relationship with wife and children—it can all be swept away, and there is always death waiting around the corner. So we turn to inward things, we practise various forms of discipline in an effort to control our minds, our emotions, and we conform to a standard of good conduct, hoping that we shall one day arrive at a state of happiness that cannot be disturbed.

Now, I see this whole process going on, and I am asking myself: Why do we seek at all? I know that we do seek. We join societies which promise a spiritual reward, we follow gurus who exhort us to struggle, to sacrifice, to discipline ourselves, and all the rest of it; so we are seeking, endlessly. Why is there this seeking? What is the compulsion, the urge that makes for seeking, not only outwardly, but inwardly? And is there any fundamental difference between the outward and the inward movement of seeking, or is it only one movement? I do not know if I am making myself clear. We have divided our existence into what we call outward life and the inward life. Our daily activities and pursuits are the outward life, and when we do not get happiness, pleasure, satisfaction in that area, we turn to the inward as a reaction. But the inward also has its frustration and despair.

So, what is it that is making us seek? Do please ask yourself this question, go into it with me. Surely, a happy, joyous man does not seek God; he is not trying to achieve virtue; his very existence is splendid, radiant. So, what is it that is urging us to seek, and to make such tremendous effort? If we can understand that, perhaps we shall be able to go beyond this restless search.

Do you know what is the cause of your seeking? Please do not give a superficial answer, because then you will only blind yourself to the actual. Surely, if you go deeply into yourself, you will see that you are seeking because there is, within each one of us, a sense of isolation, of loneliness, of emptiness; there is an inner void which nothing can fill. Do what you will—perform good works, meditate, identify yourself with the family, with the group, with the race, with the nation—that emptiness is still there, that void which cannot be filled, that loneliness which nothing can take away. That is the cause of our endless seeking, is it not? Call it by a different name, it does not matter. Deep within one there is this sense of emptiness, of loneliness, of utter isolation. If the mind can go into this void and understand it, then perhaps it will be resolved.

At one time or another, perhaps while you were walking, or while you were sitting by yourself in a room, you must have experienced this sense of loneliness, the extraordinary feeling of being cut off from everything—from your family, from your friends, from ideas, hopes—so that you felt you had no relationship with anybody or anything. And without penetrating into it, without actually living with it, understanding it, the mind cannot resolve that feeling.

I think there is a difference between knowing and experiencing. You probably know what this feeling of loneliness is, from what you have heard or read about it, but knowing is entirely different from the state of experiencing. You may have read extensively, you may have accumulated many experiences, so that you know a great deal, but knowledge is not living. If you are an artist, a painter, every line, every shadow means something. You are observing all the time, watching the movement and the depth of shadows, the loveliness of a curve, the expression of a face, the branch of a tree, the colours everywhere—you are alive to everything. But knowledge cannot give you this perception, this capacity to feel, to experience something that you see. Experiencing is one thing, and experience is another. Experience, knowledge, is a thing of the past, which will go on as memory, but experiencing is a living perception of the now; it is a vital awareness of the beauty, the tranquillity, the extraordinary profundity of the now. In the same way, one has to be aware of loneliness; one has to feel it, actually experience this sense of complete isolation. And if one is capable of experiencing it, one will find how really difficult it is to live with it. I do not know if you have ever lived with the sunset.

You know, sirs, there is a radiancy of love which cannot be cultivated. Love is not the result of good conduct; no amount of your being kind, generous, will give you love. Love is both extensive and particular. A mind that loves is virtuous, it does not seek virtue. It cannot go wrong, because it knows right and wrong. It is the mind without love that seeks virtue, that wants God, that clings to a system of belief, and thereby destroys itself. Love—that quality, that feeling, that sense of compassion without any object, which is the very essence of life—is not a thing to be grasped by the mind. As I said the other day, when the intellect guides that pure feeling, then mediocrity comes into being. Most of us have such highly developed intellects that the intellect is always corrupting the pure feeling; therefore our feelings are mediocre, though we may be excellent at reasoning.

Now, this sense of loneliness is pure feeling, uncorrupted by the mind. It is the mind that is frightened, fearful, and therefore it says, 'I must get away from it.' But if one is simply aware of this loneliness, if one lives with it, then it has the quality of pure feeling. I do not know if I am making myself clear.

Have you ever really observed a flower? It is not easy. You may think you have observed it, you may think you have loved it, but what you have actually done is this: you have seen it, you have given it a name, you have smelt it, and then you have gone away. The very naming of the species, the very smelling of the flower, causes in you a certain reaction of memory, and therefore you never really look at the flower at all. Just try sometime looking at a flower, at a sunset, at a bird, or what you will, without any interference on the part of the mind, and you will see how difficult it is, yet it is only then that there is the complete perception of anything.

This loneliness, this pure feeling which is a sense of total isolation, can be observed as you would observe the flower—with complete attention, which is not to name it, or try to escape from it. Then you will find, if you have gone so far in your enquiry, that there is only a state of negation. Please do not translate this into Sanskrit, or any other language, or compare it with something you have read. What I am telling you is not what you have read. What has been described is not 'what is'.

I am saying that if the mind is capable of experiencing this sense of aloneness, not verbally, but actually living with it, then there comes an awareness of complete negation—negation which is not an opposite. Most of us only know the opposites—positive and negative, 'I love' and 'I do not love', 'I want' and 'I do not want'. That is all we know. But the state of which I am telling you is not of that nature, because it has no opposite. It is a state of complete negation.

I do not know if you have ever thought about the quality or the nature of creation. Creativity in the sense of having talent, being gifted, is entirely different from the state of creation. I do not know if it has happened to you that, while walking alone, or sitting in a room, you have suddenly had a feeling of extraordinary ecstasy. Having had that feeling, you want to translate it, so you write a poem, or paint a picture. If that poem or that picture becomes fashionable, society flatters you, pays you for it, gives you a profit, and you are carried away by all that. Presently you seek to have again that tremendous ecstasy, which came uninvited. As long as you seek it, it will never come. But you keep on seeking it in various ways—through self-discipline, through the practice of a system, through meditation, through drink, women—you try everything in an effort to get back that overwhelming feeling of radiance, of joy, in which all creation is. But you will never get it back. It comes darkly, uninvited.

So it is the state of negation from which all creation takes place. Whether you spontaneously write a poem, or smile without calculation, whether there is kindness without a motive, or goodness without fear, without a cause, it is all the outcome of this extraordinary state of complete negation, in which is creation. But you cannot come to it if you do not understand the whole process of seeking, so that all seeking completely ceases. The understanding and cessation of seeking is not at the end, but at the beginning. The man who says, 'Eventually I shall understand the process of seeking, and then I shall no longer seek', is thoughtless, stupid, because the end is at the beginning, which has no time. If you begin to enquire into yourself and perceive why you seek, and what it is you are seeking, you can capture the whole significance of it instantaneously; and then you will find that, without any intent, without any causation, there is a fundamental revolution, a complete transformation of the mind. It is only then that Truth comes into being.

Truth does not come to a mind that is burdened with experience, that is full of knowledge, that has gathered virtue, that has stifled itself through discipline, control. Truth comes to the mind that is really innocent, fearless. And it is the mind that has completely understood its own seeking, that has gone to the fullest depth of this state of negation—it is only such a mind that is without fear. Then that extraordinary thing, which we are all wanting, will come. It is elusive, and it will not come if you stretch out your hand to capture it. You cannot capture the immeasurable. Your hands, your mind, your whole being, must be quiet, completely still, to receive it. You cannot seek it, because you do not know what it is. The immeasurable will be there when the mind understands this whole process of search, not at the end, but at the beginning—which is the continuous movement of self-knowledge.

Second Talk in Madras
13 December 1959

I f we could take a journey, make a pilgrimage together without any intent or purpose, without seeking anything, perhaps on returning we might find that our hearts had unknowingly been changed. I think it worth trying. Any intent or purpose, any motive or goal implies effort—a conscious or unconscious endeavour to arrive, to achieve. I would like to suggest that we take a journey together in which none of these elements exist. If we can take such a journey, and if we are alert enough to observe what lies along the way, perhaps when we return, as all pilgrims must, we shall find that there has been a change of heart; and I think this would be much more significant than inundating the mind with ideas, because ideas do not fundamentally change human beings at all. Beliefs, ideas, influences may cause the mind superficially to adjust itself to a pattern, but if we can take the journey together without any purpose, and simply observe as we go along the extraordinary width and depth and beauty of life, then out of this observation may come a love that is not merely social, environmental, a love in which there is not the giver and the taker, but which is a state of being, free of all demand. So, in taking this journey together, perhaps we shall be awakened to something far more significant than the boredom and frustration, the emptiness and despair of our daily lives.

Most human beings, as they live from day to day, gradually drift into despair, or they get caught up in superficial joys, amusements, hopes, or they are carried away by rationalizations, by hatred, or by the social amenities. If we can really bring about a radical inward transformation, so that we live fully and richly, with deep feelings which are not corrupted by the mutterings of the intellect, then I think we shall be able to act in a totally different way in all our relationships.

This journey I am proposing that we take together is not to the moon or even to the stars. The distance to the stars is much less than the distance within ourselves. The discovery of ourselves is endless, and it requires constant enquiry, a perception which is total, an awareness in which there is no choice. This journey is really an opening of the door to the individual in his relationship with the world. Because we are in conflict with ourselves, we have conflict in the world. Our problems, when extended, become the world's problems. As long as we are in conflict with ourselves, life in the world is also a ceaseless battle, a destructive, deteriorating war.

So the understanding of ourselves is not to the end of individual salvation; it is not the means of attaining a private heaven, an ivory tower into which to retire with our own illusions, beliefs, gods. On the contrary, if we are able to understand ourselves, we shall be at peace, and then we shall know how to live rightly in a world that is now corrupt, destructive, brutal.

After all, what is worldliness? Worldliness, surely, is to be satisfied—to be satisfied, not only with outward things, with property, wealth, position, power, but with inward things as well. Most of us are satisfied at a very superficial level. We take satisfaction in possessing things—a car, a house, a garden, a title. Possession gives us an extraordinary feeling of gratification. And when we are surfeited with the possession of things, we look for satisfaction at a deeper level; we seek what we call Truth, God, salvation. But we are still moved by the same compulsion—the demand to be satisfied. Just as you seek satisfaction in sex, in social position, in owning things, so also you want to be satisfied in 'spiritual' ways.

Please do not say 'Is that all?' and brush it off, but as you are listening, observe, if you will, your own desire for satisfaction. Allow yourselves, if you can, to see in what way you are being satisfied. The intellectual person is satisfied with his clever ideas, which give him a feeling of superiority, a sense of knowing; and when that sense of knowing ceases to give him satisfaction, when he has analysed everything and intellectually torn to shreds every notion, every theory, every belief, then he seeks a wider, deeper satisfaction. He is converted, and begins to believe; he becomes very 'religious', and his satisfaction takes on the colouring of some organized religion.

So, being dissatisfied with outward things, we turn for gratification to the so-called spiritual things. It has become an ugly term, that word 'spiritual', it smacks of sanctimoniousness. Do you know what I mean? The saints with their cultivated virtues, with their struggles, their disciplines, their suppressions and self-denials, are still within the field of satisfaction. It is because we want to be satisfied that we discipline ourselves; we are after something that will give us lasting satisfaction, a gratification from which all doubt has been removed. That is what most of us want—and we think we are spiritual, religious. Our pursuit of gratification we call 'the search for truth'. We go to the temple or the church, we attend lectures, we listen to talks like this, we read the Gita, the Upanishads, the Bible—all in order to have this strange feeling of satisfaction in which there will never be any doubt, never any questioning.

It is our urge to be satisfied that makes us turn to what we call meditation and the cultivation of virtue. How virtue can be 'cultivated', I do not know. Surely, humility can never be cultivated; love can never be cultivated; peace can never be brought about through control. These things are, or they are not. The person who cultivates humility is full of vanity; he hopes to find abiding satisfaction in being humble. In the same way, through meditation we seek the absolute, the immeasurable, the unknown. But meditation is part of everyday existence; it is something that you have to do as you breathe, as you think, as you live, as you have delicate or brutal feelings. That is real meditation, and it is entirely different from the systematized meditation which some of you so sedulously practise.

I would like, if I may, to go into this question of meditation, but please do not be mesmerized by my words. Don't become suddenly meditative; don't become very intent to discover what is the goal of true meditation. The meditation of which I speak has no goal, no end. Love has no end. Love is not successful; it does not reward you or punish you. Love is a state of being, a sense of radiancy. In love is all virtue. In the state of love, do what you will, there is no sin, no evil, no contradiction; and without love we shall ever be at war with ourselves, and therefore with each other and with the world. It is love alone that transforms the mind totally.

But the meditation with which most of us are familiar, and which some of us practice, is entirely different. Let us first examine that—not to justify or condemn what you are doing, but to see the truth, the validity or the falseness of it. We are going on a journey together, and when on a journey you can take along only what is absolutely essential. The journey of which I am speaking is very swift, there is no abiding place, no stopping, no rest; it is an endless movement, and a mind that is burdened is not free to travel.

The meditation that most of us practise is a process of concentration based on exclusion, on building walls of resistance, is it not? You control your mind because you want to think of a particular thing, and you try to exclude all other thoughts. To help you to control your mind, and to exclude the unwanted thoughts, there are various systems of meditation. Life has been divided as knowledge, devotion, and action. You say 'I am of such and such a temperament', and according to your temperament you meditate. We have divided ourselves into temperaments as neatly as we have divided the earth into national, racial and religious groups, and each temperament has its own path, its own system of meditation. But if you go behind them all, you will find in every case that some form of control is practised, and control implies suppression.

Do please observe yourselves as I am going into this problem, and don't just follow verbally what I am saying, because what I am saying is not at all important. What is important is for you to discover yourselves. As I said at the beginning, we are taking a journey together into ourselves. I am only pointing out certain things, and if you are satisfied by what is pointed out, your mind will remain empty, shallow, petty. A petty mind cannot take the journey into itself. But if through these words you are becoming aware of your own thoughts, your own state, then there is no guru.

Behind all these systems of meditation which develop virtue, which promise a reward, which offer an ultimate goal, there is the factor of control, discipline, is there not? The mind is disciplined not to wander off the narrow, respectable path laid down by the system, or by society.

Now, what is implied in control? Do please observe yourselves, because we are all enquiring into this problem together. We are coming to something which I see, and which at the moment you do not, so please follow without being mesmerized by my words, by my face, by my person. Cut through all that—it is utterly immature—and observe yourselves. What does control imply? Surely, it implies a battle between what you want to concentrate on, and the thoughts that wander off. So concentration is a form of exclusion—which every schoolboy, and every bureaucrat in his office knows. The bureaucrat is compelled to concentrate, because he has to sign so many papers, he has to organize and to act; and for the schoolboy there is always the threat of the teacher.

Concentration implies suppression, does it not? I suppress in myself what I do not like. I never look at it, delve deeply into it. I have already condemned it, and a mind that condemns cannot penetrate, cannot understand what it has condemned.

There is another form of concentration, and that is when you give yourself over to something. The mind is absorbed by an image, as a child is absorbed by a toy. Those of you who have children must have observed how a toy can absorb them completely. When a child is playing with a new toy, he is extraordinarily concentrated. Nothing interferes with that concentration, because he is enjoying himself. The toy is so entrancing, so delightful, that for the moment it is all-important, and the child does not want to be disturbed. His mind is completely given over to the toy. And that is what you call devotion: giving yourself up to the symbol, the idea, the image which you have labelled God. The image absorbs you, as the child is absorbed by a toy. To lose themselves in a thing created by the mind, or by the hand, is what most people want.

Concentration through a system of meditation offers the attainment of an ultimate peace, an ultimate reality, an ultimate satisfaction, which is what you want. All such effort involves the idea of growth, evolution through time— if not in this life, then in the next life, or a hundred lives hence, you will get there. Control and discipline invariably imply effort to be, to become, and this effort places a limit on thought, on the mind—which is very satisfying. Placing a limit on the mind, on consciousness, is a most gratifying thing, because then you can see how far you have advanced in your efforts to become what you want to be. As you make effort, you push the frontier of the mind farther and farther out, but it is still within the boundaries of thought. You may attain a state which you call *Ishvara*, God, Paramatman, or what you will, but it is still within the field of the mind which is conditioned by your culture, by your society, by your greed, and all the rest of it.

So meditation, as you practise it, is a process of control, of suppression, of exclusion, of discipline, all of which involves effort—the effort to expand the boundaries of consciousness as the 'I', the self; but there is also another factor involved, which is the whole process of recognition.

I hope you are taking the journey with me. Don't say, 'It is too difficult, I don't know what you are talking about', for then you are not watching yourselves. What I am talking about is not just an intellectual concept. It is a living, vital thing, pulsating with life.

As I was saying, recognition is an essential part of what you call meditation. All you know of life is a series of recognitions. Relationship is a process of recognition, is it not? You know your wife or your husband, you know your children, in the sense that you recognize them, just as you recognize your own virtue, your own humility. Recognition is an extraordinary thing, if you look at it. All thought, all relationship is a process of recognition. Knowledge is based on recognition. So what happens? You want to recognize the unknown through meditation. And is that possible? Do you understand what I am talking about? Perhaps I am not making myself clear.

You recognize your wife, your children, your property; you recognize that you are a lawyer, a businessman, a professor, an engineer; you have a label, a name, a title. You know and recognize things with a mind that is the result of time, of effort, a mind that has cultivated virtues, that has always tried to be or to become something—all of which is a process of recognition. Knowledge is the result of experience which can be recalled, recognized, either in an encyclopaedia, or in oneself.

Do consider that word 'recognize'. What does it signify? You want to find out what God is, what Truth is, which means that you want to recognize the unknown, but if you can recognize something, it is already the known. When you practice meditation and have visions of your particular gods and goddesses, you are giving emphasis to recognition. These visions are the projections of your background, of your conditioned mind. The Christian will invariably see Jesus, or Mary, the Hindu will see Shri Krishna or his god with a dozen arms, because the conditioned mind projects these images and then recognizes them. This recognition gives you tremendous satisfaction, and you say 'I have found, I have realized, I know.'

There are many systems which offer you this sort of thing, and I say none of that is meditation. It is self-hypnosis; it has no depth. You may practise a system for ten thousand years, and you will still be within the field of time, within the frontiers of your own knowledge, your own conditioning. However far you extend the boundaries within which you can recognize your projections, it is obviously not meditation, though you may give it that name. You are merely emphasizing the self, the 'me', which is nothing but a bundle of associated memories; you are perpetuating, through your so-called meditation, the conflict of the thinker and the thought, the observer and the observed, in which the observer is always watching, denying, controlling, shaping the observed. Any schoolboy can play this game, and I say it has nothing to do with meditation, though the greybeards insist that you must thus 'meditate'. The yogis, the swamis, the sannyasis, the people who renounce the world, go away to sit in a cave—they are all still caught in this pursuit of their own visions, however noble, which is the indulgence of an appetite, a process of self-gratification.

Then what is meditation? Surely, you are in the state of meditation only when the thinker is not there—that is, when you are not giving soil to thought, to memory, which is the centre of the 'me', the self. It is this centre that marks the boundaries of consciousness, and however extensive, however virtuous it may be, or however much it may try to help humanity, it can never be in the state of meditation. You can come to that state of awareness, which is meditation, only when there is no condemnation, no effort of suppression or control. It is an awareness in which there is no choice, for choice implies an effort of will, which in turn implies domination, control. It is an awareness in which consciousness has no limits, and can therefore give complete attention—which is not concentration. I think there is a vast difference between attention and concentration. There is no attention if there is a centre from which you are attentive. You can concentrate upon something from a centre, but attention implies a state of wholeness in which there is no observer apart from the observed.

Meditation, as we have gone into it today, is really the freeing of the mind from the known. This obviously does not mean forgetting the way to your home, or discarding the technical knowledge required for the performance of your job, and so on. It means freeing the mind from its conditioning, from the background of experience, from which all projection and recognition take place. The mind must free itself from the process of acquisitiveness, satisfaction and recognition. You cannot recognize or invite the unknowable, that which is real, timeless. You can invite your friends, you can invite virtue, you can invite the gods of your own creation; you can invite them and make them your guests. But do what you will—meditate, sacrifice, become virtuous—you cannot invite the immeasurable, that something about which you do not know. The practice of virtue does not indicate love; it is the result of your own desire for gratification.

So meditation is the freeing of the mind from the known. You must come to this freedom, not tomorrow, but in the immediate, now, because through time you cannot come to the timeless, which is not a duality. The timeless is whispering round every corner; it lies under every leaf. It is open, not to the sannyasis, not to the dehydrated human beings who have suppressed themselves and who no longer have any passion, but to everyone whose mind is in the state of meditation from moment to moment. Only such a mind can receive that which is unknowable.

First Talk in Bombay
23 December 1959

Freedom is of the highest importance, but we place it within the borders of our own conceit. We have preconceived ideas of what freedom is, or what it should be; we have beliefs, ideals, conclusions about freedom. But freedom is something that cannot be preconceived. It has to be understood. Freedom does not come through mere intellection, through a logical reasoning from conclusion to conclusion. It comes darkly, unexpectedly; it is born of its own inward state. To realize freedom requires an alert mind, a mind that is deep with energy, a mind that is capable of immediate perception without the process of gradation, without the idea of an end to be slowly achieved. So, if I may, I would like to think aloud with you about freedom this evening.

Before we go more deeply into this question, I think it is necessary that we be aware of how the mind has become a slave. With most of us, the mind is a slave to tradition, to custom, to habit, to the daily job which we have to do and to which we are addicted. I think very few of us realize how slavish our minds are, and without perceiving what makes the mind slavish, without being aware of the nature of its slavery, we cannot understand what freedom is. Unless one is aware of how the mind is captured and held, which is to comprehend the totality of its slavishness, I do not think the mind can ever be free. One has to understand 'what is' before one can perceive that which is other than 'what is'.

So let us observe our own minds; let us look at the totality of the mind, the unconscious as well as the conscious. The conscious mind is that which is occupied with the everyday events of life; it is the mind that learns, that adjusts, that acquires a technique, whether scientific, medical, or bureaucratic. It is the conscious mind of the businessman that becomes a slave to the job which he has to do. Most of us are occupied from nine o'clock until five, almost every day of our existence, earning a livelihood; and when the mind spends so much of its life in acquiring and practising a technique, whether it be that of a mechanic, a surgeon, an engineer, a businessman, or what you will, naturally it becomes a slave to that technique. I think this is fairly obvious. As the housewife is a slave to the house, to her husband, to cooking for her children, so is the man a slave to his job; and both are slaves to tradition, to custom, to knowledge, conclusions, beliefs, to the conditioned ways of their own thinking. And we accept this slavery as inevitable. We never enquire to find out whether we can function without being slaves. Having accepted the inevitability of earning a livelihood, we have also accepted as inevitable the mind's slavishness, its fears, and thus we tread the mill of everyday existence.

We have to live in this world—that is the only inevitable thing in life. And the question is, surely, whether we cannot live in this world with freedom. Can we not live in this world without being slaves, without the everlasting burden of fear and frustration, without all the agony of sorrow? The limitations of the mind, the limitations of our own thinking, make us slaves. And if we observe, we see that the margin of freedom for the individual is getting narrower all the time. The politicians, the organized religions, the books we read, the knowledge and techniques we acquire, the traditions we are born into, the demands of our own ambitions and desires—these are all narrowing down the margin of freedom. I do not know to what extent and to what depth you are aware of this.

We are not talking of slavery as an abstraction, something which you hear about this evening and then return to your old routine. On the contrary, I think it is very important to understand this problem for oneself, because it is only in freedom that there is love; it is only in freedom that there is creation; it is only in freedom that Truth can be found. Do what it will, a slavish mind can never find Truth; a slavish mind can never know the beauty and the fullness of life. So I think it is very important to perceive how the mind, by its own processes, by its addiction to tradition, to custom, to knowledge and belief, becomes a slave.

I wonder if you as an individual are aware of this problem? Are you concerned merely to exist somehow in this ugly, brutal world, muttering on the side about God and freedom, and cultivating some futile virtue which makes you very respectable in the eyes of society? Or are you concerned with human dignity? There can be no human dignity without freedom, and freedom is not easily come by. To be free, one must understand oneself; one must be aware of the movements of thought and feeling, the ways of one's own mind.

As we are talking together, I wonder if you are aware of yourself? Are you aware, not theoretically, but actually, to what depth you are a slave? Or are you merely giving explanations—saying to yourself that some degree of slavery is inevitable, that you must earn a livelihood, that you have duties, responsibilities—and remaining satisfied with those explanations?

We are not concerned with what you should or should not do; that is not the problem. We are concerned with understanding the mind, and in understanding there is no condemnation, no demand for a pattern of action. You are merely observing, and observation is denied when you concern yourself with a pattern of action, or merely explain the inevitability of a slavish life. What matters is to observe your own mind without judgement—just to look at it, to watch it, to be conscious of the fact that your mind is a slave, and no more; because that very perception releases energy, and it is this energy that is going to destroy the slavishness of the mind. But if you merely ask, 'How am I to be free from my slavery to routine, from my fear and boredom in everyday existence?' you will never release this energy. We are concerned only with perceiving 'what is', and it is the perception of 'what is' that releases the creative fire. You cannot perceive if you do not ask the right question—and a right question has no answer, because it needs no answer. It is wrong questions that invariably have answers. The urgency behind the right question, the very instance of it, brings about perception. The perceiving mind is living, moving, full of energy, and only such a mind can understand what Truth is.

But most of us, when we are face to face with a problem of this kind, invariably seek an answer, a solution, the 'what to do', and the solution, the 'what to do' is so easy, leading to further misfortune, further misery. That is the way of politicians. That is the way of the organized religions, which offer an answer, an explanation; and having found it, the so-called religious mind is thereby satisfied.

But we are not politicians, nor are we slavish to organized religions. We are now examining the ways of our own minds, and for that there must be no fear. To find out about oneself, what one thinks, what one is, the extraordinary depths and movements of the mind—just to be aware of all that requires a certain freedom. And to enquire into oneself also requires an astonishing energy, because one has to travel a distance which is immeasurable. Most of us are fascinated by the idea of going to the moon, or to Venus, but those distances are much shorter than the distance within ourselves.

So, to go into ourselves deeply, fully, a sense of freedom is necessary—not at the end, but at the very beginning. Do not ask how to arrive at that freedom. No system of meditation, no book, no drug, no psychological trick you can play on yourself, will give you freedom. Freedom is born of the perception that freedom is essential. The moment you perceive that freedom is essential, you are in a state of revolt—revolt against this ugly world, against all orthodoxy, against tradition, against leadership, both political and religious. Revolt within the framework of the mind soon withers away, but there is a lasting revolt which comes into being when you perceive for yourself that freedom is essential.

Unfortunately, most of us are not aware of ourselves. We have never given thought to the ways of our minds as we have given thought to our techniques, to our jobs. We have never really looked at ourselves; we have never wandered into the depths of ourselves without calculation, without premeditation, without seeking something out of those depths. We have never taken the journey into ourselves without a purpose. The moment one has a motive, a purpose, one is a slave to it; one cannot wander freely within oneself, because one is always thinking in terms of change, of self-improvement. One is tied to the post of self-improvement, which is a projection of one's own narrow, petty mind.

Do please consider what I am saying, not merely verbally but observe your own mind, the actuality of your inner state. As long as you are a slave, your muttering about God, about Truth, about all the things that you have learned from sacred books, has no meaning; it only perpetuates your slavery. But if your mind begins to perceive the necessity of freedom, it will create its own energy, which will then operate without your calculated efforts to be free of slavery.

So we are concerned with the freedom of the individual. But to discover the individual is very difficult, because at present we are not individuals. We are the product of our environment, of our culture; we are the product of the food we eat, of our climate, our customs, our traditions. Surely, that is not individuality. I think individuality comes into being only when one is fully aware of this encroaching movement of environment and tradition that makes the mind a slave. As long as I accept the dictates of tradition, of a particular culture, as long as I carry the weight of my memories, my experiences—which after all are the result of my conditioning—I am not an individual, but merely a product.

When you call yourself a Hindu, a Muslim, a Parsi, a Buddhist, a communist, a Catholic, or what you will, are you not the product of your culture, your environment? And even when you react against that environment, your reaction is still within the field of conditioning. Instead of being a Hindu, you become a Christian, a communist, or something else. There is individuality only when the mind perceives the narrow margin of its freedom and battles ceaselessly against the encroachment of the politician and of the organized beliefs which are called religion, against the encroachment of knowledge, of technique, and of one's own accumulated experiences, which are the result of one's conditioning, one's background.

This perception, this constant awareness of 'what is', has its own will—if I can use that word 'will' without confusing it with the will to which you are so accustomed, and which is the product of desire. The will of discipline, of effort, is the product of desire, surely, and it creates the conflict between 'what is' and 'what should be', between what you want and what you do not want. It is a reaction, a resistance, and such will is bound to create other reactions and other forms of resistance. Therefore there is never freedom through will—the will of which you know. I am talking of a perceptive state of mind which has its own action. That is, perception itself is action. I wonder if I am making myself clear!

You see, sirs, I realize, as you must realize too, that the mind is a slave to habit, to custom, to tradition, and to all the memories with which it is burdened. Realizing this, the mind also realizes that it must be free because it is only in freedom that one can enquire, that one can discover. So, to perceive the necessity of being free is an absolute necessity.

Now, how is the slavish mind to be free? Please follow this. How is the slavish mind to be free? We are asking this question because we see that our lives are nothing but slavery. Going to the office day after day in utter boredom, being a slave to tradition, to custom, to fear, to one's wife or husband, to one's boss—that is one's life, and one sees the appalling pettiness, the nauseating indignity of it all. So we are asking this question: 'How am I to be free?' And is that a right question? If it is, it will have no answer, because the question itself will open the door. But if it is a wrong question, you will find—at least you will think you have found—ways and means of 'solving' the problem. But do what it will, the slavish mind can never free itself through any means, through any system or method. Whereas if you perceive totally, completely, absolutely, that the mind must be free, then that very perception brings an action which will set the mind free.

I think it is very important to understand this, and understanding is instantaneous. You do not understand tomorrow. There is no arrival at understanding after thinking it over. You either understand now, or you don't understand at all. Understanding takes place when the mind is not cluttered up with motives, with fears, with the demand for an answer. I wonder if you have noticed that there are no answers to life's questions? You can ask questions like, 'What is the goal of life?', or 'What happens after death?', or 'How am I to meditate?', or 'My job is boring, what shall I do?' You can ask, but how you ask is what matters. If you ask with a purpose, that is, with the motive of finding an answer, the answer will invariably be false, because your desire, your petty mind has already projected it. So the state of the mind that questions is much more important than the question itself. Any question that may be asked by a slavish mind, and the answer it receives, will still be within the limitations of its own slavery. But a mind that realizes the full extent of its slavery will have a totally different approach, and it is this totally different approach that we are concerned with. You can ask the right question only when you see instantly the absolute necessity of freedom.

Our minds are the result of a thousand yesterdays; being conditioned by the culture in which they live, and by the memory of past experiences, they devote themselves to the acquisition of knowledge and technique. To such minds, Truth or God can obviously have no meaning. Their talk of Truth is like the muttering of a slave about freedom. But you see, most of us prefer to be slaves; it is less troublesome, more respectable, more comfortable. In slavery there is little danger, our lives are more or less secure, and that is what we want—security, certainty, a way of life in which there will be no serious disturbance.

But life comes knocking at our door, and it brings sorrow. We feel frustrated, we are in misery, and there is after all no certainty, because everything is constantly changing. All relationships break up, and we want a permanent relationship. So life is one thing, and what we want is another. There is a battle between what we want and what life is, and what we want is made narrow by the pettiness of our minds, of our everyday existence. Our battles, our contradictions, our struggles with life are at a very superficial level; our petty little questionings based on fears and anxieties inevitably find an answer as shallow as itself.

Sirs, life is something extraordinary, if you observe it. Life is not merely this stupid little quarrelling among ourselves, this dividing up of mankind into nations, races, classes; it is not just the contradiction and misery of our daily existence. Life is wide, limitless, it is that state of love which is beauty; life is sorrow and this tremendous sense of joy. But our joys and sorrows are so small, and from that shallowness of mind we ask questions and find answers.

So the problem is, surely, to free the mind totally, so that it is in a state of awareness which has no border, no frontier. And how is the mind to discover that state? How is it to come to that freedom?

I hope you are seriously putting this question to yourselves because I am not putting it to you. I am not trying to influence you; I am merely pointing out the importance of asking oneself this question. The verbal asking of the question by another has no meaning if you don't put it to yourself with instancy, with urgency. The margin of freedom is growing narrower every day, as you must know if you are at all observant. The politicians, the leaders, the priests, the newspapers and books you read, the knowledge you acquire, the beliefs you cling to—all this is making the margin of freedom more and more narrow. If you are aware of this process going on, if you actually perceive the narrowness of the spirit, the increasing slavery of the mind, then you will find that out of perception comes energy; and it is this energy born of perception that is going to shatter the petty mind, the respectable mind, the mind that goes to the temple, the mind that is afraid. So perception is the way of Truth.

You know, to perceive something is an astonishing experience. I don't know if you have ever really perceived anything—if you have ever perceived a flower or a face or the sky or the sea. Of course, you see these things as you pass by in a bus or a car, but I wonder whether you have ever taken the trouble actually to look at a flower? And when you do look at a flower, what happens? You immediately name the flower, you are concerned with what species it belongs to, or you say, 'What lovely colours it has. I would like to grow it in my garden; I would like to give it to my wife, or put it in my button-hole', and so on. In other words, the moment you look at a flower, your mind begins chattering about it; therefore you never perceive the flower. You perceive something only when your mind is silent, when there is no chattering of any kind. If you can look at the evening star over the sea without a movement of the mind, then you really perceive the extraordinary beauty of it; and when you perceive beauty, do you not also experience the state of love? Surely, beauty and love are the same. Without love there is no beauty, and without beauty there is no love. Beauty is in form, beauty is in speech, beauty is in conduct. If there is no love, conduct is empty; it is merely the product of society, of a particular culture, and what is produced is mechanical, lifeless. But when the mind perceives without the slightest flutter, then it is capable of looking into the total depth of itself; and such perception is really timeless. You don't have to do something to bring it about; there is no discipline, no method by which you can learn to perceive.

Sirs, do please listen to what I am saying. Your minds are slaves to patterns, to systems, to methods and techniques. I am talking of something entirely different. Perception is instantaneous, timeless; there is no gradual approach to it. It is on the instant that perception takes place; it is a state of effortless attention. The mind is not making an effort, therefore it does not create a border, a frontier, it does not place a limitation on its own consciousness. Then life is not this terrible process of sorrow, of struggle, of unutterable boredom. Life is then an eternal movement, without beginning and without end. But to be aware of that timeless state, to feel the tremendous depth and ecstasy of it, one must begin by understanding the slavish mind. Without understanding the one, you cannot have the other.

We would like to escape from our slavery, and that is why we talk about religious things; that is why we read the scriptures; that is why we speculate, argue, discuss— which is all so vain and futile. Whereas, if you are aware that your mind is narrow, limited, slavish, petty—aware of it choicelessly—then you are in a state of perception, and it is this perception that will bring the necessary energy to free the mind from its slavery. Then the mind has no centre from which it acts. The moment you have a centre, there must also be a circumference; and to function from a centre, within a circumference, is slavery. But when the mind, being aware of the centre, also perceives the nature of the centre, that very perception is enough. To perceive the nature of the centre is the greatest thing you can do; it is the greatest action the mind can take. But that requires your complete attention. You know, when you love something without any motive, without any want, such love brings its own results, it finds its own way, it is its own beauty.

So, what is important is to be aware of how one's mind, in the very process of accumulation, becomes a slave. Do not ask, 'How am I to be free from accumulation?', for then you are putting a wrong question. But if you really perceive for yourself that your mind is accumulating, that is enough. To perceive requires complete attention; and when you give your whole mind, your whole heart, your total being to something, there is no problem. It is partial attention, in which there is a withholding, that creates the problems and the miseries in our life.

About the Author

Jiddu Krishnamurti was born on 11 May 1895 in south India. He and his brother were adopted in their youth by Dr. Annie Besant, then president of the Theosophical Society, who proclaimed him a world teacher whose coming the Theosophists had predicted. A world-wide organization called the Order of the Star in the East was formed and the young Krishnamurti was made its head. In 1929, however, Krishnamurti renounced his expected role, dissolved the Order with its huge following, and returned all the money and property that had been donated for this work. From then, for nearly sixty years until his death on 17 February 1986, he travelled throughout the world talking to large audiences and to individuals about the need for a radical change in humankind.

Krishnamurti is regarded globally as one of the greatest thinkers and religious teachers of all time. He did not expound any philosophy or religion, but rather talked of the things that concern all of us in our everyday lives, of the problems of living in modern society with its violence and corruption, of the individual's search for security and happiness, and the need for humankind to free itself from inner burdens of fear, anger, hurt, and sorrow. Krishnamurti's talks and discussions flow from his own insights into the human mind and his vision of the sacred, rather than from tradition-based philosophy or religion, so he always communicates a sense of freshness and directness although the essence of his message remained unchanged over the years.

Contact Information

The Krishnamurti Foundation of America
PO Box 1560, Ojai, California, 93024, USA
info@kpublications.com
www.kpublications.com
www.jkrishnamurti.org
www.kfa.org

HOHM PRESS: Other distinguished titles can be found in our current catalog.
Write: Hohm Press, PO Box 2501, Prescott, Arizona, 86302, USA
Or visit our website: www.hohmpress.com